THE HOUSE OF HARPER

Λαμπάδια ἔχοντες διαδώσουσιν ἀλλήλοις.

THE HOUSE OF HARPER

The Making of a Modern Publisher

EUGENE EXMAN

HARPER ● PERENNIAL

NEW YORK ● LONDON ● TORONTO ● SYDNEY ● NEW DELHI ● AUCKLAND

HARPER ● PERENNIAL

A hardcover edition of this book was originally published in 1967 by
Harper & Row, Publishers.

THE HOUSE OF HARPER. Copyright © 1967 by Eugene Exman. Introduction
© 2010 by Jennifer B. Lee. All rights reserved. Printed in the United
States of America. No part of this book may be used or reproduced in any
manner whatsoever without written permission except in the case of brief
quotations embodied in critical articles and reviews. For information, address
HarperCollins Publishers, 10 East 53rd Street, New York, NY 10022.

HarperCollins books may be purchased for educational, business, or
sales promotional use. For information, please write: Special Markets
Department, HarperCollins Publishers, 10 East 53rd Street, New York,
NY 10022.

The illustration by Garth Williams on page 279 is from *Stuart Little*.
Copyright © 1945 by the E. B. White estate.

The drawing by Maurice Sendak on pages 280 and 281 is from *Where the
Wild Things Are*. Copyright © 1963 by Maurice Sendak.

The images which appear in the introduction and on page 191 are from the
Harper and Brothers Archive and Library and other collections, courtesy of
the Rare Book and Manuscript Library, Columbia University.

FIRST HARPER PERENNIAL EDITION PUBLISHED 2010.

Library of Congress Cataloging-in-Publication Data is available upon
request.

ISBN 978-0-06-193666-1 (2010 pbk.)

10 11 12 13 14   RRD   10 9 8 7 6 5 4 3 2 1

CONTENTS

PART II—PUBLISHING IN THE TWENTIETH CENTURY

INTRODUCTION

Eugene Exman's *The House of Harper* first appeared in 1967, two years after his *The Brothers Harper* was published. The earlier book traced the history of the first generations of Harpers, from 1817 to 1853. This book covers that era in some detail, but goes far beyond to the merger of Harper & Brothers with Row, Peterson & Company in the 1960s. This new edition brings back into print the story of the most important American publishing firm of the nineteenth century. As Columbia University historian Allan Nevins wrote in his introduction to *The Brothers Harper*, "Harper's was (and is) a household word among all cultivated Americans." Indeed, this history of the firm provides a fresh look at the history of American civilization from the early 1800s through the Kennedy administration.

Arranged roughly chronologically, *The House of Harper* examines different aspects of the work of the firm, including international copyright, the four major periodicals published by Harper & Brothers, the art department, and the work of editors such as William Dean Howells and Mary L. Booth. Their marketing innovation of issuing books in series began in 1830 with the *Harper's Family Library*, modeled directly on the Family Library of English publisher John Murray. This was a nonfiction series that came to include the first edition of Richard Henry Dana's *Two Years Before the Mast* (1840). It was this series that attracted Herman Melville to Harper's, since he had used a 72-volume set on board the USS *United*

Agreement made between Harper and Brothers of the city of New York, Publishers of the one part and Herman Melville of Pittsfield Massachusetts, of the other part Witnesseth That the said Harper and Brothers have agreed to publish and sell and keep for sale a certain work entitled "The Whale" where of the said Herman Melville is the author upon the following terms —
First. The copyright of the said work is to be the sole property of the said Herman Melville (subject to this contract) and shall be entered and stand in his name as author and proprietor.
Second. The said Harper and Brothers are to be the sole publishers of the said work in the United States of America during the continuance of this agreement. And in consideration of the sole right to publish said work hereby granted to them, the said Harper and Brothers hereby agree to publish said work from the stereotype plates now in the possession of R. Craighead, at their own cost and expence paying said Craighead for the cost of said plates, and to pay to said Herman Melville one half of the net profits accruing from its publication and sale of said work. Provided that at any time after the cost of the stereotype plates shall have been liquidated the said payment shall if the said Herman Melville demand it be commuted for a ____ cents per copy for all copies sold. Fourthly. Harper and Brothers agree to make semi annual settlements with said Herman Melville on the first days of February and August in each year, as long as this agreement remains in force

and the balance due said Herman Melville shall be paid by the notes of the said Harper and Brothers at three months from those dates or in cash, interest off— Fifth. this agreement shall continue for seven years from the day of publication by said Harper & Brothers; at the expiration of which time the said Herman Melville shall have the right to the possession and complete ownership of the stereotype plates of the said work on paying to the said Harper and Brothers one half of their original cost deducting a fair valuation for the wear and tear they may have sustained in their use or injury from other causes. Upon which payment which may be made at any time after the expiration of the said seven years, the said stereotype plates shall belong to the said Herman Melville as his sole property. Sixth. the said Harper and Brothers are to have the right to dispose of all copies of said work remaining on hand at the expiration of this agreement, they accounting upon the sale of said copies as herein provided. Seventh. It is distinctly understood that this agreement refers solely to the publication of said work in the United States of America. In witness where of the parties hereto have hereunto subscribed their names this twelfth day of September one thousand eight hundred and fifty one—
Herman Melville
per Allan Melville
his attorney
Harper & Brothers

Agreement

Between
Harper and Brothers
and
Herman Melville

Sept 12 1851.

The Whale / Moby Dick

To be kept by
H & B—

Copied

Herman Melville
Contract for *The Whale*
New York, September 12, 1851

This contract for Harper & Brothers publication of the first American edition of *Moby Dick* is signed on Melville's behalf by his brother Allan, a lawyer.

States when returning home from Hawaii in 1844. A similar series entitled the *New Miscellany*, begun in 1845, would include the first American edition of Charles Darwin's *Voyage of H.M.S. Beagle* (1846). As with Murray's model, a list of other titles available in the series was placed in each volume.

The importance of Harper's goes far beyond book publishing, as their story also shows the development of the periodical press, technological developments in printing and publishing, and innovative marketing strategies. Their list of firsts includes, for America, the first publisher to use cloth for book binding, the first to adopt stereotyping as a standard procedure in printing, the first to employ readers to go through unsolicited manuscripts, and the first to adopt the marketing tool of publishing in series. In addition, they were among the first in America to use horse-powered and later steam-powered presses, and to erect a large commercial fireproof building using wrought iron beams.

Harper's list of writers and their many bestsellers included the panoply of English and American literary, travel, political, historical, scientific, medical, and religious authors. Many of their publications are still bestsellers, including Dana's *Two Years Before the Mast* (1840), Charlotte Brönte's *Jane Eyre* (1848), Melville's *Moby-Dick* (1851), George Eliot's *Middlemarch* (1871), and Henry James's *Daisy Miller* (1879) and *Washington Square* (1881). Other bestsellers in their day, such as Lew Wallace's *Ben Hur* (1880) and George Du Maurier's *Trilby* (1894) are remembered today for other reasons, as Exman relates.

While the majority of Harper's authors from the 1830s until at least the 1890s were British, the brothers and their successors did their part to support American authors. One of the first bestselling women authors on Harper's lists was Catherine Maria Sedgwick, called the "Miss Edgeworth of American," and by Nathaniel Hawthorne "our most truthful novelist." Her first of nine novels published by Harper's was *The Linwoods* (1835), an account of Puritan New England home life that was sentimental but also critical. Edgar Allan Poe reviewed *The Linwoods* in the December 1835 issue of the Southern Literary Messenger, writing: "We are acquainted with few persons of sound and accurate discrimination who would hesitate in placing her upon a level with the best of our creative novelists. Of American *female* writers we must consider her the first."

Jacob Abbott
The Harper Establishment; Or, How the Story Books Are Made
New York: Harper & Brothers [c. 1855]

*(Title page, "The Power-Press" with woman working press;
see also "Sectional view of the Cliff Street building" on p. xix)*

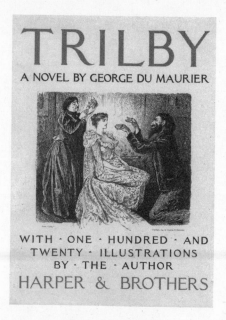

TRILBY
A NOVEL BY GEORGE DU MAURIER

WITH · ONE · HUNDRED · AND
TWENTY · ILLUSTRATIONS
BY · THE · AUTHOR
HARPER & BROTHERS

George Du Maurier
Poster for *Trilby*
New York: Harper & Brothers,
1894

Harper's issued works written by women from their early days as publishers. At first, most of these authors were British, whether men or women—including all three of the Brontës, issued under the pseudonyms of Acton, Currer, and Ellis Bell, and George Eliot—but American women were soon added to the list, including Catherine Beecher, Constance Fenimore Woolson, Ruth McEnery, Mary E. Wilkins, and Margaret Deland. In 1932, the first of Laura Ingalls Wilder's eight *Little House* books, *Little House in the Big Woods*, was issued. In 1949, Gwendolyn Brooks's *Annie Allen* appeared and won the Pulitzer Prize for poetry in 1950, the first Pulitzer awarded to an African American. These works are woven into the long tapestry of Harper & Brothers publications in this book, along with in-house details of the firm's publication of Charles Dickens, Mark Twain, Wilkie Collins, Thomas Hardy, Zane Grey, John F. Kennedy, E. B. White, Maurice Sendak, Jacques Cousteau, and many others.

Harper's published a number of works important for their social criticism, such as Fanny Kemble's *Journal of a Residence on a Georgia Plantation, 1838–39* (1863), which was influential in rallying support for the Emancipation Proclamation and in keeping Britain on the side of the Union or at least neutral in the American Civil War; Helen Hunt Jackson's exposé of injustices to the American Indian, entitled *A Century of Dishonor* (1881); and in the pages of *Harper's Weekly*, the scathing cartoons of Thomas Nast launched a devastating attack on those who wanted compromise with the South and, after the Civil War, the corrupt Tweed Ring in New York City. Later they would publish Richard Wright's *Native Son* (1940), John

Catherine Maria Sedgwick
Contract for *The Linwoods*
New York, April 1, 1835

As shown in this contract, the Harpers paid Mrs. Sedgwick $1,000 for publication of The Linwoods.

Gunther's *Death Be Not Proud* (1949), Rudolf Flesch's *Why Johnny Can't Read* (1955), and Martin Luther King Jr.'s *Stride Toward Freedom* (1958).

The story of Harper's role in the world of art, beyond the impact of political cartoons, is worth highlighting here. As Exman writes: "Joseph Penell, leading American artist and lithographer, often asserted that the growth of real and vital American art started in the department of Charles Parsons in Franklin Square." Parsons was Harper's second art editor, hired in 1863. In addition to artists working in the office itself, Harper's had a corps of author-artists in the field, sending back articles and sketches that provided the latest news and images of the Civil War, or later events such

William Nicholson
From Harper's Weekly . . . Mark Twain
New York: Harper & Brothers, 1900

as the great Chicago fire, the assassination of President Garfield, and President Grant's funeral in New York City. These artists included Thomas Nast, Frederick S. Church, Winslow Homer, Edwin Austin Abbey, Frederic Remington, Charles Dana Gibson, and Howard Pyle, among others. Their work appeared not only in *Harper's Weekly, Monthly,* and *Bazar,* but in hundreds of illustrated editions, binding and dust jacket designs, and promotional materials for Harper's books, from Shakespeare to Dickens,

Thomas Nast
Harper's Weekly Supplement, October 7, 1876
New York: Harper & Brothers, 1876

The political cartoons of Thomas Nast eventually drove Boss Tweed from power.
Ironically, Spanish officials who captured Tweed on the run used this cartoon to
positively identify him.

and from the Bible to Woodrow Wilson's five-volume *A History of the American People.*

Charles Parsons retired in 1891, and by 1893, he was succeeded as art editor by Edward Penfield, who had come to the attention of the firm while still a student at the Art Students' League in New York City. The Penfield era at Harper's lasted only until February 1901, but was to be one of the most recognizable periods in the history of graphic design. Penfield's medium was the poster, using a style that was simple, colorful, and gently ironic. As he described his design philosophy: "A poster should tell its story at once—a design that needs study is not a poster."

Harper's embraced new technology for illustrations as well as for text. For instance, in 1843, they published John L. Stephens and Frederick Catherwoods's *Incidents of Travel in the Yucatan*, the first major work to be illustrated with drawings made not only in the field but from daguerreotype photographs that they took while in the Yucatan. Harper's edition of John W. Draper's *Human Physiology* (1856) was not only the leading textbook in its field for many years, but contained the first photomicrographs ever published. And in 1885, with the invention of the "screen negative" by Frederic E. Ives, Harper's was among the first to begin using halftone photographs for illustrations instead of those made by their staff artists and wood-engraving departments.

Much has happened since the firm became Harper & Row in 1962. The collection of early Harpers archival materials discovered in 1963, that made possible Exman's two books, were given to Columbia University's Rare Book and Manuscript Library in 1975 by Harper & Row, along with Exman's working notes for this book, and Harper & Brothers's library of 2,700 of their published books. (Harper & Row's archives from 1962 through 1972 had already come to Columbia in 1973.) This material includes such treasures as the Damarest Catalog mentioned as a major source for Eugene Exman. The massive volume created by William H. Damarest provides information on all Harper publications from 1817 to 1878, arranged by author, with indexes by date, author, editor, illustrator, annotator, and subject. It also includes contracts drawn up with authors of all kinds, including, for instance, the contract signed by Catherine Maria Sedgwick and Harper's for *The Linwoods* in 1835 that paid her $1,000, as well as those with Herman Melville for the publication of *Omoo* (1847), *Typee* (1849), *Mardi* (1849), *Redburn* (1849), *White-Jacket* (1850), *Moby-Dick* (1851), and *Pierre* (1852), and ledgers giving details of employee records and equipment purchases (see pages 280 and 281).

In 1980, Chadwyck-Healey published *The Archives of Harper and Brothers 1817–1914*, a microfilm edition of the early portion of Columbia's holdings, giving access to this material on a much wider basis. For a

William H. Demarest
Compilation of Books Issued by Harper's from 1817 to 1879
New York, 1877–1880

When William Demarest retired as bookkeeper for Harpers after forty-four years with the firm, he devoted nearly three years to the creation of this great bibliographical work.

very helpful guide to the film, see Michael Winship's "The Archives of Harper and Brothers 1817–1914" (Book Review), *Papers of the Bibliographical Society of America*, Vol. 79 (1985). Other Harper records are located at the Pierpont Morgan Library, Princeton University Library, the Library of Congress, and the Humanities Research Center at the University of Texas at Austin. More recently, a number of digital projects have put a wide range of Harper's publications on the Web, such as "HarpWeek: Electronic Access to Harper's Weekly, 1857–1912," and through other subscription services such as ProQuest and the American Periodicals Series, the contents of *Harper's New Monthly Magazine* and *Harper's Bazar*, while larger-scale projects such as Google Books have digitized thousands of books published by Harper's.

Much has also happened in the publishing world since 1962. Harper & Row acquired Basic Books in 1969; the imprints of Thomas Y. Crowell Co., Inc., including World Publishing and Funk & Wagnalls Publishing, in 1977; J. B. Lippincott Company in 1978; Hemisphere Publishing Corporation in 1985; and Winston-Seabury Press in 1986. In 1987 the company was itself purchased by News Corporation Limited. Following News Corporation's 1990 acquisition of the British publisher William Collins & Sons, founded in 1819, the firm name was changed to Harper-Collins, its name today. Since 1990, it has acquired William Morrow & Company, Avon Books, and Amistad Press, and has been a pioneer in the use of digital technology, creating "Browse Inside," now an industry standard, and the "Digital Media Café," providing audio and video content to portable digital players, in 2006.

None of this more recent history is surprising, given the importance on the world's stage of the firm in its pre–Harper & Row years as described here by Exman. HarperCollins's 2005 initiative to digitize the publishing process from start to finish can here be seen as a continuum in Harper & Brothers' early embrace of the stereotyping process for all publications that might warrant more than one edition. It was the thousands of metal stereotype plates, housed in fire-proof subterranean vaults under their Cliff Street establishment, along with wood-cut blocks for the illustrations, that allowed them to rise, phoenix-like, after the great Harper fire of December 10, 1853. In this age of widely diversified media, the name of Harper's, whether Harper & Brothers, Harper & Row, or HarperCollins, still holds a major place in the cultural life of America and the world.

Jennifer B. Lee
Rare Book & Manuscript Library
Columbia University
March 2009

THE HOUSE OF HARPER

TO CASS CANFIELD

who represents Harper
in the twentieth century
as Fletcher Harper did
in the nineteenth century

FOREWORD

This book is not primarily about the writers and artists who have instructed and entertained five generations of readers. It is rather a biography of the intangible entity that can best be described as the House of Harper. It has meant many things to many people, but almost from its birth in 1817 its imprint and its image have been a reality to readers of books and of periodicals. Those who founded the House, and those who have merged their lives with it since, are primarily the concern of this narrative, even though it cannot name the countless men and women whose personal careers and loyalties have been subordinated to a loyalty to the House and to its career. Without their devoted and anonymous work there would have been no Harper history to record.

While the pages of this book often may seem to bristle with titles of books and names of authors, comparatively few have been chosen out of an estimated twenty thousand books and perhaps half that many authors published by Harper's in its 150 years. Because of the limitations of space, many who won wide acceptance or made important contributions to American life and letters have been omitted or are referred to but briefly. Even the relations of the House with its writers and artists, as revealed in their biographies and autobiographies, here are dealt with only in summary paragraphs or sentences unless an anecdote, like an importuning guest, could not be denied admittance. Thus, much that is of interest to me or might be to certain others has been sacrificed in order that the general reader might not get bogged down in detail that would delay his journey through the broad and fertile fields of American publishing. In fact, the firm's early decades are here described only briefly, because they were covered extensively in *The Brothers Harper* (1817-1853).

Fifty-five years ago J. Henry Harper chose *The House of Harper* as the title of his volume of publishing history. Its use a second time does not mean a revision or updating of what he wrote. My book is more critical than his; mistakes have been made by the House and I have endeavored to assay debits as well as credits, even though admitting a natural bias in favor of my subject. While several authorities have read the manuscript critically and have generously made suggestions for its improvement, I must take the responsibility for the views and the interpretations of fact in this book.

E. E.

April, 1967

I

PUBLISHING
IN THE NINETEENTH CENTURY

1

EARLY YEARS (1817-29)

In 1817, when the Harpers started in business, New York City had a population of nearly one hundred and twenty thousand and the nation itself nine million. The country was slowly recovering from the effects of a second war with England, and the British were still jubilant over their defeat of Napoleon at Waterloo. At Abbotsford, Walter Scott was completing a new novel, *Rob Roy,* and copies of that book would soon reach New York via the just established Black Ball Line, the first scheduled operation of packet ships between New York and Liverpool. That same year the Great Lakes were demilitarized, making a fortless boundary between the United States and Canada. To the South a new state—Mississippi—was carved out of territory abutting the Gulf of Mexico and added the twentieth star to the flag. In March, the month in which James Monroe was inaugurated President, a new sign was hung in front of a small frame house at the corner of Front and Dover Streets, New York. It read, "J. & J. Harper, Printers."

James Harper was almost twenty-two and John two years younger. Both men were experienced printers, with a reputation in the trade as diligent and skillful workmen. They had managed to save up enough money to buy two Ramage presses, a few fonts of type, and some simple binding equipment. Their father, Joseph Harper, loaned them several hundred dollars and offered to put a mortgage on his Long Island farm

3

Portrait of Fletcher Harper
by Charles Loring Elliott (1862).

to help further, if needed. Although they had to take some job printing at first, they were ambitious to become printers and publishers of books. There were then thirty-three booksellers in New York, many of whom also did some publishing; on these thirty-three dealers the Harpers pinned their hopes for survival. Business was slow and it was not till midsummer, after repeated calls all around, that they procured the first order, from a bookseller named Evert Duyckinck. It was for two thousand copies of an English translation of *Seneca's Morals*. James and John started at once to set the book in type, aided by their two younger brothers, Wesley and Fletcher. Wesley was in his sixteenth year, starting out as a printer's devil, and eleven-year-old Fletcher was on vacation from school. With this book in hand to show the quality of their work, James Harper was able to solicit a few further book orders, but business continued slow through 1818. Whereupon the brothers determined to publish a book on their own account and selected Locke's *An Essay Concerning Human Understanding*. Showing proofs to a few booksellers, they took advance orders and gave these booksellers title-page recognition. This plan worked well and set a precedent that they were to follow for several years.

Soon they were being congratulated for doing the best bookwork in town and were getting plenty of commissions. As their business expanded, they made three moves—to Fulton Street, to 230 Pearl Street, and to 82 Cliff Street. This last move was made in 1825, and the equipment and personnel housed in the four-story building turned out more printed matter than any other establishment in the city. In 1825, Fletcher Harper bought into the partnership with five hundred dollars he had saved up, as his brother Wesley had done two years earlier. The two younger brothers were now eager for J. & J. Harper to take its publishing concern seriously. While it was comparatively easy to run off editions of books sold in advance, sometimes booksellers did not order enough copies, and when they came back for more there was no stock left. Wesley and Fletcher argued that the firm had a responsibility to keep books in print. By this time the Harpers had learned how to make new editions that looked better and sold for less than those of competing firms. For several years they had been publishing the latest fiction

SENECA'S MORALS.

BY WAY OF ABSTRACT.

TO WHICH IS ADDED,

A DISCOURSE,

UNDER THE TITLE OF

AN AFTER-THOUGHT.

BY SIR ROGER L'ESTRANGE, KNT.

FIFTH AMERICAN EDITION.

NEW-YORK:
PUBLISHED BY EVERT DUYCKINCK,
NO. 68 WATER-STREET.
J. & J. Harper, printers.
1817.

Title page of the first book produced by the Harpers.

The S.S. Europe *of the Black Ball Line of America, painted in 1833 by Samuel Walton. Sailing on regular schedules after 1817, but subject to winds and tides and ocean currents, packets such as the* Europe *carried early proofs of new English books to American publishers. In his later years Fletcher Harper said that the book business was never so exciting as in the days of the sailing vessels, when publishers competed to be the first to snatch bundles of proof from the pier and quickly print and market their editions.*

from England, and booksellers had learned to expect them to be the first to come out with a new Walter Scott novel, although Scott did not publicly disclose his authorship until 1827. Once, they had printed and bound the third volume of *Peveril of the Peak* twenty-one hours after a copy was taken off the packet, a record equaled a few years later with *Memoirs of Prince Lucien Bonaparte.* In the first instance they were competing with Henry Carey, Philadelphia's leading publisher, who had got a head start by purchasing early proofs, and in the second with Frederick Saunders, who had come to New York from London to establish a branch of his father's business on the assumption that he had "property" rights in his authors even in America.

In the absence of international copyright, no publisher was breaking any law by reprinting English books. However, the competition with Carey after a few years proved to both firms that some trade courtesies should be set up, because it was profitless to "print on" each other, a phrase that meant printing a book for which another publisher claimed priority. What got to be known as the "Harper rule" worked fairly well. It had three stipulations: the purchase of advance proofs from an English publisher or author, the right to a new book by an author previously published, and the listing of a forthcoming book in a newspaper advertisement, known as a "first announcement." The competition with Saunders established the principle that a London publisher could not control American rights to his works by maintaining a branch office in New York.

Fletcher Harper carried the fight for the brothers in the battle over English reprints. He was ambitious and extroverted and humorous. During most of his adult life he wore sideburns; his hair was a brownish red and curly and his eyes were blue. Fletcher was the head of the publishing division, because he had the best sense of what books to undertake and how to get them merchandised. James Harper, the eldest brother, was also an outgoing sort of man. He was tall and affable, made friends easily, and was the front man on all occasions. He had set the pattern for his younger brothers by working in the composing room, pressroom, and bindery, and took over the direction of the manufactory. He knew all employees by name, moved among them, and often said to his foremen, "Don't try to drive men too roughly. It is so much easier to draw than push." His strong-featured face was framed with blond hair and sideburns, which in early manhood turned black and remained so till his death. From his youth on he wore steel-rimmed glasses. His eyes were blue, and by their twinkle and a certain set of the mouth those with him could tell when a good story would be forthcoming.

John Harper was massive, broad-shouldered, squarely built, and slow of movement, quiet, almost taciturn. He had been good at

The young publisher James Harper, as depicted on an ivory miniature.

arithmetic in school and liked keeping records, so he took charge of the bookkeeping, handled the finances, and drew up book contracts. In temperament he was closer akin to his younger brother Wesley, with whom he also shared a skill at proofreading. Wesley Harper was never far from the composing room and several of his early colleagues there were lifelong friends. For several years after he became a partner, he read all proofs of new books. A careful reading of reprints that passed over his desk familiarized him with much of the best of English literature. As the business of the House expanded, it fell to his lot to handle the important correspondence, and he became noted during his lifetime as the best correspondent in the book trade. R. R. Bowker, in the *Publishers' Trade List Annual, 1877,* said that Wesley Harper was "the master of an uncommonly terse, and, at the same time, finished and elegant literary style." Extant letters, including those to Edgar Allan Poe, Henry W. Longfellow, and Bulwer-Lytton, bear out this testimony.

While the duties of the four early became well defined, they worked together as a unit. No important action was taken unless there was complete agreement among them. For many years they worked without formal financial agreement; each withdrew from the common till what he thought he needed for living expenses, and no questions were ever asked. By the end of the eighteen-twenties they had built up the largest book-printing establishment in America. Their operation was carried on in four buildings on Cliff Street, one of which was the old Isaac Roosevelt mansion, which had been occupied by DeWitt Clinton when he was mayor of New York. All had married and had begun raising families. They lived frugally and their social life was largely devoted to visiting each other's homes and that of their parents, as well as those of other members of the John Street Methodist Church. The religious instruction of their parents had set a pattern for their childhood, and became for each a valid experience of maturity. From their parents, too, they had an example of integrity fostered by love and mutual respect, an example that also became precept and experience. Once, James Harper said to a friend, "Yes, sir, the basis on which we commenced was *character,* and not *capital.*"

2

"THESE EVERLASTING HARPERS"
(1830-39)

In 1830 the brothers boasted of publishing a new book a week, and by 1833, when they issued their earliest existing catalogue, they could list two hundred and thirty-four titles, of which some 90 per cent were English reprints. They started the decade with two important ventures, one of stereotyping nearly all their works, and the other of publishing a notable series of nonfiction works.

Actually they had learned about stereotyping much earlier and, almost from the beginning, had made stereotype plates from which to print important books. About 1829 it was discovered that molds made from papier-mâché reproduced the type more accurately than did those made from clay. The Harpers promptly adopted the new method and widely advertised that their books were now being printed from superior stereotypes. This advertising helped to sell their books and brought them much new business; in fact, their early success was partly due to the fact that they were the very first book publishers to adopt stereotyping as a regular procedure. While the cost of these plates was a sizable publishing expense, plates could easily be stored and the distributed type put immediately to further use.

Good books, no matter how well printed, never do a publisher any good taking up space in a warehouse. In 1830 the Harpers decided that some books would move more quickly if they were placed in a series:

new titles would advertise older ones and often a whole series would be bought as a unit. Six were promptly launched, each called a "Library," but the only one of these initial series that proved a success was Harper's Family Library. Books selected for it, all clothbound, were nonfiction titles, weighted toward biography, travel, and history. Most authors were English, although some important works by American authors were represented: J. K. Paulding's *Life of Washington,* W. C. Bryant's *Selections from American Poets,* Washington Irving's *Life of Oliver Goldsmith,* and R. H. Dana's *Two Years Before the Mast.* As Harper's Family Library grew from year to year, the books were grouped and sold at special prices. Thus in 1840 one hundred and five volumes could be bought for $46.40; in a handsome case with lock and key for $47.50; in a half-morocco binding and marbled edges for $52.50. When the series was completed in 1845, it contained one hundred and eighty-seven volumes and sold for $80.00, with single copies costing forty-five cents each. Harper's Family Library gave literate Americans—and there was a surprisingly large percentage of them in the total population—first-rate books at modest prices, and was one of the reasons it was often said that the Harpers were doing more than any single university to raise the intellectual level of the nation. John Quincy Adams recommended Harper's Family Library in 1838, but it annoyed Henry David Thoreau, who a few years later, in *Walden,* protested against the Harpers' selecting what Americans should read.

In 1830 a Harper advertisement boasted that "several gentlemen of high literary acquirements and correct taste" were reading all new works and that the public could "rest assured that no works will be published by J. & J. H. but such as are interesting, instructive, and moral." Religious and philosophical works were "examined" by George Bush, Professor of Hebrew Language and Literature of the University of the City of New York, and medical books by Dr. Sidney Doane; literary manuscripts were read by Dr. James E. DeKay, author of *Sketches of Turkey* and an intimate of the Knickerbocker school of writers. DeKay is probably the "Dr. D." referred to in a Harper letter to Longfellow as having made corrections in Longfellow's *Outre-Mer,* the poet's first important prose work.

UNCLE PHILIP'S

CONVERSATIONS WITH THE CHILDREN

ABOUT THE

WHALE FISHERY

AND

POLAR SEAS.

IN TWO VOLUMES.
VOL. II.

NEW-YORK:

PUBLISHED BY HARPER & BROTHERS,

NO. 82 CLIFF-STREET.

1839.

Title page of one of nine juvenile books by the Rev. Francis L. Hawks under the pseudonym "Uncle Philip."

Publishers' readers, who often start as bright and ambitious college graduates with English majors, are now a commonplace. To them falls the monotonous task of wading through piles of unsolicited book manuscripts (Harper's received a total of 6,355 in 1965), in the hope of finding a masterpiece. Back in the early eighteen-thirties J. & J. Harper hired the first such reader to supplement their literary advisers. He was John Inman, brother of the portraitist and later editor of the New York *Commercial Advertiser.* His employment may have indicated that the publishing brothers then felt themselves unable to judge properly the literary merits of manuscripts; it certainly showed that it was work they could delegate while they got on with other business in their small and unpretentious office (then called a counting room). Several authors did not take to the innovation of a reader. James Kirke Paulding sourly commented that the Harpers were guided by their reader's judgment and their anticipation of profit and loss, rather than by "any intrinsic merit of the work or its author," and the young Southern novelist William Gilmore Simms was upset that Inman had written critically of his second book, *Martin Faber.* (Apparently James Harper showed the reader's report to his author—always a risky thing to do.)

One of the early J. & J. Harper series was called Boy's and Girl's Library. Benjamin B. Thatcher, then a recent Harvard graduate, wrote *Indian Traits* and *Tales of the American Revolution* for this juvenile series. Its most famous title was *The Swiss Family Robinson,* this book being the first American issue of the classic. In order to bring together a collection of fairy stories, James Harper went abroad in 1835, traveling over the greater part of Europe. The *Fairy Book* which resulted, and for which Gulian Verplanck wrote an introduction, is one of the most beautiful books of the decade. A rising young engraver named Joseph A. Adams made the eighty-one wood engravings for the book, some from his own drawings and the rest from drawings by the artist John G. Chapman.

The year 1833 is a memorable one in Harper history. For one reason, a newly invented steam press was installed. The new press replaced the horsepower press, the invention of Daniel Treadwell, of Boston, which had been in use for several years. Discarding this press meant retirement to the Harper farm on Long Island for the horse that had furnished the power by walking steadily in a circular path. The horse might well have been named Treadwell, for when he found himself alone in the pasture he went to a solitary tree and walked steadily around it, from seven o'clock in the morning till six o'clock at night, with an hour out at midday, his routine directed by a nearby factory whistle.

Most important, 1833 was the year that the publishing imprint was changed from "J. & J. Harper" to "Harper & Brothers." Since the two younger brothers had been partners for several years and were responsible in part for the growing influence of the House, it was obvious that they should be included in the imprint. At first they considered "J. & J. Harper & Brothers," and then decided to drop the "J. & J." since they were all Harpers and all brothers. Thereafter anyone who asked which was the Mr. Harper and which were the brothers got the same pat answer: "Any one of us is Mr. Harper, and all the rest are brothers." The change in imprint was announced October 29, 1833, and

J. & J. HARPER, will hereafter transact business under the firm of HARPER & BROTHERS, at No. 82 Cliff street, New-York.
JAMES HARPER,
JOHN HARPER,
J. W. HARPER,
oc 29   F. HARPER.

AGREEABLY to the late act of the Legislature, the name of the firm of MILLS, BROTHERS & CO. is changed to MILLS & CO.   oc 29

IN order to conform to the law of this state, which takes effect this day, the business of FISH, GRINNELL

immediately put on the cover of a new catalogue then on press. It soon became the best-known imprint in American publishing.

"Travels sell about the best of anything we get ahold of," James Harper said in 1836. He had seen many travel stories in press, includ-

ing the first Harper ghostwritten book, published four years earlier—
A Narrative of Four Voyages, etc. by Captain Benjamin Morrell, Jr.,
the first man to sail south of the Antarctic Circle (in a 175-ton schooner)
and the first white man to be seen by many South Sea Islanders. But
Harper was probably thinking of the *Voyage of the U.S. Frigate
Potomac,* by John N. Reynolds, which had just been published. Reynolds,
who had a scientific interest in the earth's structure, went with Com-
modore John Downes in 1831-34 on the frigate *Potomac,* which was the
first American vessel to circumnavigate the globe. Thus Reynolds'
well-written book appealed to all patriotic Americans and was one
of the most widely reviewed and discussed books of the decade.

Books of fiction in the thirties were highlighted with several novels
by Simms, Catherine M. Sedgwick (called the "Miss Edgeworth of
America," after the widely read Irish novelist Maria Edgeworth), and
two by an aristocratic young Englishman, then living in New York,
named Henry William Herbert. But Herbert was lost to the firm
through one of James Harper's practical jokes. In 1838, William L.
Mackenzie, who had led an unsuccessful revolt to form a republican
government in Canada, was in New York and called on the Harpers
to talk over his indebtedness, since, as a Toronto bookseller, he owed
them several hundred dollars. During his visit the royalist Herbert
walked in, full of the forthcoming coronation of Queen Victoria, and
Harper, with a wink to Mackenzie, introduced the Canadian as a *loyal*
legislator from across the border. Mackenzie, delighted with the sub-
terfuge, talked at length with Herbert about the folly of the Canadian
rebels and how best to capture them and send them home for the
rewards that could be had. After Mackenzie left, Harper laughingly
identified his visitor. But this was no joking matter for Herbert. He left
the office using words he never dared put in a book and declared that
James Harper and none of his brothers would ever see his face or a line
of manuscript there again. This horseplay lost the Harpers a profitable
author; under the pseudonym of Frank Forster, Herbert wrote a series
of sporting books that are collectors' items and still read.

As the Harpers' list expanded, with an increasing number of works
by native authors, so did their efforts to promote their books. While it

MAJOR DOWNING'S
LETTERS.

(Fac-Simile.)

Andrew Jackson

(as seen through the "glorification" Spectacles.)

PUBLISHED BY HARPER & BROTHERS,
NO. 82 CLIFF-STREET.

Title page and frontispiece of Major Downing's Letters, *a satire on General Jackson and Martin Van Buren which was an 1834 best seller, the demand being so great that the binders*

were unable to keep up with the printers. The author, Charles
Augustus Davis, patterned his book after the "Jack Downing"
letters of the popular Seba Smith of Maine.

is known that one salesman was employed in 1833, the Harpers largely depended, as did all publishers until the middle of the eighteen-seventies, on semiannual book auctions to funnel their new books to booksellers. The auctions were known as Trade Sales and were for the most part held in New York and Philadelphia. To these publishing centers booksellers came first by stagecoach and steamboat, and later "by the rails," to bid in their stock of new books. The auctioneer supplied large quarto-sized catalogues in which publishers listed their new titles. Each title was sold in lots—say, ten copies—and the highest bid for a lot established the book's wholesale price. After the successful bidder had taken as many lots as he wished other booksellers followed suit.

Selling books by mail was equally important, since many dealers could not attend the auctions. The Harpers kept adding new accounts as book outlets increased to serve the population, which by 1840 had doubled since the brothers started in business. "Clinton's big ditch," completed in 1825, had, within ten years, canal connections to the Ohio River, so that side-wheelers and canal boats could carry printed matter more quickly and at less cost than the stagecoach. Even so, the stagecoach was still important, especially during winters when waterways froze over, and during the thirties the National Pike was extended westward into Indiana. Thus to dealers, agents, and colporteurs the Harpers mailed letters and catalogues and, receiving orders in return, sent boxes of books to far distant parts. They particularly had their eyes on Cincinnati, where two of their employees, J. A. and U. P. James, had gone in 1831 to open a publishing and bookselling enterprise that has continued to this day. The Harpers were also exporting books, shipping them as far as India, where Henry T. Hall, of Calcutta, was their agent.

Selling books to the trade has to be backed up by publicity to the reading public. The early Harpers bore down hard on newspaper editors to get them to print news about books and authors. Many newspaper editors, like Bryant and Greeley, were men of literary interests and gave space to "puffs" of books as well as to reviews. The Harpers flooded reviewers with letters about their books. In December,

1835, Edgar Allan Poe reviewed a novel by Theodore Sedgwick Fay, saying, "Well!—here we have it! This is *the* book . . . 'attributed to' Mr. Blank, and 'said to be from the pen' of Mr. Asterisk: the book which has been 'about to appear'—'in press'—'in progress'—'in preparation'—and 'forthcoming': the book 'graphic' in anticipation—'talented' *a priori*—and God knows what *in prospectu.* . . ." Unless Poe was exaggerating, the Harpers had sent nine letters to the *Southern Literary Messenger* to arouse prepublication interest.

Such sales and promotion enterprise brought them authors: W. C. Bryant with a new edition of his poems in 1836 and Edgar Allan Poe with a collection of short stories (which was declined); Richard H. Dana, Sr., with his son's seafaring "Journal" (later published as *Two Years Before the Mast*) and Washington Irving with a biography of Oliver Goldsmith. This enterprise also brought a return tide of publicity. Newspapers and magazines found the Harper success story good copy. The *American Monthly* said that they were bringing about a literary revolution in the country, and Horace Greeley wrote in the *New Yorker* that the firm's integrity was as unimpeachable as its credit. Because he was the eldest brother and the most approachable and talkative, James Harper was often singled out by reporters, and when the Book-sellers' Association dinner was held at the City Hotel on March 30, 1837, he was called on to make the most important toast (which he did with a glass of water). This was the second banquet of the century for authors, booksellers, and publishers—with no ladies invited. Fletcher Harper also acted as a toastmaster, and the brothers were so often mentioned that Dr. John W. Francis, one of the city's most respected citizens, remembered the affair, when he wrote his autobiography thirty years later, as "Harper's book entertainment."

A devastating financial panic hit the country in the spring of 1837, following in the wake of the depression of 1833-34. The earlier economic setback had hardly affected the Cliff Street operation, and the Buffalo *Literary Inquirer* had said then, "These everlasting Harpers seem absolutely beyond the influence of all ordinary courses. The iron pressure that crushes the community has no perceptible effect on the presses of Cliff Street. Banks may stop—merchants break—commerce

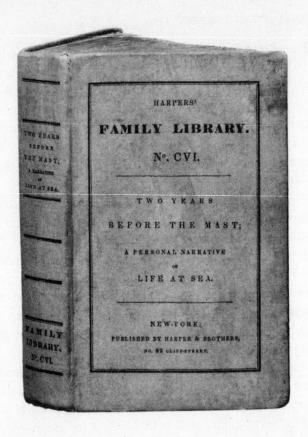

Two Years Before the Mast, *by Richard H. Dana, Jr., was published in September, 1840. It would have appeared a year earlier, but the Harper offer, in June, 1839, of a 10 per cent royalty after one thousand copies had been sold, was turned down by Dana senior, who wanted something better for his son, even though he preferred wide sales over big profits. Dana's* Journal, *as it was then called, was read by four other publishers that summer and rejected, probably because business conditions were deteriorating. The following January, Dana senior and his friend Bryant called on the brothers to ask them to reconsider publishing the* Journal. *The Harpers replied that with the trade so depressed they would not now risk a royalty contract, but they would take it on as a School District Library book if Albany approved. Bryant assured them that nothing in it could be found objectionable so the bargaining began. Harper's said they would pay $200 for the manuscript, the same amount they were paying other first authors. To be sure, it was little enough, but it was less than they could expect*

as profit on a School District Library book. Dana and Bryant argued that this was not just another such book but a work that would have a wide popular sale; furthermore the House had done extremely well with volumes of travel. Bryant proposed $500 and later he and the elder Dana came down to $300. Finally the Harpers made a counterproposal of $250, which was accepted by the author's father, who left Cliff Street disgusted with such haggling.

After reading proofs of the School District Library edition of his book, Dana junior wrote requesting a larger format for the trade edition—12 mo instead of the small 18 mo which was standard both for the School District Library and Harper's Family Library. But the Harpers were shy about investing in another set of plates. After consulting with Bryant and other "judicious friends," they made a counterproposal to Dana that his book should also be put in the Harper's Family Library. On August 20th, twelve days before the book was copyrighted, Wesley Harper wrote, "It will be quite as respectable, and certainly much more serviceable to you published in this shape than any other, inasmuch as it will take it, forthwith, before five times the ordinary number of readers. The volume, to be sure, will not be as handsome as it would be if published independently —but the price will not be more than half—and in these times especially, the cost of an article, we find, is an important consideration with all classes of the community." By the "ordinary number" Harper meant one thousand copies, then the usual size of a first printing. Thus it seems likely that Two Years Before the Mast appeared in printings of 1,250 in the School District Library and 5,000 in the Harper's Family Library.

Two Years Before the Mast was an immediate success. It was praised by reviewers, including Bryant, who gave two big puffs to the book, although one heckler wrote that Dana (just starting the practice of law in Boston) had written the book to attract clients. With an unexpected best seller on their hands, the Harpers had to eat sour pickles along with the sweet, for they were being widely criticized for buying so fine a book so cheap. Fletcher Harper wrote Dana seven months after publication to say that the papers were magnifying sales and profits, and that they had cleared to date less than paid to him. Yet the book must have earned many thousands of dollars for them until 1868, when the copyright reverted to the author. No one will ever know how many copies have been sold. The Harpers never told, saying their records were lost in the 1853 fire. That fire also destroyed Dana's letters and copies of the first two editions, if they had been saved. Recently the House purchased a first-edition copy, paying for the one copy more than twice what was paid Dana in 1840.

turn upside down—yet they still remain undaunted and unannoyed at their post, as caterers general to the literary world." But the 1837 catastrophe hit them hard. They cut back drastically on new titles, eagerly took on outside printing work to keep their plant going, and put off decisions on important books. They promised Dolley Madison in 1838 and again in 1840 that they would publish a volume of the late President Madison's papers. They held the manuscript a year hoping that times would get better and trying without success to get her to agree to publish with an equal division of profits, rather than an outright sum which she held out for.

The 1837 panic and the depression years that followed taught the brothers a sound financial lesson. As they saw fellow publishers failing, they determined that forever after they would closely watch the business thermometer. When times were bad they quickly retrenched, and when times were good they plunged ahead with alacrity. This business fixation, combined with a natural desire to hold on to a good publishing idea, got them bad publicity at times. They were said to be "famous for talking away off" by the literati, who could hardly appreciate John Harper's comment that to a merchant the commodity in which he deals is also merchandise.

What got the Cliff Street firm off the financial rocks was Harper's School District Library. During the mid-thirties school districts in New York state began assembling books for circulating among their schools, and by 1838 the Harpers had assembled a boxed set of fifty volumes which sold for twenty dollars. The following year the New York state legislature passed a law that all school districts with a population of more than ten thousand should have libraries, with half the cost to come out of state funds. Largely responsible for this action was Thurlow Weed, editor of the Albany *Evening Journal* and a leading Whig politician. Weed had worked side by side with James Harper when they were young journeymen printers, and the friendship begun then was life long. Obviously Weed was the man to speak a good word for the Harpers when they decided to go after the state business. This he was glad to do and introduced Fletcher Harper to John C. Spencer, who, as Secretary of State and Superintendent of Common Schools, had the final decision on what books were to be recommended to the school

This New England School Library was probably assembled in 1843, although most of the titles were printed the preceding year. The Library was shipped in its self-contained, 19x29-inch, pine-board cabinet, which was fitted with shelves, a lock and key, and a top piece which could be nailed to a schoolroom wall. When this cabinet and its contents were recently found in the attic of a Connecticut house, only four of the seventy-five half-leather gold-stamped volumes were missing.

districts. Fletcher Harper convinced Spencer that he and his brothers could obtain and supply the necessary books and offer them at a price satisfactory to Spencer. Harper left Albany with a commission in his pocket. That trip not only records the first "state adoption" known but also shows the importance of a sales trip. Later Spencer told Weed that Fletcher Harper was the most charming young man he had ever met.

The School District Library was continued through 1845-46, when a sixth and last series was issued. A total of 212 titles and 295 volumes were distributed by the thousands through the Empire state and to all the other states and territories. Most of the books were bound in cloth, priced at thirty-eight cents a copy, and sold to schools at from thirty to thirty-three cents a copy.

3

FROM POVERTY TO RICHES (1840-49)

"All our publishers, whether of books or periodicals, are desperately poor," a Harper author, Epes Sargent, wrote Longfellow in December, 1839. But business improved somewhat, at least for the Cliff Street brothers, during the latter part of 1840 through 1841. Then came the worst year of their history. In 1842 only thirty-six new books were issued. A work would be announced as in press and not appear until months later. They were kept in business by their two libraries and a growing series of classical textbooks by Professor Charles Anthon, of Columbia University. There were a few bright spots, all nonfiction: Dana's *Two Years Before the Mast*, Longstreet's *Georgia Scenes*, Stephens' *Central America*, and the first volumes in a series of *Notes* on New Testament books by Albert Barnes, of Philadelphia.

Hardly any new fiction was published during these three years because of the frightening challenge flung to all book publishers by the so-called "mammoth weeklies," *Brother Jonathan* and the *New World* in New York, and by large quarto supplements to several newspapers. The "mammoths" contained whole novels, mostly English reprints, and were sold as low as twelve and a half cents a copy. This competition, along with the business depression, forced some book publishers into bankruptcy. For the Harpers it was a call to warfare.

The start of this war can be dated—June 1, 1842. Early in the morning of that day someone from the *New World*, published by Jonas Win-

City Hall as depicted in a painting made in the decade in which James Harper was Mayor.

chester, broke into the Harper bindery to steal a copy of a new novel by
G. P. R. James, which the Harpers had set from early English proofs and
were hurrying to publish. On his way out the burglar set the place on
fire, and before the firemen arrived flames had spread throughout the
bindery, which was crowded into the top floors of 82 Cliff Street. All
bound stock was burned or damaged by water and some important bookkeeping records were destroyed. Insurance payments of forty-five thousand dollars enabled them to rebuild, replace machinery, and have funds
for a spirited retaliation. The Harpers immediately started their Library
of Select Novels, paperbacks priced at twenty-five cents each. In six
months they issued twelve—all at a loss. Their rivals struck again on
Christmas Day, this time to steal a copy of Bulwer's *The Last of the
Barons*, for which the Harper's had paid nearly a thousand dollars.

The most effective weapon of counterattack was nonfiction reprints
issued serially in numbers. One of the most popular was Alison's
History of Europe (1789-1815); each of its sixteen numbers ran to one
hundred and fifty pages and sold for a quarter. Lieutenant Matthew F.
Maury, then editor of the *Southern Literary Messenger,* called these
Harper efforts a public-spirited enterprise fraught with incalculable public and national advantages.

Also to fight the cause of the book and the bookseller against the
mammoth weeklies, the price of the Family Library was brought down
to twenty-five cents a volume. *Brother Jonathan* sneered at such competition by comparing the Harper enterprise to the smart fellow who turned
his money quick by purchasing apples at two for threepence and selling
them at three for twopence. A year later the same paper was complaining
that literature was a drug on the market. One reason for such despond-
ency was the April, 1843, directive from the Post Office Department that
the mammoth sheets should pay postage at book rates. That action, perhaps helped along by Fletcher Harper's taking a trip to Washington,
soon killed off the newspaper competition.

The practice of publishing new books in large paper-cover octavos
called "numbers" could not be applied to the Harpers' biggest project
of 1843, the abridged edition of Webster's Dictionary, edited by
Chauncey A. Goodrich, Noah Webster's son-in-law. It was launched that
autumn at the thirty-eighth New York Trade Sale in the unbelievably

Home of Mayor James Harper, 4 Gramercy Park. Still standing before the house are the two lamps which traditionally marked the residence of the city's chief magistrate.

large lots—for a $3.50 book—of one hundred and fifty copies. Ten years later the sales were estimated at 250,000. But it was too good to last. In 1856 the G. & C. Merriam Company, publishers of the un-abridged Webster, took over the copyright and the Harper plates of the lately revised abridged edition.

Webster's Dictionary and two other books marked the return of good times and the return of the Harpers to their main business of publishing clothbound books. First there was John L. Stephens' *Incidents of Travel in Yucatan*. This remarkable book (recently popularized in Ceram's *Gods, Graves, and Scholars*) was the author's fourth Harper title. On his earlier three his earnings had exceeded thirty thousand dollars, as had the Harpers', since the Stephens contracts called for an equal division of the profits. *Yucatan* was the first important book to be illustrated by benefit of camera. Not that halftones were used—they came nearly a half century later—but before Stephens departed for Yucatan in 1841, he and his associate, Frederick Catherwood, learned photography from Professor John W. Draper, of the University of the City of New York, who had made the first photograph of a human face by a relatively short exposure of a sensitive plate. The trip cost Stephens and Catherwood $5,707, half of which the Harpers paid. They brought back a lot of daguerreotypes, which enabled Catherwood to check his drawings of artifacts, the most exact that had ever appeared in an archeological work. Stephens and Catherwood aroused tremendous interest in pre-Columbian civilization and Stephens has been called the father of Mayan archeology.

The second noteworthy book of the year, following Webster's Dictionary, was William H. Prescott's *Conquest of Mexico*. In fact, this book was brought to the Harpers by Stephens, who, when he sent a complimentary copy of his new book to Prescott, the nearly blind Boston historian, urged that Prescott's new book be published in New York. He thought that the Harpers would effect larger sales than any other house because of their capital and business connections and their principle of small profits and large sales. He wrote that he had spoken to the brothers about Prescott and found them eager for an introduction, saying that with Prescott, Stephens, and Professor Anthon they would have the three best American authors available. The success-

An indenture for a bindery apprentice dated January 18, 1844. Between 1836 and 1848 Mr. and Mrs. Fletcher Harper lived in four different houses on Cliff Street and during this period made a home for some of the firm's apprentices.

ful publication of *The Conquest of Mexico* led to the Harpers' taking over Prescott's earlier work, *Ferdinand and Isabella,* and publishing his *Miscellanies* and *The Conquest of Peru.* In 1854 Prescott received a better offer from a Boston publisher than from the Harpers for his *Philip the Second,* accepted it, and wrote the brothers that he could never forget their long and pleasant relations in which the good understanding that should subsist between author and publisher had not once been interrupted. He said every year of their association had confirmed the opinion he had early formed of the high and honorable character of the house.

This opinion of the "honorable character" of the partners was shared almost universally. It was the chief reason that James Harper was elected mayor of New York in April, 1844. The public had been aroused by the blatant corruption and irresponsibility of both the Whig and the Democratic parties and was looking for a distinguished citizen who could clean up the mess. The American Republican Party, organized in 1843 to restore native-born Protestant-American control of the city government, shrewdly capitalized on this discontent, obtained Harper's consent to be its candidate, and elected him on the pledge of an efficient police force, economy in public expenditures, reduction of taxes, and cleaner streets. The *Morning Courier* and the New York *Inquirer* expressed the general belief that the American Republicans won because of the great personal authority of Harper and the public's desire for a city government that would consult the welfare and promote the interests of the city. His year as a reform mayor, the first in the city's history, was devoted to carrying out the party's pledges, though he disappointed its sometimes fanatical leadership by refusing to take an anti-Catholic position regarding city employees. Because of his personal popularity he might have been re-elected for another year on the Whig ticket, as many urged, but even the Whigs were defeated and Tammany Hall regained control of the city government. Harper was later urged to be a Whig candidate for Congress but refused, although a letter he wrote Thurlow Weed shows that he might have accepted the party's nomination for governor. Even so, his unwillingness to compromise his integrity, his strong temperance principles, and his lack of platform ability did not make him a good candidate for public office.

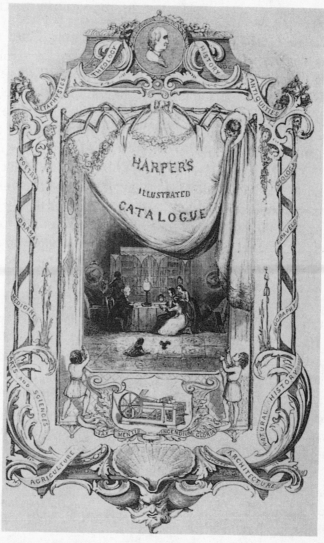

The title page used in Harper catalogues for 1847 and 1848 is dominated by a drawing of a family gathered around a library table. This family motif runs throughout Harper publishing in the nineteenth century, from the beginning of Family Library in 1830 to their admonition to Thomas Hardy in 1894 that Harper's Magazine must contain nothing which could not be read aloud in a family circle. The bust of Benjamin Franklin which tops the engraving testifies to the inspiration that led young James Harper to decide on a career as a printer, and it also appears in the portrait of him which hangs in City Hall, New York.

Shortly after he moved into City Hall, Harper was waited on by a delegation of lady officers of the Martha Washington Temperance Society. It so happened that George Wilkins Kendall, editor of the New Orleans *Picayune,* was in town for the publication of a new book and walked over from Cliff Street to pay his respects to the Mayor. After waiting awhile for the ladies to leave, Kendall decided that His Honor should be rescued, and barged in. "Come, Harper," he drawled, "let's go out and have *another* drink—it's 'leven o'clock. Ain't *you* dry ag'in? *I* am!" The ladies arose, bade the Mayor good morning, and with intemperate glances at Kendall marched out of the room. Kendall's new book, *Narrative of the Texan Santa Fé Expedition,* contained such a graphic description of the cruelty of the Mexicans who captured him and his party and marched them to Mexico City for imprisonment that the book has been called the "Uncle Tom's Cabin" of the Mexican War. A year after publication the book came out in a fourth edition, slightly revised, and soon reached a sale of forty thousand copies.

After Harper's Family Library had grown to one hundred and thirty-one titles, the series was ended and a new one—the New Miscellany—was begun in 1845. Charles Darwin's two-volume *Voyage of the Beagle* was one of the most important works issued, but from the point of view of Harperiana the most interesting is the lead title, *Elements of Morality and Polity,* by William Whewell, Master of Trinity College, Cambridge. The title page carried a vignette, drawn for the author, showing a hand passing a flaming torch to a waiting hand. This drawing, with its Greek inscription, impressed the brothers and they adopted it as the House colophon, for each of them had one or more sons who would soon be carrying the torch for them.

One of the many versions of the Harper colophon, inspired by William Whewell, with the inscription, "Holding torches, they will pass them on one to another."

At left, the original establishment at 82 Cliff Street, in 1825. At right, 82 Cliff Street (with open bulkheads) is shown after the top floors were rebuilt following the fire of June 1, 1842. By 1853 the Harpers were using the two adjacent buildings, two on the opposite side of Cliff Street, and four on Pearl Street, backing up 82 Cliff Street.

In 1843 Joseph A. Adams contracted with Harper's to make wood engravings for a large family Bible, working mainly from drawings by the artist John G. Chapman. The contract stipulated that Adams should have complete supervision of the printing and one-half of the profits from sales.

Four years earlier, Adams, concerned that his wood engravings were damaged in press runs, worked out a process whereby a copper shell could be built up for border engravings by passing an electric current, activated by batteries, through a copper solution to wax molds. Adams was thus able to find protection and support for the borders of his engravings and in doing so he discovered the process of electrotyping. Now he was concerned to get as nearly perfect a printing job as was possible and had gone to the Harpers partially because they were operating a two-roller, self-flying press recently invented by Isaac Adams of Boston. When the first form was made up, containing pages of stereotyped text and engravings, Adams took off his coat, rolled up his sleeves and began printing impressions. After each one he corrected the "overlay" of the engravings, cutting here, building up there. Hour after hour, day after day, he scraped and

---

One of sixteen hundred wood engravings made by Joseph A. Adams for Harper's Illuminated and New Pictorial Bible

rubbed, but without tangible results. The pressmen were amused and the four brothers were perturbed that an expensive press should stand idle while work piled up.

After laboring over that first form for two weeks, Adams ordered the press started. As it began to throw off the most beautiful printing ever done in America the Messrs. Harpers' worries disappeared like mist before the rising sun. They immediately decided to merchandise this work as they had never done any other. They flooded newspapers, literary periodicals, and booksellers with publicity: the Adams Bible would be issued in numbers, each to contain twenty-eight pages, with hand-sewn sheets of the best-quality paper glued to elaborate covers printed in two colors; there would be fifty-four numbers, in editions of 50,000 each, and the numbers would retail at twenty-five cents a copy. And before the first number was issued, early in 1844, nearly every American who could read knew that Harper's had ordered large new presses with which to print the lavish Bible. To satisfy the perfectionist engraver, Isaac Adams designed a six-roller press, and six of these were sent to Cliff Street for the final runs of the numbers and for a 25,000-copy edition of the Bible itself, which appeared in morocco-bound, hand-tooled, gold-embossed, and gilt-edged splendor early in 1846. It has been called the first richly illustrated book in the United States and the first attempt here to produce a fine piece of bookmaking.

Adams retired on his share of the profits, knowing that he had started a reformation of typographic art in America. The Harpers put up a new building.

In or about 1847 the Harpers lost two important authors who would have added great distinction to their imprint. One was Washington Irving. When Irving returned to New York in 1846, after serving as Minister to Spain for four years, he found that his early books, including *The Sketch Book,* were out of print. They had been published from Philadelphia by Lea & Blanchard, and when Irving talked with them about new editions, they not only refused but almost convinced him that the public had lost interest in his writings. (His fellow Knickerbocker, James Kirke Paulding, published by the Harpers, was considered passé.) Even so, Irving then went to Cliff Street to inquire of the brothers whether they would reissue his older titles along with two they controlled, short biographies of Goldsmith and Columbus. The gentle

Irving said what he really wanted was a uniform edition. The Harpers replied that they would be honored to reissue his works but were doubtful about a uniform edition. How about putting all his writings in one or two large octavos? That was the format now popular with American readers; and they showed him the ponderous volumes of Alison's *History*. But Irving did not care for two-column octavos; he left in disappointment and went to call on George P. Putnam, who was just starting up in business for himself. Putnam was prepared to risk a uniform edition and in doing so may have kept Irving from the literary oblivion that shadowed the careers of several mid-century writers. In ten years Putnam sold 575,000 volumes and paid Washington Irving royalties of $76,000.

The other Harper loss was an author more prestigious today than he was a century ago—Henry David Thoreau. In 1847 the brothers offered to publish *A Week on the Concord and Merrimack Rivers* if Thoreau would underwrite the costs. This he declined to do, but when the manuscript was rejected by several other publishers, including the Putnam firm, it was issued in Boston in 1849 on the Harper formula. Years later Thoreau had to take unsold copies—three-fourths of the edition—and wrote humorously of his large library, made up mostly of books he had himself written.

The Harpers were also having their problems about keeping stock of slow sellers. Once, in an exchange of letters with Prescott, Fletcher Harper wrote that nearly a block of storehouses were required to maintain a decent supply of each of their titles, much less than would be required if most books sold as well as Prescott's. At the end of the decade they were occupying seven five-story buildings. Nineteen power presses, besides hand presses, were printing approximately two million volumes, including pamphlets, a year. Moreover, their employees numbered nearly three hundred and fifty. They had at that time an establishment that in the numerical strength of its operation outranked any other publishing house in the world.

4

THE NEW START ON FRANKLIN SQUARE (1850-59)

The mid-nineteenth century was for Americans an exciting period of expansion. That mood had elected President Polk in 1844 and was furthered by a steady rise in the business cycle. It was strengthened by the purchase in 1848 of the New Mexico and California territories and dramatized by the forty-niners who hurried Westward for gold. But it was best exemplified in the spreading network of railroads. In 1850 there were nearly nine thousand miles of rails along the Eastern seaboard and reaching their steel arms Westward. By 1861, at the outbreak of the Civil War, railroad mileage had more than tripled and a network of tracks crossed the Alleghenies and extended to the Mississippi and beyond. A tremendous cultural development followed the railroads, for people got books and periodicals more quickly than they had been accustomed to—and at less expense because of the cheap postage law of 1851. The number of booksellers increased and young and venturesome bookmen moved Westward with the population. Charles B. Norton started a *Literary Gazette,* the first successful effort to issue a book-trade journal. In 1850 there were over twenty-three million Americans—destined to increase by over 35 per cent in ten years. And Americans were told that they were the most literate people in the world.

Many of them were reading *Harper's New Monthly Magazine,* which

Portrait of Herman Melville by Joseph Oriel Eaton.

	Costs of Plates	No. printed	No sold	Rißm England	½ profits	Total
Typee	378.52	8000	7437	$708.40	937.74	1646.14
Omoo	351.75	6500	5649	644 —	1237.50	1881.50
Mardi	564.75	3000	2291	970.65	402.25	1372.90
Redburn	279.75	4508	3695	484 —	401.36	885.36
Whitejacket	412.50	4354	3714	968 —	612.36	1580.36
Up to April 29th 1851 —				$3775.05	$3591.21	7366.26
Moby Dick	572.76	2915		703.08		703.08
				447813		$8069.34
						500
						8569.34

A memorandum drafted by Allan Melville giving publishing data on the books of his brother, Herman Melville. Moby Dick was published November 14, 1851, and when Allan Melville added that title to his list he could show no Harper earnings because Harper advances to Herman Melville then exceeded his half-profit earnings.

beginning in June, 1850, was sent out monthly across the nation. On the early covers were three gay cherubs that Benson J. Lossing drew, cherubs that he had found gracing the interior of George Washington's coach. In 1850 General Washington and the Revolutionary War were more real to Lossing than the new magazine, for he had spent two years and traveled nine thousand miles, mostly on horseback, visiting Revolutionary battlefields and studying documents and interviewing old soldiers. This trip was financed by the Harpers, who began getting their money back as they issued the *Pictorial Field-Book of the Revolution* in numbers, and later in two volumes. The text was profusely illustrated with Lossing's own drawings, many of which he also engraved on wood, and the whole job was so well done that it received scholarly approval then and is respected by antiquarians today. Because of Lossing's interest in George Washington, *Harper's Magazine* sent him to Arlington to do an illustrated article on the aging George Washington

Parke Custis, the first President's adopted son. It makes fascinating reading.

The most important piece of Americana in those early issues appeared in October, 1851 (anyone owning a copy should hold on to it). This piece was a chapter from Herman Melville's *Moby Dick*, published a few weeks later. It was issued simply as a book by the author of *Typee, Omoo, Mardi, Redburn,* and *White-Jacket.* Neither the Harpers nor anyone else knew that the classic of American fiction was being published. It is a paradox of literature that *Moby Dick* had to wait—despite being almost constantly in print—until the present century to be recognized for what it is. Melville was for many years indebted to the Harpers because of unearned advances on his books and for book purchases.

Moby Dick and all other new fiction was overshadowed when *Uncle Tom's Cabin* was published by John P. Jewett in Boston the following March. It was America's first big fiction success, with one hundred thousand sold the first year, but the English did ten times as well with more than a dozen cheap, pirated editions, bringing Mrs. Stowe fame but not fortune. It seems likely that the Harpers could have had the book, but they were opposed to the abolitionists and they would not have risked offending their Southern authors and booksellers. They soon sold the plates of Mrs. Stowe's earlier book, *The Mayflower,* to Jewett, but continued to promote her sister Catharine Beecher's book, adding two more in 1855.

The name of George W. Curtis towers above all others who were important to the Harpers in the eighteen-fifties. He gave them several books, contributed to early issues of *Harper's Magazine* and later gave his whole time to Harper periodicals. His first two books of travel were written under the pseudonym of "Howadji," the Arabic word for traveler, and were widely read. At that time nearly every publisher could boast of best sellers, for business was booming. Two new buildings went up on Pearl Street, to back up those on Cliff Street, and the counting room was moved into one of them. New presses were purchased and by December, 1853, forty-one of them were turning out an average of twenty-five volumes a minute, ten hours a day, six days a week. Annual income from sales was estimated at two million dollars, a gigantic figure for those days and, as one commentator put it, a "fresh cause for wondering and imagining." Also a cause for pride. And pride, it is said, goes before a fall. Aldous Huxley liked to put the axiom more elegantly, quoting the Greeks: *hubris* is always followed by *nemesis*.

The Harper nemesis had always been fire. Despite precautions, more determined each time, there had been four before the great conflagration of December 10, 1853. Early that Saturday afternoon a pan of camphine, used for cleaning printing plates, was accidentally ignited, and flames quickly spread throughout the complex of buildings. No lives were lost, partly because of the heroic action of Peter Rosenquest, head of the bindery, where many women were at work. But the establishment itself was reduced to water-soaked ashes, except for some contracts and business papers and plates valued at $400,000 that were stored in subterranean vaults. Losses exceeded one million dollars, with less than 20 per cent recovered from insurance. The Harpers were largely self-insured, because their intercommunicating buildings and large stocks of books and paper made insurance rates extremely high.

Before nightfall they had decided to rebuild. At first the fire seemed a heaven-sent opportunity to give up business, for they were abundantly rich. They had, in fact, never let their children know how well-off they were, Wesley Harper once remarked, for fear of spoiling their lives. However, their sons were now working their way into positions of leadership and should not be denied careers of their own. This argument, plus responsibilities to authors and magazine subscribers, led to their decision to carry on. The decision announced, telegrams began piling up offering sympathy and encouragement and even financial aid. Plans were immediately made and executed. Copy for the January *Harper's*, on the press when the fire started, was rewritten, and outside printing arrangements were made for it and for the eventual issue of the backlist and of new titles.

Eighteen months later, in the summer of 1855, the Harper phoenix had risen from the ashes in the form of two fireproof buildings. Since they opened onto Franklin Square (named for a merchant, not the statesman), this square was made the firm's address, and it was identified with the Harper operation for seventy years. Visitors flocked to see the new establishment, which became one of the sights of the city. The first and

The Franklin Square and Cliff Street buildings

The two new Harper buildings were the first large commercial buildings to make skeletal use of wrought-iron columns and supporting trusses, since the process of rolling wrought-iron beams with flanges had only recently been made possible by Peter Cooper at the Trenton (N.J.) Iron Works. John B. Corliss was the architect-builder but most of the architectural detail was planned by John Harper, who even figured exactly the number of bricks required. The manufactory was for the most part placed in the Cliff Street building (extreme right, top). The Franklin Square building housed the counting room and the partners' offices, the editorial rooms, and the artists' and engravers' quarters, with several floors devoted to warehousing. Along the top of the Franklin Square façade, between the twenty windows of the top floor, they placed statues of Washington, Franklin, and Jefferson, and over the large main entrance a large statute of Franklin.

A view of Cliff Street showing the front elevation of the manufactory (right) and a bridge leading to a building on the west side of the street which was used mainly for storage. The New York approach to the Brooklyn Bridge is depicted in this wash drawing by W. A. Rogers. Constructed of metal and brick, the buildings not only were fireproof but also embodied important architectural implications for the future. They were functional in the best twentieth-century aesthetic sense, and were constructed at a nineteenth-century cost of $350,000.

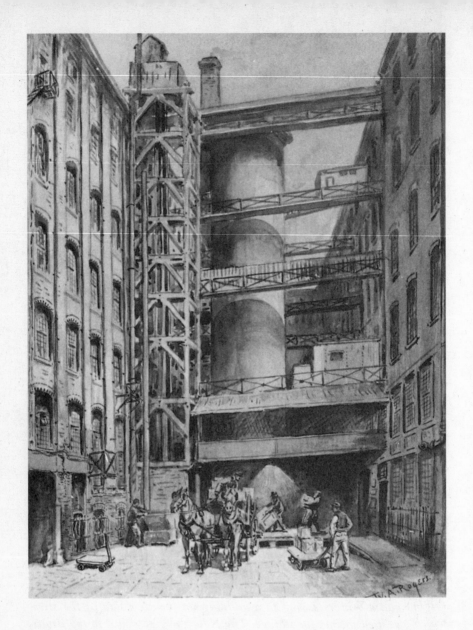

A view of the twenty-eight-foot courtyard which separated the two buildings. Alongside the Cliff Street building (left) a hoist, or elevator, raised or
lowered equipment and materials. The courtyard was dominated by a brick
tower which enclosed a spiral iron stairway. At each floor level a door from
this tower opened onto an iron landing, which in turn connected with
bridges and was the only means of entry to floors above the first. It was not
a fire escape, but a fire preventive, since it made possible the sealing-off of
each floor from those above and below.

The interior view of this stairway, also drawn by W. A. Rogers, shows what were often called "steps to fame," up which walked authors such as Henry James, Mark Twain, and William Dean Howells, and artists such as Winslow Homer, Edwin A. Abbey and Howard Pyle.

most complete of several visitors' guides, *The Harper Establishment*, was dashed off by the agile-fingered Jacob Abbott.

One distinguished visitor was the New Yorker Dr. Edwin H. Chapin, popular lecturer and minister of the Church of the Divine Paternity. He was shown through the establishment on September 27th and that same evening made his visit the basis of an address (one of the most eloquent Horace Greeley said he had ever heard) before authors, booksellers, and publishers at a banquet sponsored by the newly organized Publishers' Association. This, the third such affair of the century, was held in the Crystal Palace, a new trade exposition center, built on what is now Bryant Park at Forty-second Street. Ladies were invited this time, thirsts were quenched only by pure Croton water, and the menu and table decorations emphasized fruits—hence its name, "Complimentary Fruit Festival."

The Publishers' Association had been organized the preceding April, largely to reorganize the Trade Sales. But the venture had little encouragement from the Harpers, because they were all for the status quo. The controversy was fully debated that autumn in the *American Publishers' Circular*, which the Association was sponsoring as a continuation of *Norton's Literary Gazette*. The point at issue was whether the publishers' offerings should be limited in the quantity of any one given title offered, or continued, as before, on an unrestricted basis. Logic was on the side of the Association, which wanted a "true auction," but sales were on the Harpers' side. As a result, the Harpers held a separate auction that autumn and for a few seasons thereafter, until everyone agreed that sales were more important than proprieties.

In the late fifties the big books from Franklin Square that reached the trade included several historical works: a revised edition of Richard Hildreth's *History of the United States*, George Bancroft's *Literary and Historical Miscellanies*, John L. Motley's *The Rise of the Dutch Republic*, and the three concluding volumes of Macaulay's *History of England*, the first printing of which required forty tons of paper, with 73,000 volumes in three editions sold in the first ten days. One of the most seminal books of the time was brought to them in manuscript by their old friend Lieutenant Matthew F. Maury. Entitled *The Physical Geography of the*

Sea, it was the first scientific work on oceanography, soon in its eighth and revised edition.

Harper's Weekly, under Fletcher Harper's direction, saw the New Year, 1857, off to a good start and managed to survive the panic that swept the country that autumn. However, Franklin Square was put under extreme pressure and, lacking $100,000 in ready funds early in October, the brothers sought temporary relief, until they could liquefy assets, through a court order assigning their business to two of their sons, John W. and Joseph W. Harper. With financial affairs at sixes and sevens, the cashier, William H. Demarest, finally persuaded John Harper to institute double-entry bookkeeping. Heretofore their bookkeeping had left much to be desired and was partly responsible in the forties for a long altercation with the novelist Theodore Sedgwick Fay and a short dispute with a Philadelphia bookseller. The Harpers won when the Fay charges of financial dishonesty were arbitrated but got only bad publicity from the bookseller, who was jailed for failure to pay his debts (a pleasant practice of those days). Able to produce receipted bills, the dealer was promptly released and the matter would have been forgotten had the haughty Harpers apologized. When they failed to do so he publicized the indignity, giving credibility to the account by identifying himself as G. G. Moore.

The 1857 panic was caused by the overexpansion of railroad credit and speculation in railroad stock, a situation that led Wesley Harper to say to a friend that it was indeed a wicked world. The *Weekly* editorialized: "All this must be paid for. No fault can escape retribution; and our extravagance, like our other sins, must have its penalty. What that penalty will be we shall know better when the present autumn draws to a close."

In its early years the *Weekly* was criticized for not taking definite stands on political issues, particularly because it was namby-pamby on the slavery question. But Fletcher Harper was convinced that his "Journal of Civilization" should stand for an undivided Union. Fortunately his private conviction was also then a good business judgment.

5

INTERNATIONAL COPYRIGHT

The most significant fact about American book publishing in the nineteenth century was that the rights of English and American authors were unprotected in each other's countries. Even though the British Parliament did for brief periods permit American books to be copyrighted in England if an author lived in England or Canada or had his books first published there, the century was characterized by literary piracy on both sides of the Atlantic; the British, on the whole, were the worst offenders, often garbling American books and ignoring authorships. The widespread circulation of English works at low prices sometimes discouraged American authors, and the claim was made that the lack of international copyright discouraged the rise of a significant American literature. On the other hand, the flood of cheap English reprints did encourage book-hungry Americans to read.

The first serious effort in America to establish international copyright was started in 1837. In that year memorials urging such copyright and signed both by English and American authors were submitted to Henry Clay, chairman of the Select Committee of the Senate. Clay prepared and offered a bill which Congress turned down, largely because it was opposed by papermakers, type founders, printers, and binders. This opposition by the graphic-arts industry, including the Harpers, was based on a belief that international copyright would greatly reduce book production and put a lot of men out of work. Furthermore, despite a high tariff—thirty cents a pound in the eighteen-forties—more English books would be imported. The resultant confusion between protection of authors' rights and protective tariff was unfortunate but understandable, because protective tariff had long been a leading political issue in Washington. In 1842 Charles Dickens made his first visit to America, largely in the interest of creating public opinion for international copyright. What he said was hooted down by the newspapers, but what he read from his books was welcomed by the public, who loved him and fêted him with large dinners.

During the period that the Harpers lost money competing with the mammoths, they were converted to international copyright, and Wesley Harper joined the American Copyright Club, of which Bryant was president. A Harper signature was on a petition that went to Congress in 1844. The brothers were unwilling to take a more public stand than this, fearing the reproach of inconsistency, and thus held a median position between the Philadelphia publishers, who were consistently against copyright, and such approving publishers as George Palmer Putnam, who had no investment in a manufactory or any employees with jobs that might be jeopardized.

In 1852 Mr. Edward Everett, then Secretary of State, influenced President Fillmore to seek international copyright through a treaty with Great Britain. Knowing that he would need to have the support of the country's leading publishers, Fillmore wrote to the Harpers asking for their views. This letter was answered so equivocally that nothing came of the treaty effort. The following year the cause was set back further when Henry Carey, former publisher and leading American economist, published a widely circulated pamphlet corralling all the arguments against international copyright. In 1858, in 1868, and again in 1871 favorable bills were brought before the Congress but nothing came of the efforts of the sponsors. The Harpers dissented on the ground that international copyright would increase book prices, thus interfering with the wide education of the American people, and that British authors were being compensated by generous payments for advance proofs of new works. (This position seems surprising since Fletcher Harper had publicly stated in 1862 that he was confident his pecuniary interests as a publisher would be benefited by international copyright.) While hopes for Congressional action were being met with failure, another effort to obtain agreement between Great Britain and America was launched in 1870. Sir Edward Thornton, the British Minister at Washington, called on the Harpers to read them a draft of a treaty proposed by Lord Clarendon. It was seen to be more in the interest of British publishers than of either British or American authors and failed to get Harper support—or American support elsewhere, for that matter.

In the meantime the old-line publishers, with their gentlemen's agreements and trade courtesies, were running into trouble from abroad—an influx of cheap English books into the American market. After the Civil War high taxes on several phases of book production resulted in a sharp rise in the cost of materials (paper doubled in price), and retail prices of books had to go up. This inflation did not hit England, where the cost of labor was lower, and soon English books were flooding the New York and Philadelphia markets. Early in 1866 *Harper's Weekly* ran an editorial, "No More American Books," attacking the Revenue Law which had jacked up manufacturing costs to three times what they were in Britain. While publishers were grumbling about this competition from across the Atlantic, they discovered that they had greater cause for distress from the Midwest. Donnelly, a Chicago publisher, started the Lakeside Library, in which he placed English reprints at even lower prices than the cheap imports, offering a $1.50 book for ten cents and a $4.00 book for twenty cents. Donnelly was followed by Munro, in New York, with a Seaside Library, and soon the literary fat was in the fire. The Harpers reacted by starting, in 1878, the Franklin Square Library, and were again losing money, as they had thirty-six years earlier when they started Harper's Library of Select Novels. They even "printed on" themselves in a frantic effort to force these American pirates out of business. This they failed to do, but they continued to publish cheap books at a loss to themselves in order to maintain their position as purveyors of literature to the nation. But what made the established publishers, particularly the Harpers, most angry was a sudden influx of cheap editions of their own copyrighted books from Canada. In 1877 the Canadians enacted a law which provided that books could be copyrighted by a person domiciled there or elsewhere in the British Empire, and by a citizen of a country which had an international-copyright treaty with Great Britain. Since American books were not thus copyrighted, some Canadian firms began manufacturing American best sellers and shipping them to booksellers across the border at extremely favorable prices. The Harpers found a way to stop that competition by court action, and in doing so they apparently carried the ball for the whole industry. They brought suit against any bookseller found selling Canadian editions of their copyrighted works. In the process they may have lost some friends in the book trade, but in every case they were sustained by the courts.

Obviously something had to be done about international copyright. One could not engage in battles over cheap books at home and abroad and still carry on one's normal business. In 1875 Joseph W. Harper added up what the firm had paid for early proofs of English reprints. The sum was £50,000 (nearly $250,000)—quite as large, he estimated, as had been paid American authors for their works, other than textbooks, all of which were copyrighted. Now this English money was water over the dam. Thinking that a copyright treaty was the only hope for future security, he wrote, in November, 1878, to Secretary of State Evarts, proposing that a treaty be drafted by a commission of eighteen American citizens and British subjects, the proper governmental agency in each country naming three authors, three publishers, and three publicists. During the following months this proposal was widely discussed in the press and in the *Publishers' Weekly,* successor to *Norton's Literary Gazette.* Most publishers supported it; however, no governmental action resulted. In 1880 President Hayes advanced hopes for a treaty by suggesting that American publishers draft one that they could all agree to. He spoke to his cousin William Dean Howells, who in turn wrote to the Harpers saying that if they would initiate the treaty it would receive general acceptance. A possible treaty was written, probably by George W. Curtis and Joseph W. Harper, and circulated among authors and publishers for approval. By November sixty-two authors and thirty-four publishers, including all the important names, had signed up.

What was known as the "Harper treaty" was the most discussed liter-

ary subject for months. Charles Dudley Warner said that the only hope
was a treaty, not legislation, because the House of Representatives was
"not so friendly to the literature of the land as to its steel trade." The
proposed treaty was sent to James R. Lowell, then Ambassador to the
Court of St. James's, who in turn submitted it to Lord Granville, the Foreign Secretary. Granville wrote Lowell in March, 1881, that the British
government would consent to negotiate on the basis of the draft. The
English copyright association approved the draft "as a basis suitable for
negotiation," and Curtis wrote in the May *Harper's Magazine* that prospects for international copyright were never fairer.

But the idealistic, reforming Curtis was not a good prophet. Gradually
the feelings of British publishers, and of some authors, turned against
the proposed treaty. Their main argument, which seems valid today,
was that the terms were too favorable to American publishers, just as in
1870 the arguments of the Harpers, Appleton, and others had been directed against the Lord Clarendon treaty as favoring British publishers.
Feelings abroad were not helped any by S. S. Conant, the managing
editor of *Harper's Weekly,* when, late in 1881, he wrote angrily in the
Publishers' Weekly: "Not content with their own lucrative market,
[British publishers] want to control their authors in that of this country also; and because this grasping and avaricious demand is firmly with-
stood, they offensively stigmatize the position of American publishers
as 'selfish.' " With the treaty a dead dog, the Harpers continued to publish books in their Franklin Square Library at the rate of one or two a
week, in an effort to combat the "cheap-and-nasty" reprints. Some books,
however, were priced as low as ten cents, and for a time they merchandised the Library by making subscriptions available at ten dollars a year.
Memorandum books kept by the Harpers indicate that all English authors
received some payment for their works, and in some cases a royalty.

During the eighteen-eighties, publishers, authors, and public-minded
citizens worked diligently throughout the country to create a favorable
climate of opinion on international copyright. A copyright committee of
publishers met regularly and Joseph W. Harper was chairman of the
committee in 1884. This committee, along with the Authors' Copyright
League and copyright groups in leading American cities, finally got ac-

tion from a reluctant Congress. Late in 1890 a bill was passed by the House, which made it possible for foreign authors to obtain copyright protection in the United States. It was approved by the Senate and became law when President Harrison signed it in March, 1891. Even though this legislation has been amended several times since, the nation's copyright isolation did not fully end until 1955, when the United States joined the Universal Copyright Convention.

6

PUBLISHING ENGLISH FICTION

English novels made a publisher out of Fletcher Harper. In 1827 he launched a young writer named Bulwer, whose second book, *Pelham*, issued the following year, established him as an up-and-coming novelist. Thereafter Fletcher Harper considered Bulwer (later known as Bulwer-Lytton and Lord Lytton) his author. In April, 1835, he drafted an agreement whereby Bulwer was paid £150 for advance proofs of each new novel; it is one of the earliest—perhaps the first—known contract between an American publisher and his English author. Bulwer's early novels, *The Last Days of Pompeii* and particularly *Rienzi*, figured prominently in the eighteen-thirties, when the Carey firms in Philadelphia and the Harpers were competing for publishing leadership, and again in the early forties, when all book publishers were fighting the mammoth weeklies for sheer survival. To meet that competition, Harper's in 1843 printed 42,500 copies of *The Last of the Barons* and wrote Bulwer that "in the first fortnight there will be at least *one hundred thousand copies of the work sold!*" (Their italics.) Only the public profited from such sales, for the books were priced so low that even booksellers could not cover overhead costs. Records do not show the total amount paid to Bulwer-Lytton for his American editions, although he was paid £500 for *A Strange Story* in 1862. He died in mid-January, 1873, and *Harper's Weekly* for February 1st devoted the front cover to his portrait. It was

Fletcher Harper's tribute to the author he had launched in America back in 1827. For years Harper catalogues carried full-page listings of Lord Lytton's works, many of which had been steadily in print for more than half a century.

Next to Bulwer-Lytton, the most important English novelists that Fletcher Harper introduced to American readers prior to 1850 were the Brontë sisters and William Makepeace Thackeray. There is some question about Charlotte Brontë, since a small Boston publisher also issued *Jane Eyre* in January, 1848, and it may be that the Harpers really pirated that one. Possibly the complication arose because the three Brontës were publishing under the pseudonym of Bell. At any rate, the Cliff Street firm had *Jane Eyre, Wuthering Heights,* and *The Tenant of Wildfell Hall* well established by the end of the year. "Jane Eyre fever" was rampant in New England, where the moral climate was a bit chilly, and Bostonians talked the Old Corner Book Store into returning copies of *Wuthering Heights* to Harper's because its profanity was beyond enduring.

But Charlotte Brontë was mainly concerned with expressing truth in fiction form and dedicated *Jane Eyre* to Thackeray, whom she considered the most worthy of being named a god of truthfulness. Thackeray had made his god-like Harper début that same year with *Vanity Fair,* issued in two volumes. The popularity of his book, which he illustrated himself, helped bring him to America, late in 1852, to give readings and to visit his American publishers. He called on the Harpers just as *Henry Esmond* was being published and was surprised to hear from James Harper that G. P. R. James, a now forgotten British novelist, was the most popular author with American readers. But Thackeray—and Dickens—soon outdistanced all others. Twenty Thackeray titles were in print in various Harper editions until 1897-1900, when the biographical edition of *Complete Works,* edited by his daughter Anne Thackeray Ritchie, was issued. George P. Putnam once angled for Thackeray, who sent a letter of regret saying that Harper's had published his larger books and he was going to accept their "liberal proposal." George W. Curtis saw much of Thackeray on his two visits to America and eulogized him in the "Easy Chair" department of *Harper's Magazine.*

In the eighteen-fifties, American table talk and literary columns were spiced with comparisons of Thackeray and Dickens. Dickens had been more widely read and had visited America ten years before Thackeray. He had first been introduced to the Yankees by Henry Carey, of Philadelphia, who in 1836 issued fifteen hundred copies of *Pickwick Papers.* Fighting the mammoths a few years later, however, caused the publishers to suspend all trade courtesies. Harper's brought out *American Notes* in 1842 and *Martin Chuzzlewit* a year later in seventeen numbers, which were sold on the streets by newsboys after a James Harper pep talk.

By the mid-century, trade courtesy was again operative and the Philadelphia firm of T. B. Peterson & Brothers was known as Dickens' publishers, having taken over "rights" and stereotype plates from the Carey firm, then called Lea & Blanchard. The Harpers, however, were ambitious to serialize Dickens' forthcoming works in *Harper's Magazine* or the *Weekly* and paid good sums for early proofs from England. Some of this money they got back from Peterson by charging fees for advance proofs of their own serials and by manufacturing Peterson's stereotype plates. By 1867 Peterson had issued twenty-three editions of the novels. By 1867 Harper's had paid Dickens £3,900—nearly $29,000, in view of the high price of gold at the time. To be sure, there had been some pirating of Dickens, but most publishers respected the Harper-Peterson arrangement, partly because Fletcher Harper had squelched young T. L. McElrath, who in 1854 ventured an American edition of *Hard Times.* McElrath claimed that he had purchased early proofs and also had "rights" through issuing New York editions of *Household Words,* which serialized the novel. But Fletcher, determined to protect the Harper-Peterson monopoly, quickly issued an edition at half McElrath's price. Claiming that Harper's thus caused his new publishing business to fail, McElrath publicized the affair in a fugitive newspaper called the *Empire City,* subsequent issues of which carried communications from others who had real or fancied grievances against the Harpers. If Fletcher did, in fact, cause the failure of the son of Thomas McElrath, a long-time friend and Greeley's associate on the New York *Tribune,* he must be held responsible for that and for later retaliations made against Harper's by the *Tribune.*

In 1867 James T. Fields, of Ticknor & Fields, Boston publishers, decided to break the "trust" even though he risked retaliation and might, in turn, be pirated by those who had been envious of his having Tennyson and other uncopyrighted British authors. He had long been ambitious to get Dickens on his list. While in England and later by correspondence, he had sold himself, his firm, and his city to the Gadshill novelist. The Boston literati were all published by Fields, so why not the greatest living novelist? To this end Fields worked out a twofold strategy. He would become Dickens' authorized American publisher by offering a 10 per cent royalty and arranging a speaking tour for Dickens in America in which Fields would figure prominently.

On April 2, 1867, Dickens wrote Fields the hoped-for you-are-my-publisher letter and Fields immediately broadcast it by newspaper publicity and advertising, which in turn brought a counterblast. On April 12th, the Philadelphia *Press* ridiculed Dickens' published testimonial that the two-hundred-pound payment received from Fields on account had given him greater pleasure than any other receipt of money in all his life. How about the very large sums that the Harpers had sent him? An earlier newspaper clipping had been sent by Fields to Dickens, who replied on April 16th, "I have read the newspaper cutting you have sent me, in which it is stated that I have an interest in—have derived, do derive, or am to derive pecuniary advantage from—certain reproductions of my collected works in the United States not issued by you. Once for all, receive my personal authority to contradict any such monstrous misrepresentations. . . ." By "reproductions of my collected works" Dickens obviously meant *books,* but his financial reference was misinterpreted when the letter was released to the press by Fields. One American newspaper that reprinted the letter reached the *Pall Mall Gazette* (London), which on May 7th commented at length on Dickens' financial dealings with American publishers. Sampson Low immediately countered in a letter of protest to its editor: "Having, myself, as the agent of Messrs. Harper & Brothers, paid to Mr. Dickens many thousands of pounds for and on account of his works, when no other publishing house has paid anything, I do not think such payments should be wholly overlooked in the exuberance which he feels at being put into the possession of this additional honorarium from American publishers." The *American Literary Gazette* was much less restrained. On June 1, its editor wrote that "in our judgment [Dickens] deals with the facts in a style that is almost next of kin to dishonesty. . . we are aware of no usage of the trade which justifies an author in an endeavor to injure or drive out of the market long-established editions of his works which have been for years before the public, and which represents a heavy amount of capital."

Dickens arrived for his second American visit in mid-November and his five-months tour, from his landing in Boston until his sailing from New York, brought adulation for the man and clamor for tickets to his readings. (He netted over £200,000.) His January readings in New York were missed by a young Harper editor, Miss Lavinia Goodell, who lacked a male escort; however, she was consoled by her bosses. One said Dickens could be heard only a little way from the platform and another commented that he shouldn't care to hear him again. Miss Goodell had read in the papers that he would call at the office. He did come and for fifty years afterward authors were told, as they climbed the circular iron stairway, that they were following in Dickens' footsteps. He must have been impressed by the Franklin Square operation and by the Harper brothers, for he promised to treat with them for his next book. (Apparently Fields was not with him at the time.) The New York press gave him a banquet; Thomas Nast represented the *Weekly* and George W. Curtis the *Monthly*. Curtis was one of the speakers and some of his "graceful rhetoric" was later incorporated in an "Easy Chair" essay in the *Monthly*. He whom Curtis termed "one of the most illustrious of living men" later called on Fletcher Harper at 14 West Twenty-second Street, and a family tradition has it that Fletcher, Jr.'s, daughter Margaret sat on the novelist's lap. Aged seventeen, she must have been quite a lapful.

During 1869, two years after his American visit, Dickens was writing what was to be his last book, *The Mystery of Edwin Drood*. In November, Harper's wrote to remind him of his promise and to offer two thousand pounds for early sheets. A few weeks earlier he had read portions of it to Fields, who was then visiting him at his home in Kent. Even though the two men were the warmest of friends, when Fields spoke to Dickens about publishing the new work in America, Dickens replied that he had always been highly satisfied by his association with Harper's and considered himself bound to offer the early sheets to them. Fields only expressed disappointment then, but on his return to Boston he sent back a copy of a document Dickens had signed but forgotten about, giving Fields all rights to any new book he should write. Correspondence followed and a decision was reached that *Harper's Weekly* should have serial rights. *The Mystery of Edwin Drood* began on April 23, 1870. Seven weeks later Dickens died.

In the meantime Appleton had followed Ticknor & Fields in issuing *The Works of Charles Dickens,* and in 1872 Harper's began issuing a handsome illustrated Household Edition of sixteen volumes, matching their similar edition of Thackeray's works. Among the artists who drew the illustrations were C. S. Reinhart, Edwin A. Abbey, A. B. Frost, and Nast. The first six volumes were launched with printings of 15,000 each, the next five 10,000 each, and the last five 7,500 each. A great many people had already bought Dickens by that time.

Dickens was two years older than Charles Reade. While Reade was a university man—spending much time at Oxford, where he was a fellow at Magdalen College for more than forty years—he had a high regard for the craftsmanship of his nonacademic contemporary. Reade at first wrote plays, not turning to fiction until 1856, when he published *It Is Never Too Late to Mend.* This novel was immediately popular and marked him as a writer eager to use his graphic powers of description to expose social abuses, in this instance treatment of prisoners and abuses in prison discipline. He shared a reforming zeal with Dickens and, like Dickens, found the Harper periodicals a ready medium for introducing his novels to American readers.

Reade loved nothing more than a good fight, a phrase he used for a title of a short story in 1859. It was running in the *Weekly* simultaneously with Dickens' *A Tale of Two Cities.* Reade wrote from Oxford to Sampson Low in London: "Up to the present moment I have had every means to be satisfied with Messrs. Harper. But this time I don't feel quite satisfied. *A Good Fight* is a masterpiece. *A Tale of Two Cities* is not a masterpiece. Yet Messrs. Harper gave $5,000 [£1,000] for it, and to me one-twentieth of that sum. Now this might be just in England: but hardly just in America, where, as you know very well, I rank three times higher than I do in this country. . . ." Reade argued his case well enough to get more money, and when his short story was incorporated in *The Cloister and the Hearth,* the world of letters agreed that Reade had indeed written a masterpiece.

Ticknor & Fields had tried valiantly to get *A Good Fight.* "It is very wrong," Reade wrote, "when they know I have treated with Harper's." But James T. Fields was a charming fellow, and when he met Reade a few months later in London, he extracted a promise of a forthcoming work, to be first serialized in the *Atlantic Monthly,* of which Fields was then editor. Thus *Griffith Gaunt,* a problem novel dealing with prostitution, came out in 1866. Both author and publisher were attacked by the *Round Table,* New York's weekly journal of criticism, the book being called "a wicked, impure, and pernicious novel." Reade wrote an angry letter of protest to the *New York Times,* which the *Round Table* replied to with an editorial entitled "An English Bully." Whereupon Reade brought suit for libel in the New York Supreme Court. After hearing evidence the judge declared that what the *Round Table* had published was *prima facie* libelous, and charged the jury to determine how much Reade had suffered and the extent to which he should be compensated for his wounds. After due deliberation the jury decided that Reade should be paid six cents.

For a writer who was so concerned about his good name as an author, Reade was frequently careless about his manuscripts. Often he sent chapters of books to the *Magazine* without keeping copies, and once he sent an installment to editor Henry Mills Alden asking him to fill in one or two names of characters (clear from earlier pages) because he did not then remember how he had designated them. Such trust in an editor did not deter Reade from being an expert bargainer. He managed somehow to keep on good terms with both his Boston and his New York publishers, each of which issued editions of his works. If he received better offers elsewhere, he wangled more out of the Harpers with one hand while he wrote with the other that he would remain loyal whatever happened.

Like Reade, Wilkie Collins wanted to stay with the Harpers even though he might be offered better terms elsewhere. Once, the firm said they would go beyond a promised £750 for a novel if Collins would thereby be saved the embarrassment of rejecting a better offer from a responsible American house. In 1879 they said they had paid Collins nearly £6,000 (translated into today's dollars, about $150,000). By that time, however, Collins had passed his literary zenith. His famous detective story *The Moonstone* came out in the *Weekly* in 1867, and his novel *Armadale* is credited with saving *Harper's Magazine*. As the Civil War came to an end, so nearly did the *Magazine*. Just as Fletcher Harper was seriously considering stopping it, notwithstanding the serialization of Dickens' *Our Mutual Friend*, *Armadale* was started in the December, 1864, issue. Immediately sales increased, and by the end of the serial the circulation had reached its former level—a not surprising fact, for Collins' novel *Woman in White* had been published in 1860 and was recognized, and still is, as one of the classics of English fiction.

In 1873, six years after Dickens came to America on his second visit, Collins followed in his friend's path, with the difference that Fletcher Harper—not James Field—was his host. This visit underscores the sad lack of diaries, letters, and mementos from authors left by Fletcher Harper. All we know about his entertaining of Collins is that he was requested to serve dry, rather than the customary sweet, champagne. In honor of Collins' trip to America to give readings from his works, the firm issued an Illustrated Library Edition of his sixteen novels. Since the Harpers planned this edition in advance of his coming and wanted to preface it with a steel engraving of the author, they asked Collins to have one made, at their expense and from his latest photograph, by the best engraver in London. He replied by sending his photograph and saying that London could boast none so good as the man who had recently engraved the portrait of James Harper, an engraving he much admired. Whereupon they engaged Frederick Halpin to make the steel engraving in two months' time for two hundred and fifty dollars.

A token of the Harpers' esteem for Collins is that his works appeared earlier than those of any other novelist in their annual catalogues—always on page 7. Second in catalogue distinction but perhaps first in sales was that distinguished lady of literature George Eliot, the pseudonym of Mary Ann Evans. *Adam Bede,* published anonymously in 1859, brought her fame at once, though little cash. When John Blackwood, her English publisher, was negotiating with Harper's for the book, she counseled him not to ask more than thirty pounds, since American publishers were "very narrow-necked jars, indeed." The Harper aperture had widened considerably a year later to receive *The Mill on the Floss.* In her journal for February 29, 1860, George Eliot wrote, "G. [George Henry Lewes] has been in town today and has agreed for £300 for the *Mill on the Floss* from Harpers of New York." This £300 was exactly what Blackwood gave for *Adam Bede.*

After *Adam Bede* had become popular, George Eliot acknowledged her authorship of it and of her new novel *The Mill on the Floss.* Now known and publicized, she was deeply cut by criticism of her second book, some of it stemming from the fact that she was the common-law wife of Lewes. *Silas Marner, Romola,* and *Felix Holt* followed, with her historical novel *Romola* taken by the *Magazine* and *Felix Holt* getting one of the longest reviews ever printed in the *Round Table.* On August 4, 1866, the *Round Table* said, "There is scarcely any author to whom the reading public are [more] in debt than to George Eliot." By this time she was feeling better about reviews and publicity and making more money. In 1871, when *Middlemarch* was ready, James Osgood, who took over the Ticknor & Fields business that year on Fields' retirement, put his jar under the George Eliot pump, only to have it snatched away by Harper's. No Harper record indicates how or why, only that early proofs cost £120, and that it began as a serial in the *Weekly* in December, and was published the following year in two volumes, with a first printing of 3,000 copies. The Harpers soon found out that they had underestimated the demand, for *Middlemarch* proved to be one of George Eliot's most talked-about books. When *Daniel Deronda* appeared in 1876, after being introduced to the readers of the *Magazine,* the firm doubled the size of the first printing (two volumes for $2.50) and also issued 15,000 in paper covers at fifty cents. They paid £1,700 for the privilege. This sum George Eliot's husband termed "exceptionally large" when he wrote Blackwood that English publication should be delayed since Harper's had just telegraphed him to say that the promised sheets had not come. Lewes died in 1878 and George Eliot's artistic endeavor went with him. That year she corrected proofs of *Theophrastus Such*, a book of essays serialized in *Harper's Bazar*, but wrote no more. Two of her books are still in print with Harper's—*Silas Marner* and *Daniel Deronda*.

Several other women novelists were published from Franklin Square, including Mrs. M. O. W. Oliphant. However, none of them was such a favorite as the author of *John Halifax, Gentleman*. The Harpers never knew just how to address this lady. When she published her masterpiece in 1856, she was Dinah Maria Mulock. A few years later she married G. L. Craik, a partner of Macmillan's in London, and wrote to Franklin Square protesting that "Dinah Mulock Craik" had been printed on the title page of an otherwise "very pretty edition" of a new book; she said English women preferred to drop their maiden name when married, and requested that the title page be canceled, "and remember that on all future occasions—in books or magazines—I must never appear except as 'the author of *John Halifax*.' " Whereupon she signed herself "D. M. Craik." When Harper's published *The Little Lame Prince* in 1874, the title-page designation was "Miss Mulock," which they used in announcing the Library Edition of her twenty-one works. Sometimes they used "Mrs. Craik" in parentheses. Miss Mulock was not the only lady who caused identification problems for publishers, librarians, and readers. In 1880 the *Publishers' Weekly* wrote, under "Aggravating Ladies," how difficult it was to look up their works when they insisted on "By the author of," did not give their names, and used inconsistent pen names.

Fletcher Harper was proud to be Mrs. Craik's publisher, and proud to print in the catalogue a blurb from a Cincinnati newspaper saying her books were so desirable for family reading that it was a cause for gratitude that they were published by the house which insured their most general distribution throughout the country. When his great-grandson Fletcher Harper IV was born in 1874 she sent a charming poem, and when Mr. Harper died she sent the family another, entitled "In

Memoriam," and with it a box of English daisies and a note ending, "I liked him so!—and I hoped to have seen him again—but it was not to be." At her death the Harpers reciprocated by collecting a fund that was sent for a memorial erected in England by her admirers.

Six other English novelists of the latter half of the nineteenth century deserve mention because many of their works were first read by Americans in the Harper periodicals. They do not include George Meredith, one of the greatest of the Victorians. In 1864 he sent Harper's early proofs of his forthcoming novel, *Emilia in England,* saying, "You have done me the honour to publish *Evan Harrington* in New York. I wish consequently that you should have the early sheets of all my works. . . . I have had offers previously from Mr. Fields, of Boston, but prefer, if possible, to have my books republished by the gentlemen who first made my name known in America." But *Evan Harrington* had not sold well and Harper's rejected the new book. In so doing they lost the distinction of being the American publisher of *The Egoist.* The six additional novelists linked to Harper's are Anthony Trollope, R. D. Blackmore, James Payn, Walter Besant, William Black, and Thomas Hardy.

Anthony Trollope is now important chiefly because of the photographic accuracy with which he depicted the English social life of his time. He was critical of the Harpers because he felt they never gave him top billing or paid him enough. Perhaps the Harpers never quite forgave him for having attacked them in the London *Athenaeum* in 1862. At that time Trollope claimed that he had never received a penny from the Harpers for all his works they had published, that their London agent (Low) had declined to pay him £400 for *Orley Farm* and later bought proofs from the English publisher for £200, and that Fletcher Harper had promised him not to issue his *North America,* which he had subsequently done, despite the fact that Lippincott was the authorized publisher.

Thanks to this outburst, we have at least one published piece that Fletcher Harper wrote. He probably would not have replied in a letter to the *Athenaeum,* since his policy was not to answer criticism, except that Trollope had accused him, by name, of bad faith. Harper replied to the first accusation by saying that the London firm to which Trollope had assigned all his pecuniary rights for his earlier books had sold "early sheets" to the Harpers at fair prices. By this same token the value to them of *Orley Farm* was no more than £200. ("We do not despair of being able, some day, to pay Mr. Trollope as much as we pay Mr. Dickens or Mr. Wilkie Collins.") He went on to say that Trollope's recollection of their conversation was incorrect; he had not said they would not publish *North America* if Trollope sold the rights elsewhere. He continued, "I knew, on the contrary, that we should publish it; because we were known as his publishers; because we had money invested in stereotype plates of his previous volumes; and, because, having laid out large sums in introducing him to the American public, by publishing and advertising his earlier works, we were not likely to allow another house to step in and monopolize the market we had created. What I did say was, that we would give him as much for the early sheets as any other house would give ... or, if he preferred it, the copyright which is usually paid to American authors, ten per cent on the sales." He finished his letter with an apologia for the American comity of trade and a boast that his firm had paid, during the past thirty years, more money to British authors for early sheets than British publishers had paid American authors for early sheets since the first book by an American author was ever printed. Trollope did finally rise above the £200 plateau. For *Sir Harry Hotspur*, in 1871, he received £700. It was first serialized in the *Weekly*.

R. D. Blackmore is now remembered for *Lorna Doone*, although Harper's issued twelve other novels for him. His great Exmoor romance reached best-sellerdom slowly, and years later Blackmore wrote a special Harper introduction for a new gift-book edition containing thirty-two halftone illustrations of the *Doone* country. James Payn's prodigious output of fiction went through the Harper presses and for a while he contributed a department in *Harper's Bazar*, signed "Robert Kemble, of London." He wrote rapidly and so badly that S. S. Conant, managing editor of the *Weekly* and an expert at deciphering handwriting, was often called on to edit copy.

Some of Sir Walter Besant's novels were written with James Rice and so catalogued. Of his own work, the best is *All Sorts and Conditions of*

Men (1882), a social-problem novel depicting London's East End life. Two years later he established the Society of Authors and chaired the group through the stormy years that preceded the enactment of international copyright. As such, his opinion carried weight when in November, 1890, the London *Athenaeum* published a letter he signed, along with William Black and Thomas Hardy, testifying to "the friendly business relations" they had had with the Harpers, who were always willing and desirous of doing all they could for an English author. This letter was in response to a scathing comment by the *Athenaeum* regarding the Harpers' treatment of Kipling. J. Henry Harper was an especial friend of Black's; his history of the House contains many references to Black and the firm's social and business dealings with him.

Thomas Hardy was first published in America by Henry Holt, and *Far from the Madding Crowd* came out with his imprint in 1874. The Harpers had seen a first installment in the London *Cornhill Magazine,* where it appeared anonymously, and immediately "announced" it, but withdrew when young Holt told them he had bought American rights and that Hardy was the author. However, Holt was confronted by serials running in four periodicals, one of which, the New York *Tribune,* also issued a cheap paperback reprint. Hardy's next book, *Indiscretion in the Life of an Heiress,* came out in the *Weekly,* Holt requesting that Harper's pay the author £20. The check went off to Hardy apparently with a come-on letter, for Hardy replied, on June 24, 1878, "If at any time you should wish to make a proposal to me for including novels of mine in your [Franklin Square] series, it will be treated in confidence. I am not sufficiently acquainted with the usage of American publishers to know if an English author is held to be justified there as in England, in arranging with whomsoever he chooses for the publication of any particular book or books, irrespective of those that have preceded it."

This letter opened the door and the Harpers were not shy about walking in. What Hardy handed to them was early proofs of *The Return of the Native.* In return Hardy was promised £3 per *Magazine* page or an amount not to exceed £360. A few months later, when Holt learned of the agreement, he made at once for Franklin Square.

By virtue of trade courtesy, he reminded Joseph W. Harper, the book should carry the Holt imprint. Harper agreed amiably enough, and after Holt left he wrote the understanding reached in the firm's Memorandum Book: "Book-form offered to Henry Holt & Co. at 180; or divide book between H. & B. & Holt. Henry Holt & Co. will not divide the book-form. Prefer to do it . . . themselves alone. Will satisfy us as to payment." Eight weeks later Holt agreed to pay Harper's 10 per cent on the retail price (ten cents a copy) and not to issue the book until the *Magazine* serial, which had begun in November, was completed. Holt's royalties, plus what the *Magazine* paid, earned Hardy £472, according to Carl J. Weber, whose book *Hardy in America* covers the Hardy-Harper relationship in detail. For *A Laodicean,* Harper's paid Hardy £700 (again Holt had book rights) and George Du Maurier twenty-one guineas ($105) for each full-page illustration.

J. Henry Harper got book rights to Hardy in America by swapping William E. Morris to Holt when Holt told him that he thought Morris was the coming man. However, there was little if any profit on Hardy's books, for at least thirty-four publishers issued pirated editions. In 1887, when Harper's brought out *The Woodlanders* for seventy-five cents, the most exasperating of the pirates, George Munro, announced it three weeks later for ten cents. While Hardy lost financially by not having copyright protection in America, he did gain a vast number of readers.

International copyright came in time for a Harper royalty contract for *Tess of the D'Urbervilles,* Hardy's most famous novel, first serialized in *Harper's Bazar.* That the firm placed this work in their magazine designed for women readers seems now a daring venture, for it had been declined in England by one newspaper syndicate and two magazines, including *Macmillan's,* because it dealt with the seduction of a milkmaid. There was also criticism in America, and when Hardy wrote that he hoped the new book he was writing could first appear in the *Magazine,* the House replied that they must be assured it would be suitable for a family magazine. Hardy replied that the most fastidious maiden could not be offended. Whereupon Henry Mills Alden began *Jude the Obscure* in the December, 1894, issue only to be distressed to

hear from Hardy that the story (then called "Hearts Insurgent")
was taking an unexpected turn and might be found objectionable.
He went on to say that the serial (which dealt frankly with sexual
matters) could be stopped and the contract canceled or that Alden
could make any changes in the manuscript he thought necessary. Alden
replied on August 29, 1894. He apologized for having asked Hardy
to make changes in "work conscientiously done," and expressed appreciation for "artistic excellence" that exceeded anything he had read in
current fiction. His letter voiced the perennial problem facing an editor
who wants an author's work to find the greatest possible reader acceptance.

Jude the Obscure was Hardy's last novel. Distressed by the attacks
of "purists" (the New York *World* published a particularly vitriolic
review), he asked Harper's to withdraw the book if they thought it was
offending the tastes of the American public. Thereafter, the Wessex
author turned to poetry, but lived long enough to know that *Jude,* as
well as *Tess* and *The Return of the Native,* had taken a place among
the classics of English fiction.

7

HARPER'S NEW MONTHLY MAGAZINE
(1850-1900)

When John Wakefield Francis, the cultivated and gregarious physician, beloved of New Yorkers, spoke before the New York Typographical Society in 1852, he compared the Harper enterprise to a Cliff Street oak which had sprouted from the acorn of *Seneca's Morals* and grown into a tree, the pride of the forest, whose roots and branches ramified over the land.

Two years earlier that tree had dropped an acorn which soon took root and grew rapidly on the rich soil which nourished its parents. That sapling was *Harper's New Monthly Magazine,* and the soil from which it grew was largely imported from abroad. Ever since then, various writers concerned about American literature have complained that this rapidly-growing tree crowded out much tender native growth which would otherwise have flourished. Such criticism always smacks of the presumptuous, for no one may say what would have happened in any historical period had other events taken place.

The fact is that even though the Harper brothers had trafficked in English reprints for years, they underestimated what the American response would be to the lavish selection of the output of English authors in the *Magazine.* They printed only 7,500 copies of Volume I, Number 1. The issue, which was dated June, 1850, was soon gobbled up. By the end of the year it took printings of 50,000 copies to supply

Harper's Magazine, *Volume I, No. 1. Engraved by Benson J. Lossing.*

the monthly demand. To be sure, this circulation was aided by Cliff Street promotion and publicity, and was abetted by the confidence the general public had in the publisher. When prospective readers of a family magazine saw that *Harper,* as the magazine was known, was making good on its promise to give more reading matter (144 two-column pages) and at a lower price (twenty-five cents a copy) than any other, they subscribed through bookstores and agents or sent their three-dollar checks to the publisher.

Most of them renewed their subscriptions to read the endings of Charles Lever's *Maurice Tiernay,* Charles Dickens' *Bleak House,* William Makepeace Thackeray's *The Newcomes,* Bulwer-Lytton's *My Novel,* and George Eliot's *Romola.* American novelists could not equal them. No one, however, could better compress domestic and foreign news than the journalist Henry J. Raymond, but because of the prevalent vogue for anonymity he was not known to them either as the writer of records of monthly events or as the nominal editor of the magazine. Similarly George Ripley, a recent arrival in New York from his ill-fated communal experiment at Brook Farm, was not known as the author of the literary notices; or Donald G. Mitchell (Ik. Marvel) as the occupant of "The Editor's Easy Chair"; or George W. Curtis (even later to his biographer) as the author of an early series of eight stories satirizing American watering places. Lewis Gaylord Clark, editor of the *Knickerbocker,* conducted the "Editor's Drawer," a department named for a desk drawer in which Fletcher Harper tossed bits of humor. Later, Samuel Irenaeus Prime took over from Clark and was in turn succeeded by William A. Seaver. All these men were in their time famous raconteurs.

Thus even in the early issues American writers contributed. If their names, like the proliferating Abbott brothers', were well known they received by-lines; on the other hand, much that the more literary J. Ross Browne wrote went unacknowledged. One of the anonymous authors was Mark Twain, whose "Forty-three Days in an Open Boat" appeared in the December, 1866, issue. His delight at this recognition at the beginning of his literary career changed to embarrassment when the index to that volume revealed his name. He was listed as "Mark Swain." The drive to get native writers may have been stimulated by the start in 1853 of *Putnam's Magazine,* with its commendable effort to use home talent only. George W. Curtis was an editor of *Putnam's* during its short career and once wrote an article highly critical of *Harper's Magazine,* because it was not giving enough encouragement to American writers. At the same time Fletcher Harper was kicked from behind by a writer he was encouraging—Fitz-James O'Brien, a brilliant young

Irish American, who wrote over fifty articles as well as poems for the
Magazine. On an occasion when O'Brien was paid less than he thought
he deserved, he paraded on Franklin Square with a placard reading,
"One of Harper's authors. I am starving." Fletcher quickly called
O'Brien in and paid him what he wanted.

Curtis lived something of a double life, since while he was editing
Putnam's he was also writing the "Easy Chair" essays for *Harper's
Magazine.* What he wrote was enough to make a book a year, but only
three volumes appeared, issued posthumously, containing what Henry
Mills Alden considered the best of a forty-year output. The "Easy
Chair" writing reflected his wide range of interests, from topics of the
day (he was an early advocate of women's suffrage and the necessity
of a better understanding between capital and labor) to literature,
drama, and the fine arts. James A. Bailey, of circus fame, was one of
Curtis's admirers. Bailey once said to an acquaintance, "You know
George William Curtis? You have talked to him? Shaken him by the
hand? Well, well! When you see Mr. Curtis, tell him that a rough old
showman looks forward to the 'Easy Chair' as a treat every month.
I don't know whether this will interest him, but it will inform him as to
the wide audience he reaches and, I think, helps to civilize."

Like William Dean Howells, his colleague for a few years on the
Magazine, Curtis wrote of Emerson and the other New England literary
giants. Like Howells, he had an intimate style that invited the reader
to share a critical opinion or an informed insight almost as though it
were his own. Unfortunately none of his books is now in print and his
vast contribution to the *Magazine,* as well as that of Howells, was
inexcusably ignored when a volume of its best articles, stories, and
poems was published in 1959.

When Raymond resigned in 1856 to give full time to his recently
founded *New York Times,* Alfred H. Guernsey was named editor.
Guernsey, a Greek and Hebrew scholar, had worked on the firm's reference books and served as a reader and translator. He was succeeded in
1869 by Henry Mills Alden. Alden, like Curtis, was representative as a
man of letters of the best of New England. He was a graduate of
Williams College and of the Andover Theological Seminary. While

One of 138 drawings in Virginia Illustrated, by "Porte
Crayon," the pen name of D. H. Strother. Published in
1857, the book was made up of articles that had appeared
in the Magazine, to which Porte Crayon was one of the
highest-paid contributors in the eighteen-fifties.

Setting Type

The compositors worked from two sloping cases containing the type characters. The lower case contained the smaller letters (hence called "lower-case" letters), spaces, figures, and punctuation marks. The upper case held capitals, small capitals, and other characters. Boxes for letters were not placed in alphabetical order but in positions determined by the frequency with which letters were required. Thus the letter "z," the least frequently used, was in a small box at a far corner, and the letter "e," the most often used (sixty to each "z"), was in a large box at the center front.

A pair of cases for ordinary book composition required about 140 characters.

In setting type the compositor placed the characters in a "stick," a kind of open frame about six inches long. One side being movable, the compositor could set a line of type to fit a narrow column or a wide page. The back of the "stick" was high enough to permit about two inches of type to be composed, enough to be lifted out dexterously and placed in a "galley," a tray of metal with two sides against which the lines of type fitted securely. Type thus placed in galleys was later assembled into pages.

A skilled compositor could set 150 letters and "spaces," or word dividers, in five minutes. It was his job also to distribute used type and fill up empty boxes in his cases. His fingers were as nimble as those of a pianist, and he had as good a memory, for his eyes were always on the type. Working at ordinary speed he would distribute about 12,000 characters in an hour—between three and four a second—without making more than twenty errors in all. Hand composition was largely replaced in the eighteen-nineties by the linotype machine. Although machines for setting and distributing type had been invented decades earlier, they were costly to operate and required handwork to justify the lines—that is, to fill in spaces so that words would properly reach to the right-hand margin of each line.

These drawings of the compositor and engraver (next page) were made by W. P. Snyder for use in the Magazine *and in a* Visitor's Guide to Harper & Brothers' Establishment. *W. A. Rogers said that Snyder never appreciated what remarkable drawings they were and argued that such engravings as these carried nuances of feeling lost in the exact reproduction of a photograph by the process method.*

still in the Seminary he had two articles accepted by the *Atlantic Monthly;* this encouragement and his lack of speaking ability led him to decide against the ministry for a literary career. He was twenty-seven years old when he started to work for Harper's, and thirty-three when he became editor of the *Magazine,* a title he carried for fifty years. In his lifetime he saw and corresponded with nearly every important writer at home and abroad. He wrote two books of his own, one published anonymously, some articles, and helped countless authors with editorial counsel and in the work of revising and rewriting manuscripts.

Wood Engraving

The best wood for engravers to work on was boxwood imported from Syria. Its great value was due to its fine grain; its disadvantage was the comparatively small size of the blocks because boxwood trees never attain a large girth. Thus, if an illustration called for a double-page spread in the Weekly (sixteen by twenty-two inches), thirty-six blocks were generally required. These blocks were cut about an inch thick—to conform to the depth of the type—and were highly polished and whitened to afford a surface for pencil lines. The artist then drew a rough sketch on paper the exact size of the composite wood block. From this a tracing was made and rubbed down in reverse on the block. After the tracing was completed, one of the artists (for a large picture two, three, or four men worked together), using a pencil or a brush and India ink, laid in the main broad shadows. The composite block would then be taken apart and the artists would draw the details of the picture with pencil or brush, each being minutely careful with margins and merging tones.

As blocks were completed they were sent to the engravers, who began the laborious work of cutting out the wood not covered with pencil or brush. The engravers sat at high tables to which the blocks were securely fixed. Working under clear light and with the help of large magnifying glasses, they made their cuttings with sharp gravers and scalpels. Their work was extremely difficult when shading was required and when crossing lines required cutting at the interstices of the crossings. It would take an expert engraver ten or twelve hours to complete a wood engraving four by five inches in size. When the engravers had completed their work the blocks were reassembled, bolted together along the back sides, and sent to the press room. During the Civil War, and later, when big news events had to be covered with dispatch in order to meet the Weekly's deadline, artists and engravers would sometimes work steadily for thirty-six hours.

J. G. Smithwick, for many years foreman of the Harper engraving room, was himself an engraver whose "work added charm to the drawing it reproduced," according to W. A. Rogers. Smithwick was a tall, broad-shouldered, good-looking Irishman. A careless word of criticism of his work would drive him to anger or despair, according to his mood at the moment. In 1888 twenty-five men on his staff were earning from $25 to $50 a week. Smithwick's Saturday paycheck was $90.

When Alden became editor, he did not have the final say about what went into the *Magazine*. That decision was made by Fletcher Harper, who, according to Charles Nordhoff, made few mistakes about his public because he created it. Nordhoff worked with Harper as reader, adviser, and author, and early learned that the guiding editorial principle was to publish what would be intelligible, interesting, and useful to the average American.

From the beginning Fletcher Harper knew that his public liked illustrations. Three portrait engravings, including one of his favorite author, William H. Prescott, graced the first issue, and as circulation mounted he plowed profits back into illustrations, expending $24,000 in 1853, when 125,000 copies of each issue were being printed. (At the end of

Alden saying "no" to a lady author.

Alden worked at an old walnut desk which could not have been called beautiful even when new. Behind him were a few shelves filled with unpublished manuscripts. Dust and cigar ashes were everywhere. A chair stood by the door, and here any visitor, no matter who, was invited to sit. The only ornament to his office was the portrait of Charles Reade, willed to the House by the novelist. Although Alden had often been asked to take a larger office, considered more worthy of his editorial function, he stubbornly refused to be moved.

1865, according to editor Guernsey, the *Magazine* had printed altogether 10,000 engravings, which, with drawings, had cost $300,000.) All such expenses were paid out of sales, since advertising was not introduced until the eighteen-eighties. By the end of that decade as many as forty pages of advertising a month were being placed in the back of the book, front pages being reserved for Harper books and periodicals. Among the first author-artists to be used in *Harper's* was D. H. Strother ("Porte Crayon"), who illustrated stories of Southern and Western life. At the end of the century George Du Maurier and Howard Pyle were illustrating their own stories, and in between Winslow Homer, C. S. Reinhart, Edwin A. Abbey, Frederic Remington, and dozens of lesser-known artists made hundreds of drawings, sometimes acknowledged, which were transferred to wood blocks by any one of dozens of engravers employed by the House.

After Fletcher Harper died, Joseph W. Harper became head of the literary department and held a directing hand over the *Magazine*. He in turn was followed by J. Henry Harper. Both these men, however, gave more freedom to Alden, a gentle man with deep-set eyes and a brown beard, a man of sound literary judgment and of sympathy and understanding for all who aspired to publish in the magazine with its buff-colored cover embellished with cherubs. Under Alden's guidance the *Magazine* by 1885 had a circulation of 200,000 in America and 35,000 in Great Britain, the widest readership of any magazine of its kind, partly because of its informative articles on world concerns. Thus in the eighteen-eighties Harper's Paris agent, Theodore Child, was sent, accompanied by an artist, to Russia and South America. A decade later Poultney Bigelow and Frederic Remington went on a similar mission to Russia and Germany.

Since established writers, mostly English, were cultivated by Fletcher and Wesley Harper and their two successors, Alden found his editorial field in the greening pastures of American writers. These men and women furnished the bulk of the magazine's short stories. Many of the tales were sentimental, but first-rate stuff (stories as well as articles) came from Herman Melville, John Esten Cooke, Fitzhugh Ludlow, John T. Trowbridge, Frederick B. Perkins, Charles Nordhoff, J. W. De Forest, and from such excellent women writers as Elizabeth Stuart Phelps, Harriet Prescott Spofford, and Rose Terry.

Competition for American writers grew as the *Atlantic Monthly* (1857), followed by *Scribner's* (1870, called the *Century* after 1881), met and sometimes exceeded what *Harper's* paid for editorial matter. During the last quarter of the century the three leading quality magazines shared those who, following Hawthorne and the other great New England writers, were bringing American literature to flower. To name them in short compass is impossible, but exception should be made for such notables as William Dean Howells and Mark Twain, Henry James and Charles Dudley Warner, Thomas A. Janvier and Brander Matthews, James Lane Allen and Owen Wister, Bret Harte and Stephen Crane, Constance Fenimore Woolson and Ruth McEnery Stuart, Mary E. Wilkins and Margaret Deland, who, as the century closed, had formed closer ties with *Harper's Magazine* and with the wise and beneficent Alden than with any other editor or periodical.

8

HARPER'S WEEKLY (1857-1900)

Fletcher Harper was not a frontiersman with an axe eager to blaze new trails through the literary forest; he came later to develop land already surveyed. After *Leslie's Weekly* and other illustrated papers had shown the way and the London *Illustrated News* had furnished the format, he was ready to go. There was more available fiction than the *Magazine* could use, and all the production facilities were expanding in their new manufactory. In its first issue—Saturday, January 3, 1857—*Harper's Weekly* promised that neither labor nor expense would be spared to make it the best family newspaper in the world. It would give sound views on political, social, and moral questions; carry articles on travel, adventure, art, and literature; present well-edited news, both foreign and domestic. Thus in 1860 it fully covered the American visit of the Prince of Wales (later King Edward VII) and printed a double-page spread of the ball at the Academy of Music in Brooklyn, where one of Wesley Harper's daughters, reputed to be a great beauty, danced with the debonair Prince.

As the *Weekly* grew in influence, its editorial essays became a leading feature. That first number carried one entitled "Compromise and Union," an appeal that kept recurring for four years and one that the majority of Americans liked to hear, although leaders of opinion, particularly in the North, were impatient that a more decisive stand was not taken on political issues. But when the War Between the States began, the editorials came alive. They no longer merely reflected public opinion but strove valiantly to create it; at the war's end the *North American Review* said, "Whoever believes in his country and its constant progress in developing human liberty will understand that he has an ally in *Harper's Weekly*." The writer of that article was indirectly praising George W. Curtis, who went on the Harper payroll in 1863 and began writing the weekly political editorial.

During the Civil War the *Weekly*'s greatest contribution was its record of the conflict, the best reportorial coverage of a war up to that time. News stories, illustrated by leading artists, kept Northern families, as well as soldiers at the front, informed of the war's progress. Despite the loss of Southern subscribers the circulation mounted to 100,000. At the war's end the *Weekly* paid a moving tribute to its corps of artists and writers:

They have made the weary marches and dangerous voyages. They have shared the soldier's fire; they have ridden and waded, and climbed and floundered, always trusting in lead pencils and keeping their paper dry. When the battle began they were there. They drew the enemy's fire as well as our own.

"If success be the test of merit, this popular weekly must be awarded one of the loftiest niches in the temple of letters," the *Round Table* said in January, 1867, reviewing Volume X of *Harper's Weekly*. It noted the strong editorials, the steadily-improving illustrations, the carefully selected fiction, and the well-edited miscellaneous articles. Fletcher Harper's name was not mentioned, but despite the curtain of anonymity the reviewer probably knew that the youngest of the brothers was the man behind the *Weekly*'s success. Fletcher always had a managing editor who, with an assistant and one or more readers, made the initial selection of text for each issue. What he chose was fitted into the layout of a forthcoming issue which Fletcher brought to the office each Monday morning he was in the city, a layout that spotted illustrations and marked out the necessary space for Curtis's editorials and for advertising.

George William Curtis

Reproduced from the cover of Harper's Weekly, *September 10,
1892.*

While Fletcher Harper kept close watch over the publication of new books, he found his true métier as a publisher of periodicals, particularly the *Weekly*. Once, an editor said to him, "That is not according to precedent." Fletcher replied, "Don't follow precedent. Do what seems best today, and never mind yesterday." Though he drove himself with great force of will, he was reluctant to impose his will on a trusted associate. George W. Curtis said that in his many years of association with Fletcher Harper, with all their differences of opinion, there was never on Fletcher's part the slightest petulance or dictation. If the editorial tone of the *Weekly* showed a differing judgment from his own, Fletcher was carefully silent until the occasion passed, and never by hint or innuendo attempted coercion. At one time leaders of the Republican Party were annoyed by Curtis's editorials and publicly intimated that his publishers were not in sympathy with his convictions. Fletcher Harper's answer was to head the next issue of the *Weekly* with a manifesto that Harper & Brothers would rather not publish the paper than to do so at the sacrifice of principle or for merely partisan success.

In the seventies and eighties the *Weekly* was identified in the public mind with Curtis, the political editor, and Thomas Nast, the cartoonist. They helped to make Presidents, to bring about civil-service reform, and to break the notorious Tweed Ring in New York City.

Of the two men, Curtis was the more urbane, sophisticated, and literate. As a youth, he had lived with George Ripley at Brook Farm before traveling abroad for four years. This resulted in two travel books published in his mid-twenties, which were highly praised by critics, including Hawthorne. When *Putnam's Magazine* failed in the panic of 1857, Curtis honorably assumed its indebtedness, although he was not legally bound to do so. To this end he turned over his Harper earnings—royalties from five books, including a splendid novel, *Prue and I,* and payments for his essays in the *Magazine* and the *Weekly*— and income from lectures. Along with Emerson, Wendell Phillips, Beecher, and Greeley he journeyed in the East and the Midwest, sharing in the lyceum movement that was such a profound influence in the education of mid-century Americans. He was an early member of the Republican Party and campaigned for Frémont, its first Presidential candidate; during that campaign he was once called on for an impromptu speech and, when freed of a manuscript, realized his potential as an orator. Thus he spoke at the Republican Party's 1860 Convention in Chicago, where, it was said, "He put pandemonium to defeat, and bid the wild uproar be ruled." He worked for Seward's nomination, but when Lincoln was chosen he campaigned actively for him. For his services to the party he was offered several diplomatic posts, but he declined them all, including the ambassadorship to the Court of St. James's, proffered by President Hayes. This decision disappointed many of his friends, notably Charles Eliot Norton, of Harvard, who wrote that such a position acknowledged Curtis's real eminence. Norton wanted to dislodge Curtis from his Harper position, arguing that he was a kind of fifth wheel to a strictly commercial wagon. But Curtis knew better what he wanted to do, believed that the Harper periodicals gave him the widest possible reading public, and was characteristically humble in believing that his equally dear friend James Russell Lowell could do the job better than he.

What Curtis did of greatest national importance was to reform the civil service. When a Civil Service Commission was authorized, President Grant appointed Curtis, who was chosen its chairman. His 1871 report was a *Magna Carta* of reform, but Grant failed to obtain Congressional approval and Curtis resigned. Even so, as president of the National Civil Service Reform League, he supplied the moral and intellectual leadership that gradually forced the spoils politicians to give up what they considered their most valued prerogatives. His articulate, carefully reasoned, and persuasive editorials in the *Weekly* had a readership of half a million and were often quoted by the daily press. For nearly thirty years he exerted an influence on American political thought that was probably second to none.

Curtis's high-minded impartiality led him into frequent clashes with Thomas Nast, whose political cartoons were as popular a feature of the *Weekly* as Curtis's writing. Unlike Curtis, Nast was anything but impartial. As honest in his way as Curtis, he was eager for quick results and used his pen to satirize and punish and reform while the issue was hot. Politicians feared him and fawned on him. Once, during February and March, 1872, while Nast was in Washington, he was given an

Thomas Nast
An engraving of a photo-
graph by Mathew B. Brady,
printed in Harper's Weekly,
May 11, 1867.

ovation when he was called into the House chamber and wrote his wife about his warm welcome also at the White House, saying, "If Joe [Joseph W.] Harper is here . . . I can show what a big man I am with the President [Grant]." At that time Curtis was also in Washington. At issue between him and Nast was Nast's satirical treatment of Republican senators—all friends of Curtis—who were supporting Grant on civil service reform. "I think the Harpers will be on my side," Nast wrote, and, "I was surprised to see people think so much more of me than of Curtis," and again, "I hear that the Harpers will stick by me, no matter what will happen, and if things come to the worst Curtis will have to go."

Neither Curtis nor Nast had to go, for the Harpers realized how important both were to the success of the *Weekly*. "The *Weekly* is an independent forum," Fletcher Harper said. "There are many contributors. It is not necessary that all should agree. Mr. Curtis and Mr. Nast are personally responsible—each for his own contributions." The

Harpers loved both men, but for different reasons. Nast was something of a playboy, full of wit and charm, and a great favorite. Curtis was beloved because of his integrity, gallantry, and graciousness. He was respected for his pervasive influence and for the prestige of his name; but the firm saw little of him, for he was accustomed to work every day from nine till three in his Staten Island home, only going to Franklin Square on Thursdays. Then he went directly to the composing room, where he began writing his editorial for the week. He sat on a bench beside an old compositor, who set up the type as Curtis handed over copy.

On the other hand, the Bavarian-born Thomas Nast barged in and out of the Harper offices from the day he was hired in the summer of 1862. From the beginning Fletcher Harper took a special interest in Nast because the artist, who was then twenty-two, combined industry and competence, two qualities that in the Harper book were on a par with the Ten Commandments.

Nast's early drawings were not the caricatures that made his name famous later; they were scenes of warfare, some drawn at the front, fierce in their portrayal of conflict and alive with elemental patriotic fervor. John Bonner, then managing editor of the *Weekly,* asked Nast, "How does a field look after a battle? Can you draw that? Suppose you make it night." Soon Nast sent in a gruesome double-page spread. It was followed by black-and-white pictures of guerrilla raids, the sacking of villages, life in war prisons, and others that revealed not only the horrors of war but also Nast's intense emotional involvement. He seemed to be saying, "You, too, must become involved in this."

Then he drew a series of semi-allegorical pictures which got enormous word-of-mouth publicity and did much to make him a national figure. Now this homely pathos seems sentimental, but at that time it moved people deeply, particularly one picture entitled "Christmas Eve," showing two Christmas wreaths—in one a soldier by a campfire looks at a picture of his loved ones, and in the other children sleep peacefully in bed while their mother prays by a window ledge. This drawing brought letters from every part of the union to the Harper office with thanks for an inspired picture.

During the Presidential campaign of 1864, Nast turned to political cartoons. The Democratic Convention meeting in Chicago declared the war a failure and urged compromise. Nast answered with a cartoon, "Compromise with the South," showing Jeff Davis, President of the Confederacy, clasping the hand of a wounded Northern soldier over the grave of "Union Heroes Fallen in a Useless War." In the background Columbia is bowed in sorrow and a Negro family stands in chains. So great was the demand for this issue that an enlarged edition was printed, and the drawing was reproduced as a Republcan campaign piece. This cartoon was followed in October by an even more ferocious attack on the Democratic platform. After Lincoln's re-election, the *Weekly* claimed that the two cartoons had been "prodigious batteries" for Lincoln and Johnson in the political battle. Lincoln himself said, "Thomas Nast has been our best recruiting sergeant." General Grant went further in his praise, saying that Nast was the foremost figure in civil life developed by the rebellion of the Southern states. "He did as much as any one man to preserve the Union and bring the war to an end."

During Reconstruction, Nast became a full-fledged political cartoonist. He found in the pugnacious and politically inept Andrew Johnson a perfect target for his loaded pencil. Aligning himself with the radicals in the Republican Party, Nast drew a series of "King Andy" cartoons. These lively and satirical drawings (which Curtis complained to Fletcher Harper about) were widely commented on throughout the nation and abroad and gave the *Weekly* enormous prestige. Nast's skill in drawing directly on the wood block gave portrait likeness to his subjects. No tags were required to show who President Johnson was, or to identify Horatio Seymour, the New York politician, when Nast lampooned him during his unsuccessful attempt to beat Grant in the Presidential election of 1868. "Two things elected me," Grant said, "the sword of Sheridan and the pencil of Thomas Nast."

What really got Nast into the books of American history, however, was what he did beginning in 1869 to break up the notorious Tweed Ring in New York. William Marcy Tweed, who had gained control of the Democratic Party in New York City, was the grand sachem of Tammany Hall, and generally known as "Boss" Tweed. Peter B. Sweeny, city chamberlain, Richard B. Connolly, city comptroller, and A. Oakey Hall, mayor, were Tweed's henchmen and the four became

known as the Tweed Ring. They controlled city offices, subsidized or
intimidated the bar, and frightened the press. They defrauded the city
of amounts estimated to run as high as one hundred million dollars.
While the extent of the Ring's plunder was not then known, Fletcher
Harper decided that the *Weekly* should attempt, through cartoons
and editorials, to rid the city of its nest of vultures. He talked
with Nast, and the first of the Nast cartoons appeared in the issue of
September 11, 1869. Throughout the next year Nast hit at the Tweed
Ring. The *New York Times* joined in the fight early that year when
it published evidence of wholesale graft, revealed by M. J. O'Rourke,
county bookkeeper.

As the Nast assaults continued, the Ring became restive, for public
opinion was being aroused. Even so, Tweed was able to force the state
legislature to grant a charter greatly increasing his own power. However, he did begin to worry about the elections of 1871. The year opened
up with a devastating cartoon in which Nast showed Tweed and Sweeny,
"Tweedledee and Sweedledum," giving public money to the needy of
their followers while Tweed, wearing a fifteen-thousand-dollar
diamond, and Sweeny piled up greater sums for themselves.

"That's the last straw!" Tweed declared. "I'll show them damned
publishers a new trick!" He had already threatened the firm with a libel
suit. Now he gave orders to the Board of Education to reject all Harper
bids for schoolbooks and to destroy all on hand—more than fifty
thousand dollars' worth. The partners met to discuss what to do in this
crisis. Abner Harper, John's son, was loath to lose the schoolbook business. Others wondered whether the house might be in real danger
being so dependent on the city's facilities. The arguments grew bitter.
Finally, Fletcher Harper got up from his chair, took his hat, and said,
"Gentlemen, you know where I live. When you are ready to continue
to fight these scoundrels, send for me. Meantime, I shall find a way to
continue it alone."

They did not let him go, and the fight continued. Newspaper editorials across the country praised the Harpers for their courage, and print
orders for the *Weekly* were doubled—up to 300,000 copies an issue.
Cartoons, growing more violent from week to week, caricatured Tweed
and his cohorts as vultures, gallows birds, and men in prison stripes.

Readers of the *Weekly* identified Hall by his spectacles, Sweeny by his shock of hair, Connolly by his gross features, and Tweed by his bald head, long nose, whiskers, and protruding stomach.

"Let's stop them damned pictures," Tweed said. "I don't care so much what the papers write about me—my constituents can't read, but damn it, they can see pictures." So an agent of the Tweed Ring known to Nast called at his home and tactfully offered large sums—eventually half a million dollars—if he would give up "this Ring business" and go abroad to study art. Nast indignantly refused and closed the discussion by saying, "I made up my mind not long ago to put some of those fellows behind the bars and I'm going to put them there!"

Just before the November election, the *Weekly* printed his greatest cartoon, a double-page spread with the legend "The Tammany Tiger Loose—What Are You Going to Do About It?" Nast pictured the fat Tweed in a crowded Colosseum watching the ferocious tiger devouring Miss Liberty. It was the first time the Tammany symbol of the tiger had appeared in a cartoon. Glowering from the page, fangs bared, he was frightening to contemplate.

Going home by train that Saturday night, Nast sat behind a man who had the double-page spread open before him. "What are we going to do about it?" he muttered. Then he struck the pages a blow with his fist. "We're going to kill you." And so the voters did, that following Tuesday. Some of the Ring died in exile, some in prison. Tweed was captured, then allowed to escape; but he was recaptured because of a subsequent Nast cartoon. He died in Ludlow Street jail. In his trunk, neatly packed, were clippings of all the important cartoons Nast had drawn of him.

Thomas Nast not only popularized the Tammany tiger but he also created the Democratic donkey and the Republican elephant. In the off-year campaign of 1874 he drew the elephant to represent the Republican vote, a great and unwieldy creature frightened into a hidden pitfall by the cry of "Caesarism" against Grant. Nast first used the donkey to represent the Democrats in the *Weekly* of January 15, 1870, and a few years later it was accepted as the party's symbol and adopted by other cartoonists.

Some commentators think that Nast was largely responsible for

Horace Greeley's downfall, although in the idealistic, warmhearted, but politically ambitious Greeley, Nast had quite a different kind of adversary. For Nast, Greeley made the mistake of opposing his hero Grant. Therefore Nast turned the satire of his cartooning genius to attack Greeley during the campaign of 1872, when Greeley made his unsuccessful attempt to oust Grant from the White House.

The cartoons of Nast and the editorials of Curtis also played a significant part in the Presidential campaign of 1876. The Republican National Committee sent an official to Nast to present him a check for ten thousand dollars for his help. "You may tell the Committee that I am very grateful for the recognition," Nast said, "but I have been paid by Harper & Brothers, and I cannot accept it." (He was being paid fifteen thousand dollars a year.) What gratified Nast even more was President-elect Hayes' saying, "Nast was the most powerful singlehanded aid we had."

Nast lost his chief supporter in editorial conferences when Fletcher

A Thomas Nast cartoon which appeared in the Weekly *of November 7, 1874, uses his symbol for the Republican Party.*

Harper died in 1877, and a few months later, when a comparatively unimportant drawing was being criticized, Nast so missed Fletcher's support that he ceased for a period to send in anything at all. During this impasse Curtis made a political speech bitterly attacking Senator Roscoe Conkling, of New York, and the Senator replied in kind, ending with a taunting reference to the *Weekly* as "that journal made famous—by the pencil of Thomas Nast!"

Soon the cartoonist was again coming regularly to Franklin Square, but the issue between him and Curtis was still unresolved. It came to a head again over James G. Blaine in 1882. Nast was lampooning Blaine, who was then head of the Republican Party, while Curtis held that Blaine should not be ridiculed because it was delighting his opponents, who were opposed to principles that Curtis was advocating in the *Weekly*. Furthermore he thought that Nast was alienating their Republican friends. He saw the *Weekly* divided, with the political editor saying one thing and the political artist the opposite. He wrote to J. Henry Harper: "I think that the *Weekly* was never so powerful as when it opposed the Tweed Ring and the Greeley nomination, and the reason was that its force was undivided."

Two years later Curtis found unity for the *Weekly* by deserting Blaine and joining Nast. Their editorials and cartoons helped defeat "the man from Maine" and elect Cleveland to his first term as President. The "mugwumps," who defected from Blaine because of his compliance in railroad graft and caused Blaine's defeat in many states, were started by a group of prominent Republicans who first met in the Madison Avenue home of J. Henry Harper.

While Nast's cartoons of political subjects made his name famous, they were far outnumbered by his satirical drawings of social and economic conditions, and of domestic and foreign news events. Thus his annual Christmas pictures were saved by thousands of readers on both sides of the Atlantic, and his *Harper's Weekly* Santa Claus became the accepted type of Christmas saint. Nast was sometimes called on to draw illustrations for books, such as Dickens' *Pickwick Papers,* for which he was paid $867. After twenty-five years of service he retired from Harper's. His output of cartoons for the *Weekly* is estimated as nearly three thousand, the best of which were issued in book form. Many have appeared in other books, his work standing high among the contributors who made the *Weekly* such a rich resource for those who today write on American life in the late nineteenth century.

What distinguished the *Weekly* among the journals of its time, in addition to the work of Curtis and Nast, was its being the best illustrated and edited news weekly to be had. If the telegraph brought news on Wednesday of a disastrous train wreck in Illinois, the *Weekly*'s Chicago correspondent was instructed to get the story and photographs to New York by Thursday's overnight train. As many as twenty wood engravers would set to work to reproduce the pictures; their individual blocks joined together, the illustrated story was on the press Friday night. Thus national news events were covered along with feature stories of men, events, and places around the world. With this rich fare the *Weekly* also served up the best fiction obtainable.

When *The Cloister and the Hearth,* by Charles Reade, was being serialized, a ten-year-old Ohio River boy found an issue carrying the first installment. Frantic to read the whole story, he urged his father to subscribe for him, saying he would pay for it with the five-dollar bank note he had earned for a summer's work. To subscribe, his father sent half the bank note, as was the custom in those days, saying the other half would follow in a later mail. Weeks passed but no *Weekly* appeared. When the Harpers were asked why, they replied that the other half of the note had not come, but they were entering the subscription anyway and were forwarding back numbers. Soon the Reade story was being avidly read in that home and then passed around among families for miles around. The boy became the father of Honoré Willsie Morrow, who wrote some good stories herself, was a magazine editor, and helped her husband launch a publishing house.

Nast's place as the *Weekly*'s cartoonist was taken by Charles Green Bush, who had greater technical skill and treated themes of more general interest. He in turn was replaced by W. A. Rogers, who later wrote *A World Worth While,* an engaging autobiography devoted largely to his Harper friends and associates.

When George W. Curtis died in 1892, his editorial task was assumed by Carl Schurz, who had served the nation as a general in the Union

Army, as Senator from Missouri, and as Secretary of the Interior under
Hayes. A man of great personal charm and commanding presence, he
was also a gifted writer. His editorials continued what had become
known as "the fighting arm of the House." For six years he continued
his predecessor's policy of advocating integrity in government, civil-
service reform, and the gold standard. He was opposed to the country's
involvement with Cuba, as was the managing editor Henry Loomis
Nelson. Realizing he was out of step with most Americans, Schurz
resigned from the *Weekly,* which was disposed to make literary capital
out of the conflict with Spain. Casper Whitney was an important
correspondent for the *Weekly.* (Whitney, with Walter Camp, origi-
nated the idea of the All-American football team, and Camp himself
was on the Harper list with *American Football.*) After Whitney had
returned from a round-the-world trip to the tune of twenty-three hundred dollars, he went to Cuba as a war correspondent. To cover the
Philippine war F. D. Millet, the artist-journalist, was sent across the
Pacific by the *Weekly,* in association with the London *Times* and the
New York *Sun.* The association of these news mediums and the dual
role of Millet was symbolic of a journalistic age that was passing. In
its valiant effort to meet competition the *Weekly* had to team up with its
rivals, and Millet went not as an artist to draw pictures but as a reporter
to cable dispatches. Artistic wood engravings, the glory of the *Weekly*'s
past journalism, had given way to accurate halftones, the quick and easy
tool of the daily papers. At the end of the century it was losing money.

MANAGING EDITORS OF
Harper's Weekly

Theodore Sedgwick	(1857-58)
John Bonner	(1858-63)
Henry Mills Alden	(1863-69)
S. S. Conant	(1869-85)
Montgomery Schuyler	(1885-87)
John Foord	(1887-90)
Richard Harding Davis	(1890-94)
Henry Loomis Nelson	(1894-98)
John Kendrick Bangs	(1899)

9

THE CIVIL WAR AND POST-BELLUM YEARS (1860-69)

"I grew up under the Union and the Constitution," Fletcher Harper once said. "I am for the Union, and whoever is against the Union, I am against him with all I have in the world." Thus he was opposed to the abolitionists, and John Brown's raid and subsequent hanging received scant attention in the *Weekly*. He and the *Weekly* were criticized for not rising to the challenge of this issue. With the secession of South Carolina and other states, Fletcher's hope of maintaining the Union faded, and when Fort Sumter was fired on he saw that war was inevitable and devoted himself to the cause of the North. Editorials in the *Weekly* urged a prosecution of the war until the slaves could be liberated and "the indivisible Union of thirty-four states" be restored. "When you fight, fight!" he often said. That April, "Jack" Harper, Wesley's twenty-two-year-old son, marched off with the 7th Regiment of New York.

Fletcher Harper began to act like a general. He ordered his troops of artists to the field to depict the conflict and to send picture stories back to the *Weekly*. He circularized Northern officers, asking them to forward their own accounts of the struggle. He sent the best of his young artists, Winslow Homer, to cover the Peninsular campaign. Published drawings, some by Homer, revealing the embankments ·before Yorktown which General McClellan was besieging, angered

Harper's Weekly,

New York. Oct 8 — 1861

The bearer, Mr Winslow Homer, is a special artist attached to Harpers Weekly; and is at present detailed for duty with the Army of the Potomac. Commanding Generals and other persons in authority will confer a favor by granting to Mr Homer such facilities as the interests of the service will permit for the discharge of his duties as our artist-correspondent.

Harper & Brothers

Letter in Fletcher Harper's handwriting introducing Winslow Homer to "commanding Generals and other persons in authority."

Secretary of War Stanton. He ordered the immediate suspension of the *Weekly* and telegraphed Franklin Square that Harper's had been guilty of giving aid and comfort to the enemy (an offense carrying the death penalty), and ordered a member of the firm to proceed at once to Washington. It was obviously Fletcher Harper's lot to go, though he said jokingly that he might be shot at sunrise the next day. He went at once to see the Secretary, who was in a very belligerent mood, but before five words had been spoken Harper contrived to put Stanton on the defensive on a matter unrelated to Yorktown or the *Weekly,* and by the time the interview was over he had obtained a revocation of the suspension order. Not only that, but he spoke so convincingly of the work being done by the *Weekly* that the Secretary thanked him for such patriotic service to the country and to the government.

The war brought problems for all publishers. Reduced supplies and increased costs and taxes forced retail prices up 30 per cent. Even so, business was good and, with the war over, prospects never looked better. Textbook sales boomed and the Harpers sent a special salesman to the South. Even before the war ended, Wesley and Fletcher Harper took a trip to New Orleans to renew business and editorial contacts, and shortly after their return Fletcher took off for England. Trade sales, however, were lagging and booksellers complained of price cutting and subscription bookselling; and a plan for the formation of a Booksellers' League, a forerunner of the American Booksellers' Association, was proposed, the better to deal with such problems. At the same time, new markets were opening up. Santa Fe, for example, was now a thriving town with a well-stocked bookshop. In shortest supply were native writers; the *Round Table* often complained of this dearth but believed, as Bryant had twenty years earlier, that it was not due to the lack of international copyright. Despite their patriotism the Harpers had to continue drawing on what English writers turned out.

Even before Julius Caesar's time authors have known that people like to read about military campaigns. The first such post-bellum author for Harper's was Colonel George Ward Nicholas, Sherman's aide-de-camp on the march through Georgia. *The Story of the Great March* was the firm's most successful book in 1865, and it was difficult to manufac-

Portraits of James, John, Wesley, and Fletcher Harper, printed from steel engravings made by Frederick Halpin. The photographs from which Halpin worked were taken in their latter years, the one of James Harper just two days before his death.

ture books to supply the demand. The London *Athenaeum,* usually snobbish about American books, gave it a three-page review. Next came *Inside: A Chronicle of Secession,* by G. F. Harrington, a portrayal of life in the South during the war, with illustrations by Thomas Nast. A 7,000 first printing came out after serialization in the *Weekly. Harper's Pictorial History of the Great Rebellion,* begun late in 1862 by Guernsey and completed with Alden's help in 1868, appeared in a 6,000 first edition, in two volumes, with nearly 1,000 illustrations lifted from the *Weekly.* Herman Melville furnished the literary hors d'oeuvre for Harper's war books. His *Battle Pieces* contained seventy poems, several of which had appeared in the *Magazine.* He was a poet equally of the Confederate forces and of the victorious men in blue, but reviewers were confounded, as the House reader had been, by Melville's prodigal use of words and images, and one reviewer thought his rhymes were positively barbarous. Melville underwrote the costs of a 1,260-copy edition, of which 300 copies went to reviewers. But the hoped-for publicity moved out less than twice the total review copies, and Melville returned to literary obscurity.

In 1863 Harper's had issued *Life on a Georgia Plantation,* by the distinguished actress Fanny Kemble. This story of her experiences (1838-39) on her husband's slave plantation aroused Northern readers and influenced public opinion in England, where she was also well known. A fictional Southern lady, Lillie Ravenel, was presented four years later by J. W. De Forest, of New Haven, who had organized a company of Connecticut volunteers and led them to war, during which he rose to the rank of major and sent back vivid descriptions of battle scenes to the *Magazine.* The Harpers had earlier published a book of European travel for him, and he turned to them in 1867 for his novel *Miss Ravenel's Conversion,* which portrayed the realities of the war better than any piece of fiction before Stephen Crane's *The Red Badge of Courage.* But what Howells later called its "vigorous realism" worked against its popularity then, when the romantic novel was in full bloom.

Other noteworthy books of the decade included two nonfiction works from England, *Queen Victoria's Journal of Life in the Highlands* and Carlyle's *Frederick the Great.* The Carlyle work, for which Harper's had paid a handsome figure, was brought out in six volumes, bound in sheep-skin and in half calf as well as in cloth. However, the Harpers turned down one of the best of English books, *Alice's Adventures in Wonderland*. After warning poachers by announcing it "in press" late in 1865, they had the book read by Charles Nordhoff, who sent it to another reader, Miss Mary Titcomb. Either she reported negatively or Messrs. Appleton protested, for Harper consideration went no further. The Appletons had purchased two thousand sheets of the first Macmillan edition, withdrawn in England because the author and artist had pro-tested that the illustrations had been poorly reproduced. *Alice* had to wait four years for a proper American début, when Lee and Shepard, of Boston, brought out an edition that was widely reviewed; in the *Magazine* Ripley gave it the palm for originality of conception and called it a charming extravaganza.

Serious works of nonfiction written by American authors included Dr. John W. Draper's *Intellectual Development of Europe,* which was ap-plauded as a work worthy of the best English savants and was quickly bought by all who liked to display high-brow books on their library tables. It was soon in a second edition, published in England, and trans-lated for publication in other countries. The Beecher family got top billing through Lyman Beecher's *Autobiography* and Henry Ward Beecher's *Sermons,* each in two luxurious volumes. In many ways the most interesting work was the diverting, rambling, and unaffected auto-biography of the itinerant printer, actor, and manager, Sol Smith. He called his book *Theatrical Management in the West and South for Thirty Years,* and dedicated it to Henry Marsh, the beloved head of the Harper composing room.

Since Harper's was doing well with a monthly and a weekly, the natural expansion of the firm would have been to undertake a daily; however, a proposal to purchase the New York *World* for thirty thou-sand dollars was turned down, as was Charles A. Dana's offer in 1868 to Fletcher Harper that he join in the purchase of the New York *Sun.* Fletcher Harper saw a better means of enlarging the Harper operation without disrupting the editorial and production pattern. He proposed a weekly fashion magazine like the *Bazar,* published in Berlin and widely influential throughout Europe. But his brothers shook their heads no. Fashions were treated in the two periodicals—enough of a concession to silks and perfumes and other vanities. Fletcher argued that his concept of a *Bazar* was much more than that: fashions in good taste, with cut-out patterns, plus fiction and instructive cultural text matter that would interest a whole family. When his brothers held out against him, he asked their permission to proceed alone. "No. We have never done anything separately. We won't make this an exception," John Harper said finally. "I think brother Fletcher shall have his way, and we shall start the *Bazar*." The first issue appeared in November, 1867.

Another argument for extending the publishing enterprise was that five of the Harper sons were now carrying extensive managerial and editorial loads, work soon to be recognized by their being named junior partners. Sons were working alongside fathers: Fletcher Harper, Jr., on periodicals; Joseph W. on editorial correspondence; John W. on finances; and Philip on factory management and personnel. Abner, John Harper's second son, was handling the textbook department. The Mayor's son Philip enjoyed a special relationship with his father—that of brother-in-law. After the death in 1847 of James Harper's first wife, he married Julia Thorne, and after the death in 1856 of Philip's first wife, he married Miss Thorne's sister Augusta. Thus generations and names became scrambled. Philip's son James, by his first wife, was older than his stepbrother and uncle, James Thorne Harper, a son of the Mayor by his second wife. This mixup caused much family amusement, the Mayor often referring to Philip as his brother-in-law. The Mayor's daughter Julia wrote from Vassar to her favorite cousin and contemporary addressing him "Dear Uncle James."

Julia Harper was living at home in the early spring of 1869 and accompanied her father on his daily carriage rides. After dinner on Good Friday they drove through Central Park and down Fifth Avenue. "How well Mr. Harper looks," a fellow publisher remarked as the carriage passed. Moments afterward the pole of the carriage suddenly broke, and the horses, normally gentle, became frightened and started to run. The carriage was upset and both occupants were thrown to the pavement. Julia escaped serious injury and was carried home, but her father was taken insensible to the nearby Knickerbocker Hospital, where he died at quarter past seven on Easter night. Newspapers carried long accounts of his extraordinary career and *Frank Leslie's Weekly* said that New York had lost its most distinguished citizen.

Funeral services for James Harper were held on the following Tuesday at St. Paul's Methodist Church. The flags on City Hall and other public buildings were at half mast, and the Common Council sat in pews reserved for them. Pallbearers included Peter Cooper, A. T. Stewart, Professor Henry Drisler, and other prominent citizens. But the tribute that James Harper would have liked most was given anonymously. A Negro, unknown to anyone present, was observed weeping as he passed before the open casket. It was assumed that he was one of the boys who had regularly attended the prayer meetings that James Harper as a young apprentice printer had conducted in the home of a Negro family on Ann Street. Resolutions of respect and condolence were adopted by various groups with which Mr. Harper had been associated. The Publishers' Association, through W. H. Appleton, spoke of him as a "sagacious associate," and the Harper employees, through Henry Marsh, praised Mr. Harper's "generous character, his forbearing and kindly nature . . . his genial presence, and the kindly sympathy and encouragement with which he always lightened our labors."

10

CHARLES PARSONS AND HIS
SCHOOL OF ARTISTS

Joseph Pennell, leading American artist and lithographer, often asserted that the growth of real and vital American art started in the department of Charles Parsons in Franklin Square.

Parsons, who succeeded John Chapin, Harper's first art editor, began his Harper career in April, 1863, when Fletcher Harper hired him to manage the art department. By then he was a bearded, somewhat bald man of forty-two, and known for his versatility as a painter, particularly of landscapes and marine subjects. He had drawn illustrations for both the *Magazine* and the *Weekly,* and what Fletcher had observed in Parsons was something more than the artist—a man who was mild and unassuming, eager to praise the genuine work of others, ready to take suggestions, not irritated by criticism. In fact, he often recommended other artists, and Fletcher had learned that the men he sent in were competent. More illustrators were needed because of the full tide of work coming in from the battlefields. Furthermore, they needed an artist on their own staff to direct them.

Some time after Parsons took charge of the art department, it was moved to the second floor of the Franklin Square Building. Since these new quarters faced more to the east than to the north, the light coming through the windows was not ideal, but beside each window was the desk, drawing board, and hard wooden chair of an artist, low partitions separating each from his fellow. Parsons had a small office dominated by a desk always piled high with papers. Farther back from the windows were tables containing issues of the *Magazine* and the *Weekly,* all the foreign illustrated periodicals, book manuscripts, and proofs. There may also have been shelves and filing cabinets filled with sketches and drawings that had served their purpose, or old work may have just been stacked up. At any rate, when the art department was moved, a vast accumulation was carted off to a paper manufacturer, much to everyone's relief. What was destroyed included literally thousands of Civil War sketches and later works of Winslow Homer, Edwin A. Abbey, C. S. Reinhart, A. B. Frost, and other artists—works that would bring fabulous prices today. The art department was moved so that it could have space adjacent to the offices of the editors of the *Magazine* and the *Weekly.*

"Central-Park Winter; The Skating Pond"

This painting, made by Charles Parsons for Messrs. Currier & Ives the year before he joined Harper's, proved to be one of their most popular engravings. It was later selected by a jury of collectors as one of that firm's best fifty prints, one of three to receive a unanimous vote. Parsons was an intimate friend of both Nathaniel Currier and J. Merritt Ives and occasionally got commissions from them for the lithographer George Endicott, with whom Parsons then worked as a partner.

When Charles Parsons started his twenty-six-year Harper career, the editors of these periodicals were receiving almost daily, by mail and by messenger, articles and sketches from the corps of Harper author-artists who were covering the Civil War. Among these intrepid men were A. R. Waud and William Waud (they later covered the Chicago and Boston fires, and A. R. Waud's name was signed to many *Weekly* drawings), Robert Weir, Andrew McCallum, A. W. Warren, and Theodore R. Davis. Especially "Dory" Davis, who was the veteran of them all and stayed on for many years as an honored craftsman on Parsons' staff, drawing many of the *Weekly*'s cover pages.

Edwin Windsor Kemble was started on an artistic career by Parsons. Kemble had finished school and was working for an accounting firm when his father urged him to submit some comic drawings to Harper's. Parsons took them and asked the young man to return in a few days. When Kemble went back and asked timidly for his drawings, Parsons looked at him over his glasses and said, "You don't want to take all of them, do you? Here, take this slip of paper downstairs to the cashier." Kemble left Franklin Square with seventy dollars and walked the long way home that night, fearing pickpockets on the streetcars. The following week he gave up his accounting job.

Alfred Fredericks was one of the first staff artists whose work was featured in the *Weekly*. He was wonderfully imaginative and gave early encouragement to Thomas Nast; recognizing talent, he gave Nast some lessons, got him into the Academy of Design, and in 1859 gave him his first Harper assignment. Another close friend and instructor of young Nast was Sol Eytinge. His many humorous drawings for the *Weekly* during the Civil War years, particularly, enlivened the otherwise somber pages. His work appeared regularly with such better-known artists as Davis and Frederick S. Church, and suffers not at all in comparison. To leaf through the pages of the *Weekly* and to spot his clever work is to wish one could know more about Eytinge, who was undoubtedly one of Fletcher Harper's favorites.

Winslow Homer is now the best known of the young men who drew Civil War pictures for the *Weekly*. His Harper association had begun earlier, however, for the artist was aware of the importance of the

"*Raid on a Sand-Swallow Colony—'How Many Eggs?'*" *A wood engraving by Winslow Homer, printed in* Harper's Weekly, *June 13, 1874. This engraving is a composite of sixteen separate wood blocks.*

new periodical almost from its start. He was then twenty-one. The issue of August 1, 1857, carried his first drawings, a two-page spread of five pictures depicting student life at Harvard, one showing a football match (with some players wearing top hats). To accompany the drawing, someone wrote a short piece comparing American university life with that of Britain. This text "illustrated the illustration," as Henry James once said of a *Magazine* article he wrote which Abbey illustrated.

Thereafter Harper's took everything that Homer submitted, always giving him either full pages or double-page spreads. His work was also used in the *Magazine* and later in *Harper's Bazar*. In fact, with Cliff Street giving him so much support he left his home and studio in Boston in 1859 and set up in New York. The Harpers immediately made him a generous offer to enter their employ as a staff artist but, wanting to keep his independence, he refused. When Lincoln passed through New York on his way to be inaugurated, Homer drew him speaking from the balcony of the Astor House. He was sent to Washington to cover the inauguration for the *Weekly*. Homer had little taste for war, but, even so, his war illustrations, mostly of everyday life in camp, are among the best made by any artist. "Here were authentic types of a democratic army—gaunt Yankees looking like Uncle Sam," according to his biographer, Lloyd Goodrich, "hard specimens all, drawn with humor and keen characterization. . . . Drinking, fighting, gambling and crude horseplay were not soft-pedaled, but on the whole the picture he drew of military life was jovial." By the end of the war Homer had grown tired of being a reportorial artist and was finding a more engrossing medium in oils. In 1867 he went to Paris for a stay of ten months and sent back to the *Weekly* two drawings of dance halls. The cancan and girls kicking high were strong meat for the readers the Harpers had garnered, and the accompanying article piously stated that this was "work for the severe and steady eye of the preacher and moralist."

At the close of the war Homer had another Harper offer for a steady job, which he would take, he wrote his brother, if two oils on exhibition were not sold. Whereupon his brother promptly bought them. While Homer grumbled that Charles Parsons was cutting down the size of, and consequent payment for, some of his drawings, he continued send-

"Young Abbey and His Mentor," drawn by W. A. Rogers, who said, "Parsons worked in the shadow of the men he did so much to help."

ing illustrations to Franklin Square through 1877. Parsons often made suggestions for improvement which Homer always accepted. He would take a desk and complete his drawing on the block while Stanley Reinhart, "Ned" Abbey, W. A. Rogers, and other young artists gathered around him to watch a master craftsman work.

What impressed Rogers about Parsons was his eagerness to have the young artists study Nature and to depict honestly what they saw. Rogers observed, "Thanks to the clear vision and good common sense of wise old Charles Parsons, every man who came to Franklin Square—and it was the Mecca of illustrators in those days—was encouraged to be true to his own ideas, to develop his own style." But it was not an easy job allowing Homer, Abbey, Reinhart, Rogers, and others freedom to strike out in new paths. Once, Parsons piled on Rogers' desk a stack of letters from subscribers to the *Magazine* who had written to protest its newfangled art work, some saying they would cancel their subscriptions if this outlandish style of illustration was continued.

Homer's sincerity in seeking truth in Nature and skillfully reproducing it were qualities that deeply influenced those young artists. Homer did not attempt to "photograph" his subject. Often he used line sparsely, particularly on wood, according to W. A. Rogers, who wrote, "The boxwood color is of a light, warm tone and this Homer used as his lightest gray, deepening it with a wash of India ink and painting in one or two high lights with white. There were not more than two or three tones in the picture—just broad, flat washes and uncompromising outlines."

C. S. Reinhart came to Franklin Square in 1870 at the age of twenty-six, having just returned after two years of study with artists in Paris and Munich. From the start he proved to be one of the most dependable craftsmen Parsons ever employed. He turned out an astonishing number of drawings. His forte was that of a landscape and genre painter and his black-and-white sketches were brilliant. He would say, "A line made out of doors means as much as a dozen in the studio." He was one of the first Americans making pictures of contemporary life whose work was recognized abroad.

During his six years in the Harper art department, Reinhart illustrated several books. One of the first was *Nicholas Nickleby,* in the Harper Household Edition of Dickens' works, completed in 1872. Another was Will Carleton's *Farm Ballads,* which sold 22,000 copies in one year. The 1873 edition carries nine illustrations with Reinhart's initials, including two for the poem "Over the Hill to the Poor-House." In 1883 Reinhart's genius for line and characterization added enormously to the success of G. P. Lathrop's *Spanish Vistas,* reviewed as the best book on Spain since Irving's *The Alhambra.* He illustrated the work of at least three minor Harper novelists before teaming up in 1887 with Charles Dudley Warner for a summer's trip to famous American watering places and mountain resorts. A beautiful book, *Their Pilgrimage,* resulted. Reinhart collaborated with other artists on several books, the best joint effort—with Winslow Homer and two others—being *Songs from the Published Writings of Alfred Tennyson.*

Edwin A. Abbey was eighteen years old, and ten years younger than

Pen drawing by Edwin A. Abbey, for the de luxe edition of Goldsmith's She Stoops to Conquer.

Pencil sketch, "Center of Attention," by Charles Stanley Reinhart.

Reinhart, when he came to New York from Philadelphia to work for Harper's. He came as a result of a letter Parsons had written to Abbey's father. "Judging from these drawings of your son [which you forwarded], he will either be a great failure or one of the great American artists," Parsons wrote, and added that what the young man needed was opportunity and if he wanted to come to Franklin Square on a trial basis, he would be paid fifteen dollars a week. So he started in February, 1871, with Reinhart as his mentor. Their close association prompted Henry James to compare them. In *Picture and Text* James wrote, "With Mr. Abbey, Mr. Reinhart is the artist who has contributed most abundantly to *Harper;* his work, indeed, in quantity considerably exceeds Mr. Abbey's. He is the observer of the immediate, as Mr. Abbey is that of the considerably removed. . . . He is, in short, the vigorous, racy *prosateur* of that human comedy of which Mr. Abbey is the poet."

On occasions, if he found himself unable to concentrate on a draw- ing, Abbey would go out in the middle of the room and turn two or three cartwheels to loosen up. He rigged up a trapeze in the art depart- ment and was aloft once, "skinning the cat," when one of the Harper partners came along in his high silk hat. As the story was told later, the hat suddenly went soaring across the room to fall to the floor in a piteous condition. And the next morning the trapeze was missing.

Abbey's salary was raised to twenty dollars a week after his first year; to thirty-five at the end of the second year, and after his third year— fall, 1874—he withdrew from the art department because Parsons could not get approval of a five-dollar-a-week increase. Anyway he was am- bitious to establish his own studio and had found one on Union Square he could rent. Parsons also thought it would be a good thing for Abbey to try his wings and said to another artist, James E. Kelley, who was tempted to follow him, "If you want to go with Abbey, you will not be happy here."

But Abbey did not find it easy, as he recalled later. "That time I left Harper's and had to go to other publishers for work, I nearly died of shyness." However, there were still Harper projects for Abbey to do. The most congenial assignment that Harper's gave him was to make twenty-seven illustrations for the Household Edition of Dickens' *Christ- mas Stories*. A year later he had completed forty-five illustrations for *The Uncommercial Traveller*. But by that time, he was back working full time for Parsons. It was like coming home again. He could now ask for—and get—fifty dollars a week. And he gave that much again in help to the new fellows who were starting at Franklin Square. Henry James believed that Abbey himself profited much by his years in the Harper art department, where, he said, "the events of the day are promptly reproduced; and with the morrow so near the day is necessarily a short one—too short for general education. Such a school is not, no doubt, the ideal one, but in fact it may have a very happy influence."

Abbey's second Harper period lasted for two years and he turned out so many drawings for the Harper periodicals, especially the *Magazine*, that James said that Abbey's "whole career has been open to the readers of *Harper*." During this time Abbey did his first mural, a view of red roofs from a window—a small panel for the Harper reception room. In December, 1878, the firm sent Abbey to England after a farewell dinner at Delmonico's with fellow artists as guests. His sketches of Stratford-on-Avon (one excuse for the trip) appeared in the *Magazine* the following April. He was kept in funds by doing odd jobs for books and periodicals and by fulfilling a commission to make sketches to illustrate a volume of poems by Robert Herrick.

Abbey returned to New York for a few months in 1880-81, and the *Monthly* for May, 1881, carried some of the best of his Herrick sketches and, for the first time, mentioned him by name in the table of contents. He was back in England when Harper's brought out *Selections from the Poetry of Robert Herrick,* with Abbey's work making it "the finest illustrated book that had appeared in America up to its time," according to Professor Frank Jewett Mather. His next book, which James considered his best to date and on which Abbey had been working for four years, came out in 1886. It was the oversized richly embellished *She Stoops to Conquer,* Goldsmith's drama, lavishly illustrated with Abbey's black-and-white drawings. Ten of the full-page illustrations were reproduced by photogravure at Abbey's insistence.

Harper's then commissioned Abbey to illustrate the plays of Shakespeare, and a salary journal shows that Abbey was paid £250 in 1888, and beginning in November of that year and continuing through December, 1889, he earned over $12,000, at the rate of $325 a page, for work on five of the *Comedies.* All fourteen were illustrated by 1895 and issued in four volumes. For such an expensive undertaking (it cost nearly a thousand dollars a volume just to make and print the engravings), it is surprising that only fifteen hundred copies were printed. The set of books—one of the most handsome ever issued by the house—was sold by subscription. The illustrations for the *Tragedies* were never printed in book form because of the difficulty of fitting them into book format.

Some connoisseurs consider *Old Songs,* published in 1889, as Abbey's best book, while E. V. Lucas, his biographer, votes for *The Quiet Life,* issued a year later. *Old Songs* contained seventeenth- and eighteenth-century lyrics that Abbey illustrated in moods varying from rapture to

waggishness and with sentiments ranging from dolorous love to acid-
ulous common sense. Sixteen drawings from *Old Songs* received a First
Class medal when they were shown in Paris, and won for the artist an
accolade from Joseph Pennell, "the greatest living illustrator." Abbey
lived the rest of his life in England and spent years painting "The Quest
of the Holy Grail" for the Boston Public Library.

Among the young artists whom Abbey helped was W. A. Rogers.
Rogers found the Harper art department like a country school where
young "scholars" like him listened to the older ones like Abbey "recite"
under the guidance and direction of Parsons. Parsons had a gift for dis-
covering the good points of the recruits and carefully developing them.
For example, he found that Rogers was adept at drawing very round
wheels, and Rogers saw himself in danger of being handed down to
posterity as the wheelwright of the *Weekly*.

Finally, a year later, Rogers got his first big assignment—to draw
sketches of the visit of President Hayes to the Minnesota State Fair. As
he finished his work, regretting his return to New York, he was called
to the office of one of the directors of the Fair. "How would you like to
see the real Northwest?" a grizzled old soldier asked him. "You are a
long way from New York. Why not go a little farther? With that pencil
of yours you can make a [valuable] record of your trip."

Rogers wired Parsons of his opportunity to depict wildlife on the
plains, but Parsons was unimpressed and wired Rogers to return to his
round wheels, back to the grind of Franklin Square. Still, New York
was a long way off and here he was at the gate of the Northwest. He
went, carrying letters to commanders of military posts, owners of stage
routes, post traders; he had a map showing the upper Missouri and the
new country of Manitoba. From Bismarck, North Dakota, which in 1878
was the end of the Northern Pacific Railroad and the "jumping-off
place" to the Northwest via the famous Deadwood stage, Rogers wrote a
long letter to Parsons describing his experiences. Parsons replied with a
telegram that eventually caught up with Rogers: "Come back at once.
Harper & Brothers." From the wilderness Rogers replied, "Please send
me one hundred dollars."

He had played hooky often enough as a boy to know what sort of
reception awaited him three months later at the Franklin Square

school. Parsons told him that he was grievously disappointed and that the House was extremely dissatisfied; however, he would go downstairs and put up as strong a plea as he could. "While that kindly gentleman was pleading my cause below," Rogers said, "I plastered his sanctum from ceiling to floor, covering desk, table, chairs with sketches of everything I had seen on my runaway trip. I was just opening another mud-stained packet when Mr. Parsons, who was very near-sighted, returned. There was a sorrowful expression on his sympathetic face, which suddenly changed to a dazed one. Then as he saw the mass of material I had brought back, his whole countenance cleared and the enthusiastic spirit of the man shone in his face. We planned pages and double pages and more pages for the *Weekly*."

Rogers covered the assassination of President Garfield in 1881. He obtained a picture of Guiteau, the assassin, made from it a drawing for the *Weekly,* and returned to Washington to make sketches in and around the White House, where the President lay dying. He finally succeeded in getting to Mr. Garfield's secretary. Rogers argued that history was being wasted unless the occasion was accurately portrayed in *Harper's Weekly.* This plea for honest journalism made sense to the physicians and the Garfield family, and Rogers was admitted early one hot July morning to the room in which the President lay sleeping. For half an hour Rogers sketched the bedroom scene, with Mrs. Garfield and her eldest son occasionally looking over his shoulder as he worked. Later in the day, Rogers laid out the drawing for a double-page spread in the *Weekly,* and at nine o'clock the next morning he stepped into the art department. Parsons jumped to his feet. "My dear boy," he exclaimed, "why did you leave Washington? Postmaster General James is working to get you into the White House, and we are sure he will be able to do so before this week is over. You must return at once." Rogers replied by opening his bundle of sketches, and word of his scoop was soon known throughout the establishment.

By 1888 Rogers was being paid $5,500 a year, drawing cartoons for the *Weekly* and illustrations for books, and eventually he turned altogether to cartooning. In the mid-nineties he drew devastatingly of William Jennings Bryan and the silver issue, his cartoons backing editorial

matter in the *Weekly,* and he delighted Theodore Roosevelt, who was
then Police Commissioner of New York City, with drawings that favored
his zestful policies. About 1900 Rogers left Harper's, at the urging of
James Gordon Bennett, to become the New York *Herald*'s cartoonist.

Of the many artists who worked under Parsons at Franklin Square,
some are known only by initials that appeared on engravings or by names
appearing in a payroll ledger. From six to eight artists were always
needed for work on the periodicals and books, including histories, geog-
raphies, readers, and other textbooks, which made up a large segment
of the Harper business. A few of these achieved sufficient recognition as
artists on their own account to deserve mention; with one exception they
were about the same age and were in the art department while Rogers
was a freshman under Parsons: John W. Alexander, A. B. Frost, William T. Smedley, F. V. Dumond, and Charles Graham. Graham was
the highest-paid artist on Parsons' staff, earning by 1883 the top salary
of fifty dollars a week. (Parsons was then being paid one hundred and
twenty dollars a week.)

In addition to artists who were on the Harper payroll, there were
many who worked in their own studios and submitted their pictures to
Parsons or worked on commissions he gave them. Of these the two most
famous, in addition to Homer, are Frederic Remington and Howard
Pyle. Both men first saw printed reproductions of their work in the
Weekly. Both men were authors as well as artists.

Remington was a tall, blond, and handsome fellow with a rugged
physique. After studying at the Yale School of Fine Arts (at Yale he
played football with Walter Camp) and the New York Art Students
League, he went to the Rocky Mountain country for adventure—and
for art. After he had composed a picture he thought worthy of sending
to the *Weekly,* he sketched it on a piece of wrapping paper, crammed it
into a small envelope, and posted it to Franklin Square. Parsons had
often opened packages containing sketches well protected by cardboard
and neatly tied with ribbon, but nothing as informal as this. He was
intrigued and curious about the Wyoming postmark. And when he
spread out the crumpled sheet he was impressed.

Shortly afterward Remington, in Wyoming, received a larger en-

Ink and wash drawing. "Mounting a Wild One," by Frederic Remington.

Ink and wash drawing. "The Old Flute Player," by Howard Pyle.

velope from Harper's enclosing a check and a tear sheet with his printed sketch. Seeing his work in print soon brought him to New York with a portfolio of sketches. Parsons introduced him to Alden, who asked him to try his hand at writing an article to accompany his drawings. This he did, and acceptance brought payment for both text and illustrations. It was the first of several articles and stories by him published in the *Magazine.* The House also published five books for him, beginning with *Pony Tracks* in 1895. His style was vigorous and lucid, and his illustrations unmatched—even today—for delineation of Indians, frontiersmen, and cowpunchers on horseback.

Howard Pyle had to work harder to gain Harper recognition. During 1877 he sent in his first drawings. Parsons thought they had strength but lacked technical skill, and had them redrawn. One day Pyle took in a rough sketch called "A Wreck in the Offing," and begged Parsons not to turn it over to Abbey, Reinhart, Frost, or another of his "young Olympians." Parsons reluctantly agreed but said that if the finished picture was not acceptable he would pay Pyle ten or fifteen dollars for the idea. After six weeks Pyle returned, and later wrote what happened:

I think it was not until I stood in the awful presence of the art editor himself that I realized how this might be the turning point in my life— that I realized how great was to be the result of his decision on my future endeavor. I think I have never since passed such a moment of intense trepidation—a moment of such confused and terrible blending of hope and despair at the same time. I can recall just how the art editor looked at me over his spectacles, and to my perturbed mind it seemed that he was weighing in his mind (for he was a very tender man) how best he might break the news to me of my unsuccess. The rebound was almost too great when he told me that Mr. Harper had liked my idea very much and that they were going to use it in the *Weekly*. But when he said that they were not only going to use it, but were going to make of it a double-page cut, my exaltation was so great that it seemed to me that I knew not where I was standing or what had happened to me. . . . I found a friend and I took him to Delmonico's, and we had lunch of all the delicacies in season and out of season. . . .

Pyle was a big man, with wide shoulders, who had more of the appearance of the scholar than the artist. He held his head high, so that he often gave the impression of looking down on people. His face betrayed pride and ambition. Yet his writing and drawings revealed him as an artist whose concerns were idealistic, humanistic, and religious. Of his nine Harper books, *Men of Iron* was most popular. First published in 1892, this story of the times of chivalry in the England of Henry IV has remained constantly in print, with nearly 200,000 copies sold. Several of his books were first serialized in *Harper's Young People*. He also illustrated many other books, including two by Woodrow Wilson— *George Washington* and *A History of the American People*. In sending the manuscript for his life of Washington to Alden, Wilson wrote requesting that Pyle be asked to illustrate it. Pyle eagerly accepted and undertook intensive research to make his drawings correct. He did not hesitate to question the Princeton professor on his facts, and Wilson wrote that he welcomed such probing. These drawings now hang in the Boston Public Library.

In his later years Pyle taught art in a school he established in Wilmington, Delaware, the city of his birth. Here, among others, he had Maxfield Parrish, N. C. Wyeth, and Frank Schoonover as students. Despite his extraordinary influence on young artists, he failed to help them develop their own characteristic styles. They were too dazzled by the Howard Pyle convention. The death in 1911 of his early Harper mentor and dear friend Edwin A. Abbey saddened him greatly, and his own death followed a few months later in Florence, Italy.

Knowledge of what Parsons paid his artists can only be pieced together from various sources, since his record books were assumed to have no historical value and were not kept. In the eighteen-eighties, according to Rogers, artists were being paid $75 for an illustration. In the eighteen-nineties, Pyle received $100 for a page illustration in the *Magazine* if the drawing was returned to him—$150 if it was retained. Sometimes the firm recouped this additional amount by selling reproduction rights, as they did one of Frost's to a calendar concern. The *Magazine* paid Laurence Hutton $250 for each of his six "Landmark" pieces on literary cities, while F. V. Dumond was given $2,500 for accompanying illustrations. Hutton was not bothered by this seeming discrepancy, for he was then on the staff of the *Magazine* and familiar with policy, and also knew that the author retained book rights. F. D. Millet experienced the same thing in the dual role of artist and author. He submitted an article entitled "Cossack Life" to Alden, who said he would gladly accept it if it was illustrated. Millet found in his sketchbook several drawings of Cossack people, places, and activities. With this material, he drew the necessary illustrations in half the time he had given to the writing. As a writer he received $100, as an artist $300.

Two other artists were being paid at the rate of $100 for a *Magazine* illustration, F. S. Church and T. de Thulstrup, although Thulstrup's drawings were more often used in the *Weekly*. Thulstrup was a dependable workhorse, moreover, and was often called on to draw the *Weekly* cover, particularly when scenes depicting large crowds of people were called for. These he could do with a mastery of detail that would panic

HARPER'S WEEKLY.
JOURNAL OF CIVILIZATION.

Vol. XXIX.—No. 1495.
Copyright, 1885, by Harper & Brothers.

NEW YORK, SATURDAY, AUGUST 15, 1885.

TEN CENTS A COPY.
WITH A SUPPLEMENT

GENERAL GRANT'S FUNERAL.—MAJOR-GENERAL HANCOCK AND STAFF AT THE HEAD OF THE PROCESSION.—DRAWN BY T. DE THULSTRUP.—[SEE PAGE 534.]

almost any other artist working against a deadline. When President Grant died in 1885, the *Weekly* staff decided to devote most of the August 15, 1885, issue to his life and work, with copious illustrations. Parsons asked Thulstrup to do the cover, which would show the procession to the General's temporary resting place. Since Thulstrup had to draw background material ahead of time, he tinted the sky in a way that would be appropriate for rain clouds, and he spotted a few umbrellas among the crowds of people he drew—umbrellas that could serve as protection from sun or rain, and in either event could cover the art department. Fortunately it was a clear day.

Ingenuity and enterprise had been accepted for nearly thirty years as a necessary routine in the publication of a weekly news magazine. Elkins, the superintendent of the cylinder press room, could quickly run off an edition, for his men were operating the latest and best of the Hoe presses. But the inventive genius that revolutionized printing had not been paced by improvements to speed up the reproduction of pictures. Smithwick, of the engraving room, and Parsons, of the art department, were still working with material and equipment that went back to the days of the hand press.

If Frederic E. Ives, of Philadelphia, read that Grant memorial issue of the *Weekly*, as he very likely did, he probably mused that such a method of reproducing illustrations would soon be a thing of the past. That year Ives was developing a revolutionary new "process method" of reproducing pictures. He placed cross lines, finely and expertly drawn on glass, in front of a negative on which a subject—a drawing or photograph—was reproduced. The resulting "screen negative" could then be made into a halftone electroplate by processes known since 1839, the year Daguerre's invention became known. In the early nineties this form of engraving replaced wood engraving, and with its use staff artists and wood-engraving departments could be dispensed with. Even Parsons was dispensable. In 1889 he was sixty-eight years old. He had taken nearly a 20 per cent cut in salary. Times were changing. Perhaps he should retire.

Late in 1889 the House gave a dinner at Delmonico's honoring Parsons on the eve of his retirement. Those present included the partners, the editors of the periodicals and their staffs, and many contributors and artists. Joseph W. Harper spoke for the House and Parsons replied. Charles Dudley Warner paid a tribute for the contributors. Curtis spoke for the editors, but apparently the artists were not given a chance to speak their piece, for the following April a committee composed of Harper artists organized another testimonial dinner for Parsons. Abbey was toastmaster and presented Parsons with a portfolio containing drawings, water colors, sketches, and letters from his old associates.

Parsons was flattered to know that Abbey never drew a picture without wondering what Parsons would think of it, that Pyle looked up to him as the best critic in the United States, and that Remington signed himself "Your Discovery." However, it was enough to know that he had done something to influence art in America through a generation of artists that had passed through his Harper school. He had lived through the transition of the House from the four brothers to their sons and grandsons and had shared in its widening influence. But while he said his goodbyes tearfully, he was thinking of the future as well as of the past. He would now have unhurried years for still another career, time to work seriously with his water colors.

11

HARPER'S BAZAR (1867-1913)

Fletcher Harper chose Mary L. Booth as editor of the *Bazar*. She had achieved considerable notice as a translator of several books from the French, especially Gasparin's *The Uprising of a Great People* (1861), which she translated in a week of nearly solid work. It received enormous word-of-mouth advertising, and Miss Booth had a letter of thanks from President Lincoln for her help in strengthening the spirit of the American people. She was also known to Harper's as the author of the first complete history of New York.

The first issue of *Harper's Bazar* appeared on Saturday, November 2, 1867, and after its first six weeks it had gained a circulation of 100,000 copies, owing, a trade journal said, to its brilliant illustrations, clever text, and a new, unrivaled field. While it tried not to be merely a magazine of fashion plates, these were its primary feature and by the second year color plates were printed. For many years plates of the fashion pages were purchased from the Berlin, Germany, *Bazar*. George W. Curtis, using the pseudonym of "An Old Bachelor," wrote many light and amiable articles called "Manners Upon the Road," and Harriet Prescott Spofford was the *Bazar's* most frequent contributor of stories and poems. Feature columns came and went, such as "Diets for Invalids," "Sayings and Doings," and "Women and Men," the latter written by Colonel Thomas W. Higginson, a popular essayist prominent

121

in literary circles. Paris fashions and New York fashions were reported regularly, as was gossip from England and Washington.

Each issue carried illustrations, several by Winslow Homer and other protégés of Charles Parsons. European royalty was frequently depicted and life in various foreign countries was written up. The *Bazar* ran seven or eight serials each year—written mostly by the Victorian novelists. Much attention was given to household management, recipes, diets, and health. Most readers, apparently, had servants and could live in houses costing from seven to ten thousand dollars, and Miss Booth counted on them to be churchgoers (mostly Protestant), faithful to a strict moral code, and eager to improve their etiquette and broaden their knowledge of public affairs. Subscribers could cut out patterns for all sorts of clothing or write to the publishers for more.

Books came out of *Bazar* articles, several carrying the *Bazar* name— of decorum, of health, of the household, of cooking recipes, and of a half-dozen other subjects. These and other Harper books were advertised regularly, proving Fletcher Harper's argument that periodicals were a tender to the book business of the House. By 1880 the *Bazar* had a circulation of 150,000 and boasted a readership of half a million, and the Boston *Transcript* said that to dress by it would be the aim and ambition of the women of America.

At that time the ladies could have breakfast caps fashioned for every type and contour of face, and corsets were more comfortable than they had been, because the weight of the clothing was carried from the shoulders and whalebones were slanted instead of being straight, thus causing no unpleasant breaking at the hips. The *Bazar* never objected to women going to bathing beaches, and actually published a drawing by Winslow Homer showing them decorously grouped, stockings and all, around a seashore rock.

Miss Booth took her editorial job with considerable realism. She tackled the problems of the ugly girl and the girl who was quiet but not stupid. She knew there were unhappy wives and saw to it that they were counseled to do something positive about their condition rather than gather with *bonnes camarades* to bewail their fate. Concerned that single women were generally pitied and often patronized, she charged at the

A typical cover of Harper's Bazar.

single man. He, she said, should be laughed at. If she could have had her way, unmarried men as a class should not even be allowed to vote. But, married or not, men needed to be informed about changing styles in shirts and suits, the best materials for waistcoats and what to wear on special occasions. Almost every week she and her advertisers saw to that.

Being a single woman herself did not deter Miss Booth from living a full social life. Although she was not beautiful, she had lovely large brown eyes and a warm engaging smile. People commented on her "majestic bearing" and her "hands as exquisite as if carved in ivory." She was often seen at lectures, concerts, and the theatre. Out of her salary of fifty dollars a week she entertained friends, many of them authors, at her home on Fifty-ninth Street. After the poets Alice and Phoebe Cary died and their home was no longer open to the New York literati, Miss Booth and her friend Mrs. Wright began having open house on Saturday evenings. Margaret Sangster was often there and wrote later of the famous people who came to share tea and wafers along with witty and sophisticated talk. Once, she gave a reception for Louisa May Alcott, who had written a serial for the *Bazar*. Laurence Hutton came late in the evening and talked with Miss Alcott so long that Miss Booth came up to present another guest. "Oh, don't take this young man away," Miss Alcott said. "He is the only person who has not mentioned *Little Women* to me tonight."

Miss Booth's Franklin Square office was small and fitted only with a desk, a small sofa, and two chairs. She had neither typewriter nor secretary and, of course, no telephone. She was treated with deference and respect by the Harper partners not only because of the success of her magazine but also because she had a masculine grasp of business and the quick decisiveness of a man of affairs. And she could not be pushed around.

In 1888, to honor her on her twenty-first year as editor of the *Bazar*, the House sent her on a four-month trip abroad. She died in March, 1889, and both the *Bazar* and the *Weekly* carried accounts of her career. J. Henry Harper asked Margaret Sangster to become the new editor. She replied that she had slight interest in clothes and spent as little time as possible with milliners and dressmakers, an argument Harper disallowed since Miss S. H. Shanks had for years taken care of the fashion department. With the help of this attractive, Kentucky-born fashion expert, Mrs. Sangster directed the *Bazar* for ten years, when she retired. She shared the ability of her predecessor for tactful refusal of manuscripts.

Three of Mrs. Sangster's favorite authors were Olive Thorne Miller, who wrote about home pets, chiefly birds, and how to keep them happy, Marion Harland, and Mrs. Candace Wheeler. These and other writers were women of many interests, and well known at the time, so that their names helped to popularize the *Bazar*. Marion Harland was the pen name of Mary Virginia Hawes Terhune, the mother of Albert Payson Terhune, whose dog stories made him a greatly beloved and profitable author for Harper's a generation later. Mrs. Wheeler wrote a "Distaff Series," which later made a book; she designed and directed the Woman's Building of the Chicago World's Fair. On the nearby campus of the new University of Chicago, William Rainey Harper had brought together a distinguished faculty, including eight college presidents. His ability to negotiate such talent inspired a wit to call the University "Harper's Bazar."

Mrs. Sangster used less fiction than her predecessor and, under the influence of Howells, attempted to play down the romantic story and play up the realistic. English fiction made up half of her output, and she had the honor of introducing Hardy's *Tess* to American readers; however, decisions about what periodical issued a particular novel were made by J. Henry Harper. The new technology, which eventually replaced wood engravings with halftones, made its bow in the issue of April 18, 1891. Thereafter photo reproductions appeared in the *Bazar* more frequently than in the other Harper periodicals.

The Harper hierarchy greatly impressed Mrs. Sangster. She was always pleased to take visitors to the front door past the railing, behind which sat the sons and grandsons of the four brothers whose engraved portraits hung on the wall of her office. She thought the descendants resembled their forebears in looks, honesty, sincerity, and kindness. She told the story of a messenger boy who was sent out on an errand in below-zero weather. Noticing that the boy wore no overcoat, one of the Harpers asked why. "His father is dead and his mother is very poor," he was told. Later that day, Mr. Harper asked the boy to come to his desk. He put a key in his hand, saying, "I am going home now. Wait a few minutes till the other boys have gone, then open that door and in the closet you will find a coat that doesn't fit me. Put it on and wear it."

This paternalism reached across the sea. "Our Paris Letter" was written for the *Bazar* by Katherine DeForest. One day she received a letter from an unknown reader saying that a friend who was traveling abroad was ill in a Paris hospital. Could Miss DeForest spare the time to see her, for she was also a *Bazar* subscriber? Miss DeForest looked up the woman, found that she was very ill with pneumonia, and badly in need of a friend and interpreter. The patient did not recover from her illness, and when she died it was Miss DeForest who notified friends and relatives in America. Reader identification with the Harper enterprise was nothing new. Shortly after the Civil War, Joseph W. Harper opened a bulky package for which the mail clerk had paid postage. It contained not a manuscript but letters of recommendation of a lady's boarding house written by Union soldiers. Could the Harpers help by telling others of the good board and room she provided?

In 1899 the sixty-fourth volume of the *Bazar* was completed, and a bound copy was placed in the Franklin Square library alongside its predecessors. Here was a repository of the changing fashions of American women during nearly a third of a century. The new volume was the last that Mrs. Sangster edited. She was replaced by Miss Elizabeth Jordan, a university graduate, who had worked for ten years on the New York *World* and written a book, *Tales of the City Room*. Miss Jordan, who insisted that her name be pronounced with the stress on the last syllable, began to stress economies and, beginning with the May, 1900, issue, reduced the magazine's trim size. However, she found that she could not compete with other women's periodicals, some with a million-dollar backing, that gradually forged ahead of the *Bazar*. In 1913 it was sold to William Randolph Hearst for $10,000 cash. Hearst had plenty of money to revive it and a wife eager to edit it; he kept the Harper name in the title but added an "a" to *Bazar*.

"THE OLD ORDER CHANGETH"
(1870-79)

The first partnership agreement that the four brothers drew up was signed in May, 1860, after Fletcher Harper returned from a nine-month sojourn in Europe. The time had come to put values on the participation of each partner and to designate heir-apparents. After the Mayor's death a second agreement was drafted which recognized equities of each in equal amounts of $312,500. The eldest brother's estate was paid $250,000 over four years (with unpaid amounts receiving interest at 6 per cent) and the balance, $62,500, retained for Philip Harper's one-sixteenth interest in the business now capitalized at one million dollars. The other partners and their equities were as follows:

John	$187,500 (3/16)
John W.	62,500 (1/16)
J. Abner	62,500 (1/16)
Wesley	187,500 (3/16)
Joseph W.	125,000 (2/16)
Fletcher	250,000 (4/16)
Fletcher, Jr.	62,500 (1/16)

In case of the retirement of any one partner, the remaining partners had the option of buying his interest. Furthermore no partner could draw out in any one year more than 10 per cent of his equity unless by common agreement and on a pro-rata basis—thus limiting four of the junior partners to an annual income of $6,250. As before, any differences that could not be settled by the partners themselves were to be arbitrated by a board of six men.

When Wesley Harper signed the second partnership agreement, he knew that he had not much longer to live. On the day before James's accident his three brothers had gone to Brooklyn Heights to see Wesley. It was their last time together. Although Wesley did return to Franklin Square a few times thereafter, his visits were short and largely devoted to meeting with his old cronies, the compositors and pressmen with whom he had worked when important books were being put through. He always counted on his presence and example to inspire good work. "His step is light, his motions rapid," a reporter once wrote. "Nothing escapes the glance of his eye. He moves like a man who has work to do." When an employee's work or behavior called for correction, he spoke to the man privately; his authority was his integrity and his known conscientiousness. As George W. Curtis put it, "He controlled without commanding." This control through example lived on as a Franklin Square tradition long after Wesley Harper's death on February 14, 1870.

The publicity that he shunned during his lifetime shone around his figure after he died. Newspaper and magazine editors printed anecdotes about him that portrayed the man, such as the anecdote that revealed the feelings of his domestic staff after the 1853 fire. Returning home that evening, he was met by a spokesman who said that they had agreed to continue at reduced wages or none at all till he could recover from the heavy loss. "I stood everything very well up to that time," he said, "but that broke me down." Another editor wrote of Wesley's last illness, which confined him to his home, "Toward the last he expressed a wish to see as many as possible of his old employees. They came, one by one—editors and artists, men from the composing room, and women from the binders. . . . To one, who had been a compositor, proof-reader, and literary assistant, he said, 'I have always loved my work. I have loved my fellow workmen. I have tried to do right. I have tried to do right.'" This man was one of four employees that Wesley chose to be his pallbearers;

In the seventies the noisy, smoky elevated railway brought employees,
authors, and visitors to the Harpers (left). In 1883, when the Brook-
lyn Bridge was completed, they came over it from Queens County more
conveniently than by ferry. The picture at the right shows the Manhattan
abutment of the bridge which, on its completion, became one of the
sights of the city and the subject of a Harper book by W. C. Conant and
Montgomery Schuyler.

the other four were fellow deacons of the Sands Street Methodist
Church; of the employees the youngest had been with him more than
thirty years and the oldest almost fifty. A reporter noted that among
those who stood tearful at his funeral was the old piewoman who sold
her wares throughout the establishment.

When J. & J. Harper began printing and publishing books, their work
carried little in the way of kudos. Such men were considered drudges,
a tail to the kite of the politician and the author. But John Harper
lived to see the climate of opinion change completely. In November,
1874, the New York *Evening Post* began a series of articles entitled
"The Bookmakers: Reminiscences and Contemporary Sketches of American Publishers," probably written by Parke Godwin. The first article
related the Harper story, carried a picture of John Harper, and said,
"The extraordinary ability displayed by a few men of small begin-
nings, like the Harpers, who chose their own course at the outset as

leading to honor as well as to wealth, has caused a remarkable change in public opinion. The example of this great house imparted new life to the book trade in this country, and, as subsequent papers in this series will show, many of the best educated and ablest young men have determined to devote their lives to promoting literary education as publishers, rather than to risk their characters and fortunes in the more glittering but less substantial efforts of authorship and statesmanship."

After the death of his brother James, John Harper rarely visited the office. He continued, however, his favorite recreation, that of driving a spirited team of horses hitched to a light carriage. He knew a good horse, was a skilled driver, and enjoyed impromptu races on Harlem Lane with such other enthusiasts as Robert Bonner and Cornelius Vanderbilt. A paralytic stroke incapacitated him, however, and during the last year of his life he remained in his home at 234 Fifth Avenue. He died on April 22, 1875, at the age of seventy-eight.

During the decade of the eighteen-seventies booksellers continued their fight for survival, and their state was so forlorn that the *New York Times* ran an editorial in 1872 prophesying that bookstores would soon be a relic of the past. In the Chicago fire of 1871 booksellers suffered total losses and in the Boston fire of 1872 booksellers lost a quarter of a million dollars. Some failed in the panic of 1873 and the resulting depression, but they suffered mostly from ills peculiar to their trade. They complained of the competition of door-to-door selling of subscription books (a lot of them trash, but including *The Adventures of Tom Sawyer* in 1876) and of the widespread discounting of books. Forty per cent was a common discount, fifty not infrequently given, and as much as sixty on "special sales." Often these discounts were in part passed on to customers, who alone profited by cutthroat competition among wholesalers and retailers.

Most publishers, including the Harpers, agreed that booksellers had cause for complaint, but countered by saying that dealers were not enterprising enough to fight subscription selling by going out after customers and selling their services, and had neglected books for "fancy goods"; hence the only means of marketing expensive art books and sets was

The thick, nine-by-fourteen-inch, leather-bound ledger into which William H. Demarest copied his compilation of Harper books issued between 1817 and 1879. Demarest retired in 1877 after forty-four years with the firm and devoted nearly three years to this bibliographical work, which is one of the most important historical records of the House. In July, 1876, the New York Tribune referred to Demarest in a long editorial, saying that the firm had "many of the characteristics of Dickens' 'Cheeryble Brothers,' including a veritable Tim Linkinwater in the cashier, Demarest, who does pretty much as he pleases, abuses the firm from senior to junior, whenever he feels like it, and is one of the best-natured and best-hearted and most popular fellows in the world. In revenge the firm occasionally conspire to play such practical jokes on Tim as banishing him for summer trips to Europe with $5,000 for expenses, 'only to get rid of him.' Altogether it is a very happy commercial family."

Other historical records held by the House include memoranda books summarizing late-nineteenth-century editorial and business transactions, and many of these entries are in the handwriting of J. F. Phayre, who was Joseph W. Harper's assistant. During most of the Harvey regime, Phayre was the liaison between the Harpers' literary past and the new century. For a brief period he represented the firm in England. Phayre's complement on the commercial side of the House was Fred A. Nast, related to the cartoonist; both men began their Harper careers near the end of the Civil War. Nast knew all phases of the business operation, could find anything no one else could, from the musty basement vaults to the dusty files on the top floor of the old Cliff Street building. His mind was a kind of index of Harper information, and he helped compile Harper's Book of Facts (1894), which was largely scissored from the four periodicals.

Several two- and three-generation employees have been associated with the House, the most notable being the Rosenquests. Captain Peter Rosenquest was followed by his son Fletcher Harper Rosenquest, whose son Lewis retired in 1947.

through subscription agents. The Harpers stopped advertising post-free books to individuals, and joined with other publishers in urging a reduction in retail prices through lower discounts, a maximum of 25 per cent, with jobbers getting only slightly more. But no bookseller would swallow such a small discount, having tasted the sweets of 40 per cent and more. So the arguments continued with one happy result, the establishment in July, 1874, of the American Book-Trade Union, with 400 bookseller members, at Put-in-Bay on Lake Erie. The long-established Trade Sales died a natural death the following year and publishers' salesmen, with their trunks packed with new books, were taking to the rails to call on the trade.

And trains were dashing across the countryside at astonishing speeds. On September 16, 1875, the New York Central started daily overnight runs between New York and Chicago. Leaving New York at 4:15 P.M., the iron monster reached Chicago the following morning at 6:27 A.M. Beginning about 1880, Colonel John H. Ammon began riding this train as Harper's trade representative at $5,000 a year. Harper subscription book agents also called on some booksellers, and the junior partners covered leading trade accounts. When Joseph W. Harper was competing with Fields & Osgood in the publication of Charles Reade's *Put Yourself in His Place,* he thought it would be great fun to have the Harper edition piled up under the nose of his rival. He wrote Boston's leading bookseller, Lee and Shepard, approving a 50 per cent discount and promising that the two editions would be "published simultaneously, same day, same hour and minute. A gun will be fired when the book goes off in June and flags will be displayed at all military stations and from the Boston State House on the 4th of July."

When the spectacular Philadelphia Centennial Exposition opened in 1876, the Harper space in the Main Building's exhibit hall was not, the *Publishers' Weekly* noted, in consonance with its standing in the trade. Acting true to form, the firm held off from cooperating with other publishers until a late hour and then took second best. In the front section of their exhibit were imposing ranks of handsomely bound volumes of the three periodicals and editions of English classics and American books in cloth or half calf. Charles Nordhoff's *Politics for Young Amer-*

icans, called "the best Centennial book a-going," was stocked up with a patriotic dress of red, white, and blue. An original drawing on wood by Thomas Nast was prominently displayed, as were illustrations from *Harper's School Geography.* Harper's received two awards at the exposition, one in Paper, Stationery, Printing, and Bookmaking, and one in Education and Science.

Fletcher Harper was not in the vast throng that enjoyed the Exposition but suffered from Philadelphia's July heat. It was cooler at his summer home in Irvington-on-Hudson, from which he wrote to A. D. F. Randolph, head of the Publishers' Association, "I am very much touched by your remembrance of an old fellow like me, but I am too great an invalid, just now, to incur the excitement of accepting your invitation to be personally present at the convention." Fletcher's declination was a disappointment to all bookmen, for he was "Mr. Publisher," the one most often pointed to and eulogized. Paul Du Chaillu, the noted explorer, dedicated the last of his seven African books to Fletcher. Always shy of such honors, he could hardly deny the emotional Du Chaillu, who wrote requesting the dedication, "not only as a token of the profound respect I have for you and the great friendship we entertain toward each other, but also as a token of the high regard I have for every member of the House, so that when years shall have passed away and [you and I] have gone to our rest some may know how the humble traveler of Equatorial Africa and his publisher thought of each other."

More impressive is what his employees thought of Fletcher Harper. Two of them named sons for him and another testified that he treated all employees with such confidence and respect that none was ever afraid to go to him for advice or aid in time of trouble. Or for a raise in salary. Miss Lavinia Goodell, at the time assistant editor of the *Bazar,* once wrote her parents that she had asked for an increase, though hardly expecting it. "I found Mr. Harper very kind and considerate and 'open to conviction,' and didn't have to present near all the arguments I had concocted before he surrendered. He is just as kind and good as he can be, and I think ever so much of him." Lavinia's salary was raised to fifteen dollars a week.

After Henry J. Raymond died in 1869, Curtis was asked to replace him as editor of the *New York Times* at a salary double what he was receiving. He showed the letter to Fletcher Harper with the remark that he had decided not to accept the offer, but that he felt Mr. Harper ought to know the offer had been made. "Don't decide rashly, George," Fletcher replied. "This is a great compliment to you, and a very serious matter. Take the letter home with you and sleep over it a night or two, and talk it over with Mrs. Curtis." A day or two later Curtis showed Harper his written reply—a polite refusal. "Is this final, George?" he was asked. "Yes," Curtis said, "it is final. I have been with you a long time, I have been very happy here, you have been very good to me, and I cannot go." Fletcher Harper said nothing, sealed the letter, stamped it, and gave it to a messenger to post. He then asked Curtis to stay for a moment, led him to the cashier's desk, and said, "Dating from the first of January last, Mr. Curtis's salary is to be increased a hundred per cent."

Such a decisive act was typical of the man. He had a strong instinct for the right course, and could rarely be talked out of it. To those who spun out elaborate arguments for a certain action, his common reply was "If you talk metaphysics I can't follow you." His own logic was intuitive and direct. His first question about a man was "Is he honest?" and about conduct "Is it right?" and about an assertion "Is it true?" That logic led him to forsake the Democratic Party at the outbreak of the Civil War.

As both Curtis and Nordhoff pointed out, Fletcher Harper had the qualities of a diplomat. He would have gone far in politics, for he was at his best in managing a difficult situation. In July, 1871, a mob threatened the Franklin Square Building because of the strong stand the *Weekly* had taken on Boss Tweed and Tammany Hall. Fletcher Harper immediately took command. "Take down the shutters," he ordered to those who in panic had just put them up. He had the entrance barricaded with piles of paper from the stockroom and placed employees where they could meet rioters, should they come (which they did not), with hot spray from hose attached to the water tanks.

After John Harper died, Fletcher seldom went back to Franklin Square. He divided his time between his New York home and his rural Westchester retreat. He traveled some, for his greatest relaxation for thirty years had been the steamship voyages that had taken him almost annually on editorial trips to England. In the winter of 1876 Fletcher became seriously ill; he died on the morning of May 29, 1877. Three days earlier the firm had issued another edition of *Seneca's Morals* (in Latin), and so it happened that the first title printed by the Harpers was the final book issued while the last of the brothers lived. On Memorial Day those publishers not away for the holiday met in the New York Trade Sales rooms to commemorate him who was their best-known colleague.

Fletcher Harper's warmest friend among his authors was Dr. John McClintock, first president of Drew Theological Seminary. Dr. McClintock died in 1870, five years before the completion of his major work, undertaken with James Strong, an eight-volume *Biblical Cyclopaedia*. Sold only through agents for many years, "McClintock and Strong" became a byword among seminary students and clergymen. It was one of several scholarly works that made this a golden decade of theological literature for Harper's. Phillip Schaff's three-volume *Creeds of Christendom* was praised alike by Catholic and Protestant scholars, and an imprinted edition was sold to Messrs. Hodder & Stoughton, of London. Revised twice, the 2,337-page work has continued in print until today. Similarly long-lived was a huge volume of sermons by F. W. Robertson, of Brighton, England, and clergymen still go to it for homiletical help. Dr. Albert Barnes had written the last volume of *Notes* on books of the Bible, and it was reported that over a million copies of these commentaries had been sold, of which a large number had been pirated in England; however, American sales earned $75,000 for him and a like amount, probably, for Harper's. A few years later Bishop John F. Hurst, who founded the American University in Washington, D.C., gave the Harpers *A Short History of the Christian Church,* which stayed in print for more than fifty years.

Of interest to the general public as well as to the religious market was David Livingstone's *Last Journals,* the third of his books of missionary travels to be issued from Franklin Square, and Henry M. Stanley's greatest book, *Through the Dark Continent.* While the Harpers probably earned back what they paid for rights—and more—there was much

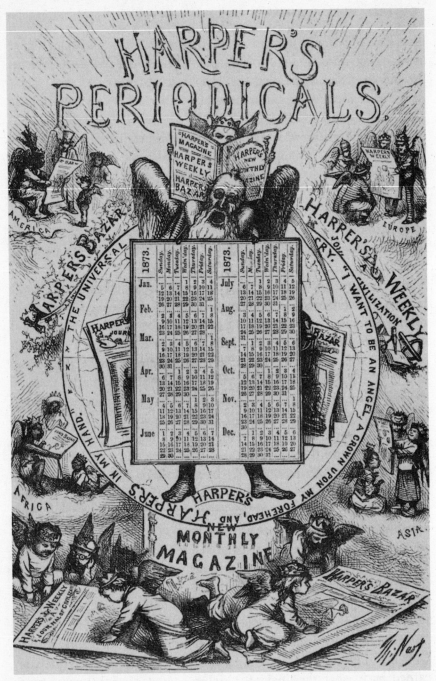

"*The Universal Cry,*" *a drawing by Thomas Nast which appeared in* Thomas Nast's Almanac, 1873, *and decorated the back cover of a textbook catalogue.*

pirating, with Stanley's American citizenship debated. They were paying royalties to English authors more frequently, as typified in a 10 per cent royalty on Green's *History of the English People*. For this standard work and for the unparalleled scientific work *The Voyage of the Challenger* (a study of biological life in the depths of the sea), they also purchased plates from Macmillan in London, who gave the Harpers a first refusal on the latter book, saying they were not interested in sending sheets to their agent G. E. Brett, at 21 Astor Place. Also on a royalty basis Macmillan and Harper began publishing the famous English Men of Letters series, edited by John Morley. In return, Macmillan was given rights to several American books, including *Popular Astronomy*, by Simon Newcomb, the country's leading mathematical astronomer.

Thomas Nast's Almanac brightened the depression years of 1873-75, with 30,000 copies printed each year. Many were sold as a result of Nast's lectures in the season of 1873-74, a seven-month tour that earned $40,000 for the cartoonist-lecturer.

Published three months too late for the Philadelphia Exposition, Charles Carleton Coffin's *The Boys of '76* hardly needed that springboard. The first edition was increased in size before going to press, an augury of the book's popularity, for it has been steadily listed in Harper's catalogues until recently and read by three generations of boys. In addition to Coffin's book, other leading titles in Harper's nine-page advertisement in the *Publishers' Weekly* for Christmas, 1879, were *Art in America*, by S. G. W. Benjamin; *The Rime of the Ancient Mariner*, with illustrations by Doré; and a new edition of the best-selling *The Land and the Book*, by Thomson, for which the Harpers had sent artists to Palestine to make new drawings. And to honor a beloved author, recently deceased, they devoted a whole page to Jacob Abbott's seven series of books, a phenomenal output of 72 volumes. In 1879 the house issued one hundred and seventy-one new books and new editions and its 322-page catalogue described almost 3,000 volumes. And to get the next decade properly launched, they began in December to publish their fourth periodical, another weekly, *Harper's Young People*.

HARPER'S
YOUNG PEOPLE
AN ILLUSTRATED WEEKLY.

VOL. V.—NO. 218.   PUBLISHED BY HARPER & BROTHERS, NEW YORK.   PRICE FIVE CENTS.

Tuesday, January 1, 1884.   Copyright, 1883, by Harper & Brothers. $1.50 per Year, in Advance.

"SUCH FUN GETTING INTO BERTIE'S OLD CLOTHES."

BERTIE'S BOX.
A Christmas Story.
BY LOUISA M. ALCOTT.
I.

"HERE'S a letter for you, mamma, and, please, I want the red picture on it," said little Bertie, as he came trotting into the room where his mother and aunt sat busily putting the last touches to their generous store of Christmas gifts.

"Do read it, Jane; my hands are too sticky," said Mrs. Field, who was filling pretty horns and boxes with bonbons.

"Whom do you know in Iowa?" asked Aunt Jane, looking at the postmark.

"No one. It is probably a begging letter. As secre-

A typical cover of Harper's Young People.

13

HARPER'S YOUNG PEOPLE (1879-99)

The fourth of the Franklin Square periodicals, under the editorship of Kirk Munroe, began its weekly career on Tuesday, November 4, 1879. It was a laudable attempt to give young people better reading material than the popular dime novels, but from the start it had strong competition from *St. Nicholas* magazine, edited by the able Mary Mapes Dodge. It started modestly as an eight-page paper, but six weeks later the Harpers doubled the number of pages, increased the page size, and boasted in the *Publishers' Weekly* of "unprecedented success." This success was due to someone's bright idea of sending the first thirty issues free to all subscribers of the other three journals, along with subscription blanks. When these blanks piled up, the publishers not only expanded the paper but also got busy lining up the best authors they could and adding departments and illustrations.

The old Harper standby, Benson J. Lossing, contributed pieces of American history. W. O. Stoddard, who probably set an all-time record writing boys' books, was given the greatest amount of linage, and Thomas W. Knox ran him a close second with "Boy Traveller" stories; they eventually made fifteen books, all illustrated. The best of the lot was James Otis, whose *Toby Tyler* began in December, 1880. Munroe picked W. A. Rogers to illustrate it and its sequel, *Mr. Stubbs's Brother.* Rogers enjoyed making the pen-and-ink illustrations for these books

Toby Tyler as drawn by W. A. Rogers.

more than for any others he ever did, and was chagrined when they were
thrown out during the year-end housecleaning of the Harper art department. The drawings so impressed an Indiana boy subscriber named
Booth Tarkington that he decided he wanted to become an artist. (He
did attempt some pictures, but soon found his pen could do better
with words.) Abbey, who read the Otis stories while he was abroad, told
Rogers the pictures made him homesick, and the homely details of
American dooryards were so true that it was his boyhood all over again.

The story of the poor boy and his ten weeks with a circus was so be-lievable that children sent letters to the editor enclosing money to help Toby Tyler buy something to eat. Rogers also illustrated several of Kirk Munroe's stories for young people. He admired Munroe for his in-sistence on factual detail and for his ability to see the world as a boy sees it while understanding the world as a man.

Howard Pyle wrote and illustrated *Men of Iron,* which ran early in 1891, the year following *A Boy's Town,* by Howells. But good as such writing was, it could not keep circulation from falling off, and money was being lost on every issue. The trouble seems to have been that the paper attempted to cover too wide an age group and to appeal equally to boys and girls. No boy would dare be seen carrying an issue with an article telling how to make lace embroidery, and no girl would be fascinated by an article on ice hockey. Mrs. Sangster conducted the most popular department for many years, "The Post-Office Box," aimed at "little readers." But little readers soon became big enough to lose interest in the periodical, and the consequent drop-off in renewals and the cost of getting new young subscribers caused a dwindling sub-scription list. To meet this challenge, the Harpers decided to direct the paper to older boys and girls and changed the name to the *Round Table.* It did little good and two years later it became a monthly, with the reading matter extended to forty-eight pages. Losses continued until October, 1899, when they could no longer conscionably be accepted, and the paper was discontinued.

14

TOP OF THE MOUNTAIN (1880-89)

At Fletcher Harper's death, Philip Harper became head of the House with a continuing responsibility for the manufactory. He commuted to Franklin Square from Hempstead, Long Island, where he and his family lived in the Thorne Mansion, a building still standing.

Joseph W. Harper, Jr., known in the family as "Joe Brooklyn," had full charge of the literary department and lived in a large house at the northwest corner of Fifth Avenue and Forty-sixth Street. Here he and his wife, the former Caroline Sleeper of Boston, often entertained authors. The home was crammed with Victorian furniture and servants and stiff formalities. Harper was a graduate of Columbia, class valedictorian, and a long-time trustee of the college. The fact that he was a college graduate was helpful to the author of a long historical article on publishers in the *National Quarterly Review;* he argued that publishers were mendacious and dishonest in proportion as they were illiterate, and honest, liberal, and courteous as they were educated. Since none of the four brothers was a college graduate, he had to resort to Joseph W. Harper, Jr., to sustain his thesis. He rated Longman and Murray highest in England, and in America Ticknor & Fields and Harper's. His two American favorites did not resort to practices he despised—publishing cheap stuff for quick profit, exaggerating the merits of their books, and objecting to unfavorable reviews. Messrs.

142

Joseph W. Harper.

Scribner, Putnam, Appleton, and Holt might equally have merited such distinction. They were, with the Harpers, remembered by Frederick A. Stokes, when he started in business in 1880, as so friendly that they dined together regularly and drank from a loving cup engraved with their names.

A somewhat different version of the loving cup was remembered by Henry Holt, but he agreed that these houses were incapable of petty or ostentatious things, and would not go for another's author any more than for his watch. And when Walter Hines Page wrote *A Publisher's Confession* in 1905, he spoke nostalgically of this period when the lead-

ing publishers respected each other's relations with authors. According
to Holt, "Joe" Harper would approach an issue by talking all around
Robin Hood's barn, and if he did not know his man he would affect
pigheadedness until the issue was clarified; Holt considered Harper an
intimate friend and a business genius.

Harper was the front man on all public occasions. He presided at the
frequent House dinners at Delmonico's given for authors, artists, and
retiring personnel. He, not Alden, went to Boston to speak at the
Atlantic Monthly's "breakfast" honoring Oliver Wendell Holmes on his
seventieth birthday. He spoke with ease and on occasion with a subtle
wit. Once his humor backfired, when, at a dinner given in New York for
William Dean Howells, Harper mistook another guest, the sculptor
Quincy Ward, for Artemus Ward, the humorist.

Charles Scribner and Harper stopped passing the loving cup in 1887
and got into a dogfight over which one had the American rights to
Carlyle's *Reminiscences.* Scribner claimed the work because it was edited
by J. A. Froude, who was Scribner's author by virtue of trade courtesy.
The Harpers contended that Carlyle had been identified with them since
1848, when they purchased plates of Carlyle's early work from Putnam, and because of later books they had paid for. Furthermore Carlyle
had agreed, before his death in 1881, that the Harpers should have his
memoirs in return for a royalty and a £250 advance. Scribner countered
by saying that Froude was Carlyle's literary executor and had done
much work on the manuscript, an argument that Froude himself used
in London when the newspapers there aired the difference between him
and Carlyle's niece, who held for the Harpers and cashed their royalty
checks. It was an embarrassing issue for the *Publishers' Weekly,* which
had to print page ads from the rival publishers and to editorialize on
the unhappy incident.

What turned out to be most embarrassing for the Harpers, however,
was the result of their casual treatment of Rudyard Kipling in 1890. They
took six of his stories, including some they had paid for and used in the
Weekly, and issued them, without asking Kipling's permission or
giving him the opportunity of revising them, as No. 680 in the Franklin
Square Library. They sent Kipling a token payment of £10, which he

spurned in a letter that ranks high in that literary *curiosa* of what angry authors think of publishers. If such a book is ever compiled, it should include a small item on Putnam that Kipling had privately printed on toilet paper. A more offensive—and unprintable—letter was sent to Joseph W. Harper's desk in 1890, written by the half-blind Lafcadio Hearn, author of three successful books. Much of what he had written, including a marvelous account of the French West Indies, was first serialized in the *Magazine* after Alden had befriended and encouraged the shy and sensitive author. Even before Hearn left for Japan to do more articles and a book or two, he knew that C. D. Weldon, the artist accompanying him, was to receive more money than he could expect, but after arriving there he became so upset over his financial prospects that he wrote not only to consign Harper's to the Devil but also to relieve his feelings by comparing their actions, in earthy monosyllabic words, to activities normally confined to the bathroom.

Joseph W. Harper took over from his Uncle Fletcher the pleasant responsibility of scouting trips to London. He sold the Clarendon Press of Oxford a set of plates of *Harper's Latin Dictionary,* the editorial work on which had cost nearly $20,000. And at no risk, for it was a thorough revision of the old *Andrews Latin-English Lexicon,* which had been a gold mine for forty years. The 2,023-page work went out of print only a few years ago, and a redaction made for schools by one of the editors, Charlton T. Lewis, is still catalogued by the American Book Company. This prestigious contact with Oxford and a later deal on Liddell and Scott's *Greek Lexicon* was flattering to Harper, who was himself something of a classicist. He paid Professor Henry Drisler and two other scholars handsome sums to edit the *Greek Lexicon,* and to have their work accepted at Oxford was an atonement of a kind for his Uncle Fletcher's having pirated the work back in 1846.

He arranged with Kegan Paul, Trench & Co. to take some of their books on a royalty and a *quid-pro-quo* basis. With Murray he negotiated the sale and purchase of plates of books easily salable in both countries. Harper probably valued his London association with John Murray III more than any other he had. He entertained for Mr. Murray's son when he came over to the Centennial Exposition, spoke fraternally

with John Murray III of third-generation Harpers now at Franklin
Square, and talked him into writing an article which was published in
the *Magazine* for December, 1883.

A sister of Joseph W. Harper married John W., making the cousins
also brothers-in-law, and thus creating still another problem for family
genealogists. John W. was noted for a magnificent handle-bar mustache.
Unlike his father, he was a gregarious, outgoing sort of man, much
given to hospitality. Even so, he was well trained in his father's conservative fiscal policies; he served many years as a director of the Bank of
Manhattan and was an incorporator of the Lincoln National Bank and
the Lincoln Safe Deposit Company. So conservative was he, in fact, that
once, just after the Civil War, he advised an employee to hold off buying
a new watch until the price of gold came down. He lived most of each
year at Sands Point, Long Island, and his home, "The Knoll," received
plush treatment in a 262-page book issued in 1877 by the Long Island
Railroad Company. A full-page engraving depicted the house, another
revealed its spectacular view of Long Island Sound, and a third, lifted
from a *Harper's Magazine* article, showed what Sands Point looked like
from the water.

Since the nearest Long Island Railroad Station was more than eight
miles distant, the Sands Point Harpers commuted to Manhattan via
the steamboats that made regular stops along the north shore. One day
in 1884 young Horatio Harper fell to talking with an alert, intelligent
lad he had observed working on one of the boats. He asked him what he
wanted to make of his life and, reaching for his card, said he would
be glad to talk with him sometime about a publishing job. The boy
followed up this lead promptly and was hired as a clerk at four dollars
a week. His name was Henry Hoyns. Born the year before Mayor
Harper died, Hoyns, a perfect Horatio Alger prototype, lived to be
head of the House.

John W. Harper was two years older than his brother Abner, who
was born the year the firm's name was changed to Harper & Brothers.
Abner's house in New Windsor, near Newburgh, New York, is no
longer standing, which is a pity, because it was Hudson River Gothic at
its most grotesque. Abner's loving brother described it as a mustard-

plaster and pumpkin-pie house. Abner retired there in 1889 after nearly forty years with the firm. His chief responsibility, in addition to running the textbook department, had been the commercial side of the operation, and his opinions on publishing costs and problems were often quoted in the trade journals and newspapers. As a person, he was jovial and easygoing and optimistic. He filled his home with paintings and objets d'art which he soon tired of and auctioned off. In many ways the happy, somewhat fat Abner Harper was the most likable of the second-generation partners.

The cousins' interest in the family business was less evidenced by Fletcher Harper, Jr., and his brother Joseph Wesley (differentiated from "Joe Brooklyn" by being called "Joe 22nd Street"). The latter worked at Franklin Square only a few years and went into the foreign service; at his death he was U.S. Consul at Munich. Fletcher, Jr., was given every opportunity—was made a partner with Raymond when the *New York Times* was established, and, at about the same time, a special partner with H. W. Derby & Co., leading Cincinnati booksellers. But he lacked his father's drive and enjoyed the life of a rich, cultivated New Yorker.

Knowing that his sons were not likely to furnish second-generation leadership, Fletcher Harper had talked his favorite grandson out of going to college, the more quickly to enter the business. So J. Henry Harper matriculated in the composing room instead of at Harvard. He was only twenty-nine when he was made a partner and advanced to assistant head of the literary department, taking full charge when Joseph W. was absent on trips abroad. His job was to improve the quality of the book production and he was credited with the handsome format and binding of the most notable Harper works of the time. He also had an aptness for composing titles, the despair of many editors. He loved going to dinners, entertained a lot in his home on Murray Hill, and eventually succeeded his second cousin as head of the literary department. The two books he himself wrote (*The House of Harper*, 1912, and *I Remember*, 1934) are discursive and disorganized but are valuable records of the House, his publishing career, and the authors he dealt with. He has a significant place in Harper history also because he was the first of the third generation to be made a partner.

There were six other third-generation Harpers in the business by the early eighties. These six, along with James Thorne Harper, the son of the Mayor's old age, were called junior partners. After topping off their formal education by a year's travel abroad, each of them had been given an apprenticeship in the composing room. They were bound by the same ties of affection, mutual trust, and comradeship that had been character-istic of the association of their parents and grandparents. They were also carrying the torch and proud to be associated with the House that had made their name famous throughout the world. Closer ties linked two of the second cousins when they married daughters of Colonel Richard Marsh Hoe, whose inventive genius produced the high-speed printing presses that revolutionized the printing industry and brought the modern newspaper into being. The junior partners had great fun together, as their family letters reveal. They once gave a kids' party for their seniors, with artists, including Abbey, and authors, including Du Chaillu, as guests—appropriately dressed. Miss Amelia Harper, daugh-ter of Horatio, remembers her embarrassment, as a little girl, at seeing her parents—her father dressed as little Lord Fauntleroy—go off to one of the annual Christmas parties that Mrs. James Harper, the Mayor's widow, gave at No. 4 Gramercy Park.

During the eighteen-eighties the House grew to its maximum size and influence. Nearly eight hundred employees were paid over half a million dollars annually. Joseph W. complained of a business "grown to be in-conveniently large" in a year marked by an annual volume of around four million dollars derived from the sale of four periodicals and four thousand or more books in print. What profits accrued to the partners came largely from the manufacturing operation and from the periodi-cals, since on the sale of books they allowed themselves only 10 per cent for overhead and profit. They figured that for a $1.00 book, the dealer took 40 per cent, the manufacturing 40 per cent, and the author and the publisher 10 per cent each, the last reminiscent of the old Harper half-profit contracts. Out of their small overhead they presumably paid for advertising, with annual expenditures in the eighteen-eighties averag-ing more than $45,000, most of which was spent to promote the periodi-

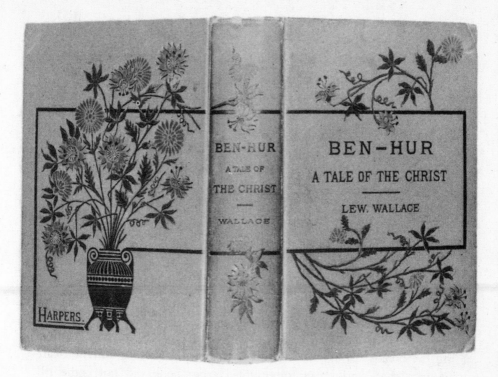

Front and back boards and spine of the first edition of Ben-Hur.

cals. Once, the advertising agents Lord & Thomas wrote from Chicago soliciting business, and Joseph W. penciled across the letter, "No hurry. We had better walk our advertising horse for the present."

The Harpers employed many readers, chief of whom, after George Ripley's long tenure, were George Cary Eggleston, brother of the novelist; Charlton T. Lewis, the Latinist; and Laurence Hutton, literary man-about-town. Lewis was paid $40 a week, a low rate compared to today's payments, when the dollar buys less than twenty cents did then. By the same token, typists charged Harper's the unbelievably low rate of four cents a hundred words for manuscript work.

One of the last manuscripts that the aging George Ripley read, and could hardly bring himself to recommend for publication, turned out to be the best-selling book to carry the Harper imprint in the nineteenth century. It was *Ben-Hur,* by General Lew Wallace, published in November, 1880, and announced in the *Publishers' Weekly* with a modest one line at the head of their list of new novels. This muted trumpet and a first printing of only 2,500 copies probably reflected Ripley's concern that the book was not "legitimate literature," although both he and Dr. Lewis thought that Wallace's bold and imaginative and reverent treatment of Christ's life might fascinate a multitude of readers. But the multitude was slow in assembling, as indicated by these disposal figures:

$$1880\text{-}1881 — 4,187$$
$$1882\text{-}1883 — 9,085$$
$$1884 — 26,496$$

Seven years after publication *Ben-Hur* had sold over 230,000 copies and earned royalties (10 per cent on the retail price of $1.50) of nearly $35,000. Even so, the 1887 catalogue boasted no such figures, and tucked in the back section was a sixth of a page containing reviews following the book's listing. The usual assortment of leather and half-calf bindings that marked an important Harper book did not come till later, along with an illustrated two-volume edition. In 1913 Henry Hoyns concluded negotiations with Sears, Roebuck & Co. for their purchase of 1,000,000 copies, which was the largest sale of any one title ever made by a book salesman. While deliveries, scheduled over a period of years, did not finally reach that figure, they did boost the total sale to over 2,500,000 copies. Royalties and income from dramatic rights (in which the House shared) made a fortune for the Hoosier General and his heirs. The manuscript of *Ben-Hur,* lacking the first twenty-nine pages, has long been in the possession of the University of Indiana; the missing portion was recently found in a Harper box of old papers and was presented to the University at the 1960 dedication of the Lilly Library of rare books and manuscripts.

"Legitimate" fiction from American authors included *Washington Square,* by Henry James, his fifth book for Harper's (the former ones, including *Daisy Miller,* were short works available separately and in one volume); also several novels by Constance Fenimore Woolson, a close friend and fellow expatriate of James's. Miss Woolson, a great favorite of Alden's, is downgraded by critics today, but her stories, such as *Anne* and *For the Major*, enjoyed acclaim and were widely read. Henry James wrote an introduction to a volume of thirteen "tales" by Guy de Maupassant. (Its title, *Odd Number*, later named a series of books.) It was credited by Frank Luther Mott in *Golden Multitudes* as the best seller of 1889, and has continued on the Harper list ever since. The novel *King Solomon's Mines*, by H. R. Haggard, was one of the three best sellers of 1886, the Franklin Square edition having to compete with three other editions selling for twenty cents each. A distinguished novel of the decade was *The Bread-Winners*, published anonymously in a first printing of 7,500 copies. The authorship was a well-guarded secret; however, William D. Howells knew that John Hay of Cleveland had written this satirical novel attacking labor unions and defending economic individualism, since Hay had asked Howells if he might dedicate the book to him. Howells, a liberal, declined the honor, although he did not think that Hay assailed work-ingmen as a class. With such fiction being published, it is not surprising that Harper's had thirty-three titles—almost twice as many as any other house—when *The Independent* of July 5, 1888, printed a list of 173 superior novels published within a period of three or four years.

Howells began his long Harper career in 1885, although he had earlier written for the *Magazine* and had contributed a farce to *Harper's Christmas* (1882), that gay symposium compiled by the Tile Club, an association of writers, architects, and artists. Other important books were Ignatius Donnelly's *Atlantis,* which went through twenty-one editions (reissued in 1949); Helen Hunt Jackson's exposé of injustices to the American Indians entitled *A Century of Dishonor;* Henry Cabot Lodge's 550-page *A Short History of the English Colonies in America;* John Fiske's *American Political Ideas*; Charles Eliot Norton's *Historical Studies of Church Building in the Middle Ages;* and *The Life and Letters of Horace Bushnell,* a kind of testament of America's leading nineteenth-century theologian.

Two further books are noteworthy of themselves and illustrative of a perennial publishing problem. The Harpers were committed to issuing the works of Borden P. Bowne, of Boston University, founder of the so-called philosophy of personalism. When they were about to bring out his *Philosophy of Theism,* a rising young philosopher named John Dewey submitted his *Psychology* with the stipulation that Harper publish no other book in this field at the same time. Since the Dewey book was obviously important, his request caused considerable editorial worry —unnecessarily so, apparently, for both books were issued. The problem must have arisen often and is frequently given as the reason for rejecting manuscripts. When George Cary Eggleston wrote his autobiography (published in 1910 by Holt), he said that during his time at Harper's every important writer tried first to get his book published from Franklin Square.

(15)

WILLIAM DEAN HOWELLS AND
MARK TWAIN

"I am mighty glad you are with Harper's," Mark Twain wrote to William Dean Howells. "I have noticed that good men in their employ go there to stay." This was in October, 1885. Howells had written to Mark Twain confirming what he assumed his friend had read in the papers. It was news that the former editor of the *Atlantic Monthly* and author of the recent and widely read novel, *The Rise of Silas Lapham,* was pulling up publishing stakes in literary Boston to hazard new fortunes in commercial New York. Howells had been left without a publisher when James R. Osgood & Co. failed early in May, 1885, and he was disinclined to continue with Ticknor & Co., who took over that firm, or to join up with Houghton Mifflin & Co. He did confide to his friend Charles Fairchild, who sold paper to Harper's, that he would consider an offer from them. (Alden had rejected his latest novel, *The Minister's Charge.*) Letters and telegrams were exchanged, and an extremely urgent wire from Fairchild early in October led to Howells' being invited to come to Franklin Square for a talk. He had lunch with Joseph W. Harper in his office. The two men talked over possible arrangements, with Harper making digressions from the topic, as he loved to do, before coming down to terms. They agreed that Harper's would pay Howells a weekly salary based on $10,000 a year, in return for which he would write one novel and one farce; in addition to this compensation they would pay a 12½ per cent royalty on his books, with Howells paying for the plates. Finally Howells agreed, with considerable reluctance, to conduct a department in the *Magazine,* to be called the "Editor's Study," in which he would treat of the literary scene in somewhat the fashion that Curtis discussed the social scene in the "Easy Chair." For this he was paid an additional $3,000. The "salary" paid to Howells was in reality compensation for serialization of what he wrote based on a rate of $50 per 1,000 words in the *Magazine* and $30 in the *Weekly.*

Howells was assured that he would be given freedom to write his monthly department as he chose, although he should watch out for whatever "rang a little bell." Howells understood what he meant: the little bell would tinkle when such subjects as women's suffrage or capital punishment begged for discussion; the Harpers were not reformers enough to take advanced positions on such issues. The following year, when the Haymarket riot broke out and the Chicago anarchists were not given what Howells thought a fair trial, he wrote letters of protest to the New York *Tribune* and the Chicago *Tribune.* He did not write of the controversy in the "Editor's Study," but his wife feared that the publicity would lead the Harpers to cancel his contract. However, this fear was groundless and he said later that he was treated by them with "magnanimous forbearance."

During the six years he conducted the "Editor's Study," Howells was mainly concerned to speak his mind about the sentimental and romantic fiction that pervaded the closing decades of the century. The best of his pieces were published in a book, *Criticism and Fiction.* This fight against romanticism and for realism, both he and Harper's believed, reacted against the sale of his own books. Even so, he made his greatest contribution to American critical thought in this department, which he had reluctantly agreed to undertake. Among his early Harper novels, *A Hazard of New Fortunes* ranks highest. After appearing serially in the *Weekly,* it was published in November, 1889, in paper covers, and two months later in a two-volume cloth edition. Deeply concerned with the meaning of civilization, particularly in America, Howells wrote a realistic story of the rich and the poor, of trade unions and strikes.

He was living in New York when he wrote the book; Basil, his fictional hero, also moved from Boston to New York to be near "the painting and writing fellows." The "painting fellow" who illustrated the book was W. A. Rogers. Howells wanted Rogers to draw Fulkerson, the syndicate man, with side whiskers, as that was the way Howells, the realist, had known this character. Rogers disagreed, because men by that time had ceased wearing burnsides, but he could only win his point by trimming back the whiskers week by week till at last they were barely discernible.

The farces that Howells wrote each year—amusing pieces of light humor—were collected in several volumes; *The Mouse-Trap* was especially popular, and amateur dramatists found the plays easy to put on. Altogether Harper's published through 1891 nine books for Howells, including *A Boy's Town,* delightful reminiscences of his Ohio childhood. That year, for his contributions to Harper periodicals—not including royalties on books—Howells probably received $15,000, according to R. W. Watts in his doctoral thesis on the Howells-Harper association. In March, 1892, the last of his "Editor's Study" pieces appeared. Howells had become restive under the burden of editorial work and asked for a release from his contract. He spent a sleepless Saturday night that first week without a check from Harper's, but, as he wrote later, "They remained my most frequent customers for serial rights, and they remained the publishers of all my subsequent books."

Other sleepless nights must have followed since Howells suffered, as nearly everyone else did, in the three business depressions of the nineties. There was a brief flirtation with *Cosmopolitan* magazine in 1892, and in 1896 he accepted a proposal from the *Weekly* to write an occasional "Life and Letters" piece at $100 for a minimum of 2,000 words (later published as *Literature and Life*). He agreed to write four short stories for the *Magazine* at the rate of $50 a page, and in 1899 he contracted to write *Their Silver Wedding Journey* with the understanding that the *Magazine* would run no other serial. By making this promise Harper's had to give up H. G. Wells, for whom they had published four books, including *The War of the Worlds*. The handsome and ambitious young Wells submitted *Love and Mr. Lewisham* through his agent Pinker only to be told that while the Harpers were favorably impressed, the *Magazine* was "fully filled." He refused their counter-offer of the *Weekly* or the *Bazar,* plus a usual 12½ per cent book royalty.

The financially vicious nineties also caused Howells to worry about troubles facing his most intimate friend, Mark Twain, who was then living abroad. In April, 1893, they had a reunion in New York to talk over family affairs and business concerns, one of which was Mark Twain's publishing house, then under pressure from the banks. Most of the American sales of the Mark Twain books had been made by subscription and, in recent years, by a company headed and named for his niece's husband, Charles L. Webster, in which both Mark Twain and his wife, Olivia L. Clemens, had invested heavily. In April, 1894, the firm was forced into bankruptcy, and except for the bargaining ability of his friend Henry H. Rogers, an officer of the Standard Oil Company, Mark Twain would have lost all of his copyrights, which he assigned to Mrs. Clemens. As it was he was saddled with a liability of $80,000, which he hoped to repay through the profits to be made on the Paige typesetting machine in which he had invested $190,000. But by the year's end this fantastically complicated and cumbersome invention turned out to be another failure and unable to compete with the new linotype machine.

Despite his embarrassment and despair because of the failure of his business enterprises, Mark Twain set to work to pay off his debt. His first effort was directed to rounding out several literary projects. The manuscript of *Joan of Arc* was completed in France, in January, 1895, and sent to the *Magazine,* where serialization began in April. Mark Twain spent March in New York largely to consolidate his publishing properties. In the preceding November *Pudd'nhead Wilson* had been issued in Hartford by the subscription book concern the American Publishing Company, which had brought out the first Mark Twain books. Now Mr. Rogers was attempting to make an arrangement whereby Harper's could publish a trade edition of it and of the earlier titles. The Hartford people were stubborn about allowing Harper's to issue a uniform edition that might compete with their own, and Harper's was stubborn about sharing book rights on *Joan of Arc* and *Tom Sawyer Abroad* in a new edition containing "Tom Sawyer, Detective." Mark Twain told Harper's that he thought he could eventually convey rights to all the books and asked them to draft a contract to that effect, which Mrs. Clemens could sign. He was going back to Paris and she would return with him in May. He now had a project in mind that might liquidate his indebtedness. This glorious scheme was a round-the-world trip in which Mark Twain would emulate Charles Dickens by reading from his own works.

Several years earlier Mark Twain's friend Joseph H. Twichell was being shown around Chester Cathedral in England and remarked to the clergyman-guide that this was something America could not boast of. "Yes," was the reply, "but then you have things we have not [for instance], Mark Twain and *Harper's Magazine.*" Now the Harpers had Mark Twain—at least a part of him. When the Clemenses arrived in New York, they went at once to Franklin Square, where on May 23, 1895, Mrs. Clemens signed the first of the many Mark Twain contracts that cram a large file in Harper's offices. This contract gave Harper's book rights on ten titles and provided that similar rights on six more would be conveyed by Mrs. Clemens at the "earliest possible date." The Harpers agreed to publish a uniform edition of these works at their own expense and to pay a royalty of 15 per cent of the retail price to 5,000 copies, and 20 per cent thereafter. In August they began setting *Huckleberry Finn,* with five more books strung out over the year in which Mark Twain was making his famous tour. Without his being on hand to bring pressure on Frank Bliss, head of the American Publishing Company, the Harpers could not do much to advance their uniform edition. In fact, when the world trip ended in England, Mark Twain had little heart to return to America, for his twenty-four-year-old daughter, Susan, had died there before the family could be reunited. He stayed on in London trying to solace his grief and self-condemnation by writing *Following the Equator,* a book based on his world tour. "Will healing ever come, or life have meaning again?" he wrote Howells, who a few years earlier had suffered a similar bereavement. Later he wrote further, "If you were here now I think we could cry down each other's necks, as in your dream. For we *are* a pair of old derelicts drifting around, now, with some of our passengers gone and the sunniness of the others in eclipse."

In the meantime *Joan of Arc* was published in May, 1896, with *Tom Sawyer Abroad* following in November. Thus before the end of that year Harper's had these two and four other titles set in the uniform edition; then the firm endeavored to get more by entering into a series of three-way contracts (American Publishing Company—Olivia Clemens —Harper & Brothers), whereby the Hartford people could issue subscription editions of Harper titles. With great hopes but no promises, Harper's launched the first of the uniform edition early in 1897, and Howells wrote a long review in the *Weekly* of February 13th.

Harper's did not share in publishing *Following the Equator* the following November. "Notwithstanding the belief that the sale of single subscription volumes had about ended, Bliss did well with the new book," Albert Bigelow Paine wrote in his biography of Mark Twain. "Thirty or forty thousand copies were placed without much delay, and the accumulated royalties paid into Mr. Rogers's hands." Added to income from his lectures, these royalty earnings enabled Mark Twain to write Howells in January, 1898, that the financial corner had been turned, and a month later to say there was now no undisputed claim that could not be "cashed." In 1899 the American Publishing Company brought out Mark Twain's *Complete Works* in uniform edition, while Harper's limped along with fewer titles, now labeled New Library Edition. Both Mark Twain and Howells had pieces in the December *Magazine*: "The Man That Corrupted Hadleyburg" is perhaps the best short story Mark Twain ever wrote, and *Their Silver Wedding Journey*, which was completed that month, is one of Howells' most charming stories. It was a symbolic linking of the two most famous men of American letters then living. Years earlier Mark Twain had written Howells, "You are really my only author," and as the century drew to a close, Howells could return the compliment: "You are my shadow of a great rock in a weary land, more than any other writer."

16

THE HARPER LONDON OFFICE
(1834-1900)

When the Harpers first employed a London representative is not known. In 1832 they attempted to place Paulding's *Westward Ho!* with a London publisher by sending proofs to the English novelist E. L. Bulwer. Two years later Bulwer sent the corrected proof of his new book, *The Last Days of Pompeii,* to New York in care of Obadiah Rich. It seems reasonable to assume that by that time the Harper brothers had arranged with the American-born, Harvard-educated Rich to be their London agent. He had recently opened a bookstore at 12 Red Lion Square, and was supplying American scholars and college libraries with foreign books. In 1835 Rich printed 250 copies of *Bibliotheca Americana Nova* with his and the Harper imprint and shipped 150 copies to New York for sale in America. A recently discovered cache of Bulwer-Harper correspondence contains several references to Rich's acting for Harper's, one as late as 1842. Such a representative was especially needed to negotiate the purchase of proofs of important books and to speed them to Cliff Street on clipper ships before bound copies could be forwarded to other houses on vessels sailing later.

After the advent of the steamship and the establishment of trade courtesies among the leading American publishers, the work of Harper's London agent changed somewhat. He continued to watch out for new titles and dispatch proofs promptly, but he was increasingly important in placing American books with English publishers and acting for them between the London visits of one of the Harper partners. The first known trip that Fletcher Harper made was in 1846-47. That winter or spring, he saw Sampson Low in Lamb's Conduit Street and arranged to have the British publisher act as the firm's literary agent. Either Rich was too involved in his bibliographical work to give the necessary time or Harper's felt that they should now be represented by one of the leading publishers. Low had the high regard of the London publishing fraternity and was for many years editor of *The Publishers' Circular,* a trade journal established in 1836 by a committee of British publishers. The partner of his latter years, Edward Marston, said that from the time of Sampson Low's appointment to the time of his death Harper's interests were absolutely identified with his own. This loyalty and affection were shared by his New York associates. In 1876 Western Union customers were permitted to register one word that would represent a firm's full name and address. The Harpers coined a word that would include Low's name as well as their own. That designation, "Harpsam," is still in use today. About that time Matthew Low, the youngest of Sampson Low's eight sons, came to America and was given an apprenticeship in Franklin Square. His father requested that Harper's pay Matthew one pound sterling per week and charge it to his private account.

Because of increasing age (he was born in 1797), Sampson Low had often requested that he be replaced, and in 1880 the Harpers attempted to employ the Boston publisher James R. Osgood, who had just resigned from a partnership with H. O. Houghton and George Mifflin. When Osgood said he was ambitious to set up in business for himself, Harper's turned to R. R. Bowker, who was editor of the *Publishers' Weekly.* One of Bowker's first assignments was to arrange for an English edition of *Harper's Monthly Magazine.* From the beginning the *Magazine* was popular in England and soon outsold its competitors, including the American *Century* and the English *Illustrated Magazine,* which was started in 1883 to dislodge such rivals from overseas. In fact, the launching of an English edition of *Harper's Magazine* worried the London *Bookseller,* which suspected that Harper's next step would be to publish books in England as well. It queried, "What is to prevent the Harpers from competing with the Longmans for the control of the works of future Macaulays?"

Bowker returned to New York after two years and continued on the Harper payroll as an assistant to Alden until 1885, when he returned to his first love, trade journalism. His work in London was taken over by William M. Laffan, one of whose important contributions was to replace the editor of the London *Harper's Magazine,* Lillie, with Andrew Lang, a most distinguished man of letters in Britain. Laffan was not too satisfactory a representative, since he was also acting as agent for the New York *Sun.* In 1885 the Harpers found that they could at last employ Osgood.

"James R. Osgood failed," Howells once commented, "although all his enterprises succeeded." After thirty years as a Boston publisher handling the works of all the distinguished New England writers, either as a partner with Fields or Houghton or on his account, Osgood was forced into bankruptcy in May, 1885. He failed because business conditions were bad and because publishers, including the Harpers, priced their books too low; the *Publishers' Weekly* editorialized on May 12, 1883, that half the books being published failed to return their costs and that half the remainder made no profit. Osgood announced his new association in a letter to the Boston *Daily Advertiser,* saying in part, "I expect to remove to New York and to become connected with Messrs. Harper & Bros., who upon learning of my recent business misfortune, with characteristic hospitality, renewed an offer made me several years ago." After spending a few months at Franklin Square familiarizing himself with titles and procedures, Osgood went to London at a salary of $10,000 a year. Amiable, loquacious, and greatly beloved by all who knew him, Osgood was the best representative the House had had since Low, partly because Osgood's previous scouting trips had made him well known to British publishers and authors.

In 1891 Harper's sent Clarence W. McIlvaine to London to help Osgood carry the load and to fulfill the prophecy of the London *Bookseller,* for with the immediate establishment of Osgood, McIlvaine & Co., Harper's had set up an English publishing house. McIlvaine had

come to Franklin Square looking for a job shortly after being graduated from Princeton in 1885. He soon proved his worth in the literary
department. Like Osgood, he was a bachelor and could easily pull up
stakes and welcome a life in literary London. They opened an office at
45 Albemarle Street, only a few steps from the well-known address
of John Murray. They have been credited with the honor of being the
publisher that first used the book jacket to display the author's name and
the title and to advertise other books. They not only represented Harper's but also ventured books in which the New York office had no
direct concern, such as assembling all of Hardy's works from several
British publishers for a uniform edition.

All such plans were halted in May, 1892, when Osgood died after a
short illness. Thomas Hardy wrote to his wife after the funeral: "We
buried Osgood this afternoon. . . . McIlvaine and Laffan (an American
friend who happened to be in London) walked as Chief Mourners, and
Black and myself next—behind us came Abbey, Boughton, Du Maurier,
etc. The grave was in wet clay—and before we left it was more than half
filled in. Very sad. . . ."

Osgood's obituary with an engraving of his photograph appeared in
the *Weekly* of May 29th, and some time later in the *Magazine* Howells
paid his tribute to a friend and former publisher. Of Osgood's junior
partner Howells had earlier written Henry James, "McIlvaine is an admirable fellow." However admirable, the junior partner did not have
Osgood's experience, wisdom, or drive, and by 1897 the firm ceased
publishing for English authors. McIlvaine stayed on at 45 Albemarle
Street as Harper's London representative. He had a competent clerical
assistant in Frederick W. Slater, and to cover the London trade he hired
a promising young man named Jonathan Cape.

17

HARPER TEXTBOOKS IN THE NINETEENTH CENTURY

Among the first books published by Harper's were medical books written by physicians and surgeons of England and France and edited for use in American medical schools by American authorities. Hooper's *Lexicon Medicum,* edited by Dr. Samuel Akerly, came out in 1829 and stayed in print for more than fifty years. Dr. Martyn Paine, the first head of New York University's Medical School, wrote a philosophy of medicine that he kept revising until 1870. Other medical textbooks were translated, edited, or written by six of his associates. Books for use in theological seminaries were also featured in early catalogues.

The firm's actual start in the textbook field, however, was made in 1835, when Charles Anthon, the first Jay Professor of Greek and Latin Languages of Columbia College, signed a sixty-four-word agreement whereby he became editor of a series of Classical and Auxiliary Works. For nearly thirty-five years he turned in an average of one manuscript a year, and the fame of his books, as well as his teaching and lecturing, made him the most influential classicist in America in the mid-nineteenth century. There was probably not a college or an academy during that time that did not use one or more of his Latin and Greek grammars, his readers, and his translations of the ancient classical authors. What made the last so popular were Anthon's notes and explanations, a new and desirable feature, and the excellence, for that period, of the

163

From Columbia College, Charles Anthon, James Renwick, Sr., and other professors had only a few blocks to walk when they went to 82 Cliff Street to see their new books through the press.

typography, printing, and binding. His early editions of Sallust, Cicero, and Caesar were widely pirated in England and adopted at Oxford and Cambridge, and blurbs from English sources were featured in catalogues and promotion pieces.

His students nicknamed their professor "Bull" Anthon because of his large head and massive build, feared him for his strict discipline, loved him for his devotion to classical studies, and respected him for his industry. He turned out a phenomenal amount of literary work, lectured and tutored at the college, and also directed the grammar school run by Columbia. Since the college was then only a few minutes' walk from Cliff Street, Anthon was often there reading proofs, checking on the presswork, and pocketing his semiannual payments. He did not receive a royalty but shared the profits on his works equally with the Harpers. This arrangement, often made by the House in the eighteen-thirties and forties, specified that after manufacturing costs were determined, 33⅓ per cent of that amount, plus a few cents to cover bad credit and losses of stock in shipment, was added as overhead. The remaining "profit" was equally divided and generally earned for an author the equivalent of a 15 or 20 per cent royalty. It earned for Anthon more than $100,000.

An old record escaped the 1853 fire and showed printings of various Harper books from mid-1842 to early 1853. Printings of several of the Anthon titles reveal how sales pyramided as the depression years of the early forties gave way to good times, as the number of educational institutions and students increased, and as the popularity of Anthon's books grew. In 1842, Cicero was printed twice, in quantities of 500 and 750; ten years later, in September, 1852, an edition of 2,000 copies was printed, followed by another 3,000 in six months; a total of nearly 25,000 copies were sold in eleven years. Sales of Caesar called for printings of nearly 31,000 in the same period and for 13,000 of Anthon's fat *Classical Dictionary*. Anthon received much editorial help from Professor Henry Drisler, who succeeded to Anthon's chair at Columbia and was twice acting president. He was an intimate friend and adviser of the Harpers, and his son and namesake was a long-time employee. Nearly all the Anthon and Drisler books were still in print at the end of the century.

In 1856 John W. Draper, of the University of the City of New York, published *Human Physiology*. For years it was the leading textbook in its field and also noteworthy because it contained the first photomicrographs ever published. Equally long-lived textbooks were written by Professor Elias Loomis, of Yale University. For forty years, beginning in 1847, Loomis wrote and revised more than twenty mathematical texts, ranging from elementary arithmetic through algebra, geometry, trigonometry, and calculus to astronomy and meteorology, with *Elements of Natural Philosophy* added to cover the field. Several catalogues printed an *"incomplete* list" of ninety-six colleges and universities that were using the Loomis texts in whole or in part. It is a roster of nearly all the important ones, from Massachusetts to California. His semiannual royalty checks enabled Loomis to bequeath $300,000 to Yale, the largest single donation the college had received up to 1890.

Until the middle of the century, colleges and academies comprised the chief market for Harper textbooks. According to the 1850 census,

The geography was big enough, when propped up, to hide the latest issue of the Tip Top Weekly.

the country had 6,000 academies, enrolling one out of eighty-eight of the population. But the public school movement was spreading fast from the New England states, which first adopted the concept of a school tax, to all the Northern and Central states. In 1854 there were 60,000 common schools, costing taxpayers six million dollars, most of it spent in Massachusetts, New York, and Pennsylvania, and in 1868 three times that amount was being spent for textbooks alone for an estimated school population of five million children. By that time the Harpers had put themselves in a good competitive position to get their share of the elementary school business.

Professor Loomis's colleague Dr. Worthington Hooker, of the Yale Medical School, helped the Harper educational department get into the schoolbook field. Of his texts, *Child's Book of Nature* (1857) was the most popular. Up to that time about all they had was the old warhorse, Morse's *School Geography,* sired in New Haven by Jedidiah Morse back in 1784. The Harpers began with the twenty-seventh edition in 1844. Completely revised in 1847, it sold by the thousands. It was replaced in 1875, when the lavishly illustrated *Harper's School Geography* began its spectacular career. City and state superintendents of schools approved adoptions and wrote letters of commendation to the publishers. Teachers found the books teachable and pupils found them interesting.

The best sellers of all schoolbooks were readers, as was demonstrated by an Oxford, Ohio, professor named William Holmes McGuffey, who in 1836 published the first two of a series of *Eclectic Readers.* Ten years later the Harpers ventured a *New York Class Book,* but with little success. In 1859 they signed up Marcius Willson, of Astoria, Long Island, to write a series of readers and spellers in return for a royalty of 8 per cent and a salary of $1,600 a year for help in promoting the readers. First editions of 15,000 copies were printed and by the mid-seventies the Willson series had grown from a primer through three spelling books to five readers. They were the firm's best-selling books, adopted in many states, and earned $20,000 a year for Willson. In 1871, Willson became angry with Harper's because of a series of editorials in the *Weekly,* written by Eugene Lawrence, attacking the Roman Catholic Church for apparent efforts to influence and control political power and to weaken the public school system. Fletcher Harper upheld Lawrence, who had become one of his most intimate friends. Lawrence was a competent writer, filled in for Curtis on the *Weekly* and the *Magazine* when Curtis was away, and wrote three books for the firm.

There were two reasons for the popularity of Hooker's natural science books, the *School Geography,* and the Willson *Readers*: first, they were written in line with the current vogue for "object teaching," the pedagogical theory that children wanted practical information—facts, not generalizations; second, the books were copiously illustrated. No other publisher had the Franklin Square resources of artists and engravers and few had their printing facilities. About 1854 a St. Louis man named Witter began to publish schoolbooks in the German language. (A million German immigrants came to the States during the next ten years.) His early reprints of German works compared unfavorably with the American output, and for several years Witter tried in vain to get cuts from other publishers. When he applied to Harper's in the summer of 1864, according to a trade journal, they cheerfully offered the free use of all their woodcuts.

To round out the schoolbook line, the House signed up Professor William Swinton, of the University of California, for a language series and Dr. John H. French to write a series of graded arithmetics. These arithmetics, the Hooker's course in natural science, and the Loomis series were advertised on the back of Harper envelopes during the eighteen-seventies. On the front cover, with just enough room left for a stamp and the correspondent's name and address, were printed the publisher's name and address, a large cut of the Franklin Square building, and a listing of the three Harper periodicals and the Willson *Readers*. It may have been good advertising, although of questionable taste, but it is evidence of what the House then considered were its foremost publications.

Abner Harper worked with other leading schoolbook publishers to bring order out of the chaos of textbook adoptions during the eighteen-seventies and eighties, when handsome bribes and fancy discounts demoralized the business and some states threatened to publish their own books. In 1881 the Harper discount plan was favored by the *Publishers' Weekly*, because it established a "solid, one-price system." Boards of education and reputable booksellers were given a discount of 25 per cent of the list price. "Exchange prices," given with the first purchase of Harper books for an equal number of old books in prior use, varied from 33⅓ per cent to 40 per cent. Working under Abner Harper was J. C. Jones, who managed the department of schoolbooks and directed the

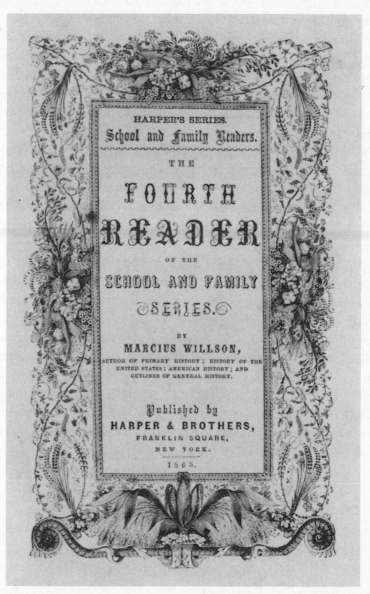

The Willson Readers were the firm's most popular nineteenth-century schoolbooks. There were five basic readers and three intermediary readers, as well as a primer and three spellers.

work of five agents, of whom the highest paid received $5,000. On the 1888 payroll at $2,500 was James Baldwin, an Indiana Quaker, who had been hired to develop a new line of *Readers* which, in 1889, had been adopted in New York City and a hundred other cities and towns. On September 25, 1889, the Harpers sent their last known letter to Herman Melville, along with a complimentary copy of "our new *Fifth Reader* published today." It contained a selection from *Moby Dick* on the capture of the whale.

The firm's biggest project in English literature was begun in 1870 with the help of Dr. William J. Rolfe, who developed a series of English Classics for School Reading. Rolfe was a Massachusetts educator, credited with having introduced regular instruction in English literature into the state's high school curriculum. His main contribution was to annotate Shakespeare's plays and sonnets, which were published in forty volumes. "Rolfe's Shakespeare" became a byword in academic circles, was praised by Dr. Furness, editor of the New Variorum Shakespeare, and is remembered by some still living who first studied Shakespeare's works with the help of Rolfe's notes.

In 1889 the country's schoolbook business was estimated to be five million dollars. What Harper & Brothers then earned on their total textbook operation can only be guessed—perhaps a quarter of a million dollars a year in gross profits; i.e., income over manufacturing costs and royalty. Their books ranked among the best in terms of quality and were priced as low as possible to get maximum distribution. Good books at low prices had for seventy years been a Harper maxim.

18

THE TRAGIC END OF A LONG STORY
(1890-99)

The closing decade of the nineteenth century was marked by economic upheavals and banking crises and business upsets. The gold standard was attacked by those who advocated the free coinage of silver, causing foreign investors to sell securities and withdraw great chunks of capital. During 1893 nearly five hundred banks and three times as many commercial firms failed, and by 1897 a third of the total railroad mileage was in the hands of receivers. If the four brothers had been alive then, they would have retreated and retrenched, for they respected economic records as much as they did the Bible. But their descendants pushed ahead with undiminished zeal. Their chief financial concern was to cover the withdrawal of capital because of the retirement or death of second-generation partners. To meet these contingencies no funds had been set up in reserve.

When Abner Harper retired, his son John replaced him as a partner. Whether or not Abner withdrew money is not known. Apparently Philip did not when he retired late in 1890, since he was succeeded by his son James, and his will directed that his Harper interest should be retained by his estate. However, the death of Fletcher Harper, Jr., was something quite different, for he had the largest single holding and no heir-apparent. When "Junior," as he was called, died on May 22, 1890, he was survived by his eighty-three-year-old mother; a daughter, Mrs.

171

Hiram Sibley; and many nephews and nieces. The day following his death, a meeting of the surviving partners was called by Philip to see where they stood financially. They were faced with the necessity of amortizing the largest equity of any one partner. Before the meeting broke up, Joseph W. said that consideration should also be given to his desire to retire four years hence, and asked approval of his plan to leave half of his total equity of $296,000 in the firm to cover the partnership of his son (Henry) Sleeper Harper and to receive $148,000 in four annual installments, with unpaid balances receiving interest at 6 per cent. His partners agreed.

Such drains on capital had been in part anticipated earlier in the year when Fletcher, Jr., had become seriously ill. Just as they were trying to figure out where the money would come from, they were asked by General Barnes, of A. S. Barnes & Co., to sell their schoolbooks to a new firm being organized (later called a trust) that would include those of A. S. Barnes & Co., D. Appleton & Co., Ivison Blakeman & Co., and Van Antwerp, Bragg & Co. After considerable dickering, the sale was consummated early in May, 1890. Harper's agreed to $400,000 for publishing rights, plus $150,000, the actual cost of plates, sheets, and bound stock, the total amount being paid over a five-year period, backed by interest-carrying notes. From this polygamous mating, with the Harpers an important but somewhat reluctant parent, the American Book Company was born.*

Since John W. Harper was in charge of finances, he was the logical one to be named the new head of the House, even though he was a year younger than Joseph W. Soon, however, the House was in trouble. Drains on capital, plus the depression, plus the lack of textbook income, plus declining periodical revenues, quickly depleted Harper's resources. And more. In 1896 the Harpers faced the necessity of borrowing large sums of money to keep going. Thinking that J. P. Morgan & Co. might give them the help they needed, the Harpers asked William M. Laffan to approach Mr. Morgan on their behalf. Besides serving briefly in the London office, Laffan had worked in the Harper literary depart-

---

* *Harper's School Geography* stayed in print until 1920 and the *Harper Readers* lasted through 1940, despite a new series of *Baldwin Readers,* launched in 1897, which eventually replaced the *McGuffey Readers.*

ment, advised them on art, and had written *Engravings on Wood* for them. In 1896 he was closely associated with Charles A. Dana on the New York *Sun* and was counseling Mr. Morgan on art purchases. The negotiations resulted in the termination of the seventy-nine-year-old Harper partnership and the reorganization in November, 1896, of Harper & Brothers as a stock company. Equities were translated into a $2,000,000 issue of capital stock. Mortgage bonds valued at $3,000,000 were also issued. Taking all but $250,000 of these bonds as collateral security, J. P. Morgan & Co. loaned $850,000 to the Harpers, between November, 1896, and August, 1899. Out of this amount they had to pay the art critic Laffan a fantastic commission of $100,000 for his services.

In the preceding July Joseph W. Harper had died, four months after the death of his cousin Philip. Because Philip was Mayor Harper's son, and had been head of the House, his death was covered in long obituary articles and editorials in scores of newspapers across the country. The Cincinnati *Commercial Gazette* said that since 1817 many money panics had swept the country, toppling giant banking and commercial enterprises, but Harper & Brothers had weathered all storms. The San Francisco *Bulletin* noted that the five sons of the founders had retired with fortunes and made way for their own sons who now conducted the business. Almost all accounts praised what they assumed to be the impregnable financial position of the firm and commended its eight-decade contribution to the commonwealth. "It is not too much to say," editorialized the New York *Commercial Advertiser*, "that this publishing house has equipped more men and women for their active duties than any combined score of colleges in the United States." Many of these editorial writers remembered the Family Library and had gone to school with *Harper's Geography* and Harper's *Readers*. The Harper periodicals came regularly to their homes or offices. They had read the Harper best sellers.

The most recent best seller had come out in September, 1894, after being serialized in *Harper's Magazine*, where it was so popular that the circulation increased by 100,000 copies. It was Du Maurier's *Trilby*, the gay, sad story of a remembered youth, evocative of art student life in Paris. Trilby, an artist's model and the creature of Du Maurier's imagina-

Trilby, as drawn by George Du Maurier for his novel Trilby.

7. *under the apple tree, with*
the Prince & fairy.
Part I. p. 9 - (Peter Ibbetson)
G. du Maurier

Illustration drawn by Du Maurier for his novel Peter Ibbetson.

tion, was adopted by Americans as one of their own. There were Trilby dolls and Trilby shoes and Trilby luncheons. Clergymen used the story to point a moral and judges quoted from it in their decisions, and nine companies toured the country to dramatize the tale. However, the book that was being read from Provincetown to the Golden Gate did not altogether follow the *Magazine* serial. No sooner was the March issue out in London than it was read by James McNeill Whistler, who was infuriated because the artist Joe Sibley was obviously a fictional portrayal of himself. He stormed into the office of McIlvaine, Harper's London agent, and demanded that the sale of the *Magazine* be stopped. Since the firm was fearful of a libel suit (the controversialist Whistler had once sued Ruskin because of an unfavorable review of his art), the issue was stopped in New York and a letter of apology was sent to

Whistler. Laurence Hutton, whose ear could detect literary gossip miles away, made immediately for Franklin Square. "I want a copy of that issue," he demanded. "You can't have it. It has been suppressed." Hutton was not to be put off. "But I'll buy it," he said. The Harper he was addressing glared at him a moment, then said, "We can't sell even one more; but—damn you—you know where they are!" The section that offended Whistler was rewritten for the book, beginning with page 142. That March, the manuscript of *Trilby* was sent to the composing room with instructions to print 6,500 copies. Before publication, it was increased three times: to 10,000, to 25,000, and to 35,000. Eventually more than 1,000,000 copies were sold. When the sales began to mount up, Harper's began paying Du Maurier royalties; this was their original proposal, which he had declined, preferring a lump sum for all rights. He and his estate also shared in dramatic rights.

With all its success, *Trilby* was not as good as Du Maurier's *Peter Ibbetson,* the first novel of the famous artist who late in life turned to fiction. Howells loved this book, calling it "a glamorous, haze-hung romance, the fond, gentle tale of an exile from Paris." The book was made into a play starring the Barrymore brothers and into an opera by Deems Taylor, with a première at the Metropolitan Opera House. Harper's published Du Maurier's last book, *The Martian,* with a first printing of 50,000 copies, but the author did not live to see a copy. He died in October, 1896, the month serialization began in the *Magazine.*

A. Conan Doyle, too, was being widely read in the early nineties, also with copyright protection and a 15 per cent royalty. His *The Adventures of Sherlock Holmes* held hosts of American readers in weekly suspense during 1892 until the serial was completed and the book was issued. It was not the first Sherlock Holmes tale but the one that made him famous. The Harpers quickly brought out two earlier books and followed with *Memoirs of Sherlock Holmes,* and *The Refugees.* Conan Doyle was represented by the agent A. P. Watt, in London, who, as the author's popularity sky-rocketed, pushed the price of each of the *Weekly*'s installments up from £30 to £150. And there was competitive bidding from America, chiefly from S. S. McClure, a young entrepreneur from the Middle West who had never heard of a publisher's loving cup. The

Poster drawn by Edward Penfield to advertise the August, 1896, issue of *Harper's Magazine*

Edward Penfield eventually succeeded Parsons as art editor for Harper periodicals. He served the house with intelligence and distinction for eleven years before he resigned, at the age of thirty-five, to devote his entire time to his own work. He is best remembered for his poster art. He was, W. A. Rogers believed, the first man to make posters works of art. Penfield illustrated a few books, including The Dreamers, *by John Kendrick Bangs, and two of his own books were issued from Franklin Square.*

detective story vogue that Conan Doyle started had literary repercussions, not the least of which was "Tom Sawyer, Detective," included in Mark Twain's second Harper book.

In 1895 a list of "Best Sellers" made its début, published in the *Bookman.* That first list of ten fiction titles carried four from Harper's, including Richard Harding Davis's *The Princess Aline.* It was illustrated by Charles Dana Gibson, a kind of American Du Maurier, whose girls flounced in and out of Harper periodicals and books for many years. Beginning in 1890, Davis was managing editor of the *Weekly* for several years and was sent abroad on numerous reportorial missions, some of which made up his six nonfiction titles catalogued in 1900.

John Kendrick Bangs hit the best-seller list in 1896 with *A House-Boat on the Styx.* Bangs was employed by Harper's the same year Davis was and began editing and writing humor for the periodicals. He managed to pull a lot of funny stories from the squeaky "Editor's Drawer"; for his own jokes he paid himself one dollar and for others, including the only one Remington ever wrote, two. The best of his own were published in several collections, one of which came out in the Harper Black and White Series, entitled *Coffee and Repartee.* More than 50,000 fellow jokesters bought copies, among them Conan Doyle, who struck up a friendship with Bangs when Conan Doyle came to America to give readings. Despite his friendship for Mark Twain, Howells claimed that Bangs, as a humorist, had the field to himself. His humor was often satirical and always distinguished by a sense of literary value. The latter quality led to his being asked in 1898 to write "Literary Notes" for the *Magazine* and to edit the American edition of *Literature,* a weekly paper of literary criticism published in association with the London *Times.* At Franklin Square, Bangs did *Magazine* chores along with Thomas Nelson Page, Charles Dudley Warner, and Howells, the last also helping with *Literature.* Once, Bangs polled readers for their choice of the ten best living American writers. Howells headed the list, with Mark Twain second. Whereupon Clemens wrote Bangs, "Do you think you could persuade Mr. Howells to come out of that polling-booth and let me keep game for a while?" Bangs was an intimate friend of J. Henry Harper's. The story of the close business and personal relations among the members of three generations of the Harper family and the Bangs family would make a book of itself.

In 1895 Howells took note in his *Weekly* "Life and Letters" department of the "broad-shouldered, six-foot verities of Owen Wister's wild, Western world." The book he reviewed was *Red Men and White,* published in November. By accepting Wister's first Western story, "Hank's Woman," Alden was responsible for Wister's decision to represent the West in fiction as faithfully as his friend Theodore Roosevelt had in factual reporting or Remington had through drawings. Because Remington was the obvious artist to illustrate Wister's stories, the Harpers sent him out West to collaborate. "Mr. [J. Henry] Harper is paying me high wages," Wister once wrote, and again, "I corrected proof [in New York] and lunched with Alden and Charles Dudley Warner." Another book of Western interest was *Boots and Saddles* by Elizabeth B. Custer, widow of General Custer, who told the story of life in a frontier garrison in the midst of Indian perils and alarms. A real bit of Americana, it has sold over 100,000 copies and is still in print.

Howells plugged for Mary Wilkins Freeman, who wrote, realistically and with pathos, quaint humor and homely tragedies of New England life. *A Humble Romance* and *A New England Nun* were her best books. Margaret Deland began her long connection with the House about this time. Her *Old Chester Tales,* illustrated by Pyle, was long in print.

The letters of the beloved poet and distinguished citizen James Russell Lowell were published posthumously in 1893. They were edited by Curtis's close friend Charles Eliot Norton and carried the highest royalty ever paid by Harper's up to that time, 20 per cent to 2,000, and 25 per cent thereafter. The manufacturing order specified "extra good" paper with deckle edges and printing "with very great care." The following year, at the urging of Howells and after the book had been declined by four publishers, the firm issued *Wealth Against Commonwealth,* by Henry Demarest Lloyd. Lloyd was the first and one of the best muckrakers, and in this book he dealt with the trust system, using the Standard Oil Company to illustrate what Howells called "the evilest phase of the century." Lloyd was widely read by the Populists, who were then in their most vocal period. What is called a landmark in historical writing, *His-*

tory of the United States from the Compromise of 1850, was launched in 1893 with the first two volumes of what eventually became a seven-volume work. Its author, James Ford Rhodes, was a brother-in-law of Mark Hanna.

A "first author" to be credited to Alden was Henry van Dyke, who was sent in 1879 to do a magazine article about the big wheat farms on the Red River and in Manitoba. Later van Dyke wrote four books for Harper's, the best known of which is *The Story of the Other Wise Man.* Issued in 1895 in a first printing of 2,500 copies, the book has sold over three hundred times that number. When I was nine years old, a copy was given to me by an aunt, and it was my first introduction to the Harper & Brothers imprint. Henry van Dyke left the pastorate of New York's Brick Presbyterian Church in 1899 to become Professor of English Literature at Princeton. There he became a warm friend of Woodrow Wilson, a professorial colleague, whose biography of George Washington, illustrated by Pyle, came out in 1896. When Wilson became President, he sent van Dyke as U.S. Minister to the Netherlands. Wilson's interest in international affairs prompted the Harpers to send him a complimentary copy of Captain Dreyfus's *Letters to His Wife,* which purported to give convincing proof of his innocence in the celebrated case in which he was wrongly condemned for treason because of the anti-Semitism of many French army officers.

By 1895 a frost was on the leaves of the *Magazine,* with circulation down and advertising gross falling off badly. Along with the *Atlantic* and the *Century* it was losing out to the new *McClure's* magazine, which could be bought at newsstands for fifteen cents a copy compared to their thirty-five cents. S. S. McClure was not only competing for their best authors, many of whom were won over by his big newspaper syndicate, but was also ambitious to turn serials into books. To this end he took on young Frank N. Doubleday, who had managed Scribner's subscription book department, and started publishing books as Doubleday & McClure. Their enterprise was well known to Laffan, who, after Dana's death, was in full charge of the New York *Sun.*

With the Harpers unable to meet interest payments on their loan, Mr. Morgan called in Laffan early in 1899 to discuss the worsening of affairs on Franklin Square. Laffan recommended McClure as the best publishing doctor to take care of such an ill patient and found McClure eager to extend his practice. Whereupon the Morgan attorney notified Harper's that accountants would be coming in to look over their books and that they and their attorneys should be prepared to discuss reorganization, with McClure in full charge. There was nothing sugar-coated about that pill, but they swallowed it. McClure agreed to take over the direction of the House on the basis of the purchase of 67½ per cent of the stock, for which he would pay $692,000 over a period of ten years.

By summer McClure had taken over. He commandeered John Finley, the young president of his alma mater, Knox College, to edit the *Weekly*, and Thomas Nelson Page, then editor of the *Atlantic*, to help with the Harper business. To Page he wrote, "I have got the earth with several things thrown in, and am eager to see if you don't want one or two kingdoms for yourself." But he failed to give enough territory to the ambitious Doubleday, who saw himself ruling in one of only the minor kingdoms. Doubleday balked and left McClure, taking Page along with him to start a new publishing company. Meanwhile McClure had not succeeded in his efforts to get enough capital to swing the Harper deal, and on his return from a European trip in October he was forced to cancel his Harper agreement.

By that time the Harpers had accepted the fact of outside leadership and asked Colonel George M. Harvey if he would take over control. Harvey, a small-town boy from Vermont who had made good in the big city as Pulitzer's managing editor of the New York *World*, was a genius at publicity and was the new owner of the venerable *North American Review*. Harvey was interested and, with Mr. Morgan's approval, moved into Franklin Square. What he discovered appalled him—sales for the year down to $676,000 and a loss for the year to date of more than that amount. He said that unless the Harpers among themselves could bring in enough funds to stave off creditors, complete reorganization was called for. Sums brought in were comparatively small, but represented a heroic sacrifice on the part of several, including Philip's son James and wife, Lillie—hardly the crippled Harpers' "death wish," a phrase applied to them by Peter Lyon in his recent biography of McClure.

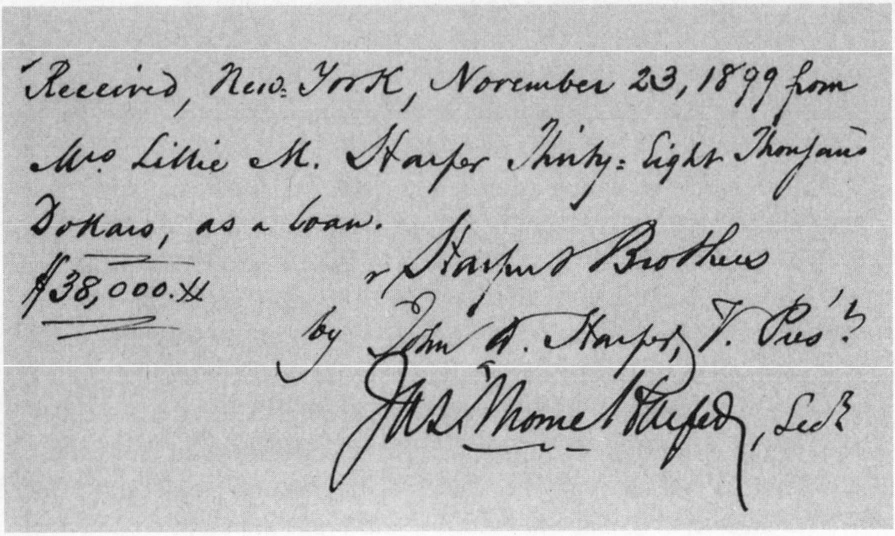
Received, New-York, November 23, 1899 from Mrs Lillie M. Harper Thirty-Eight Thousand Dollars, as a loan.

$38,000.xx

Harper & Brothers
by John A. Harper, V. Pres't
Jas. Thorne Harper, Sec'y

Four days later, along with five other directors of the company, James Harper signed his name to a letter to Mr. Morgan. They said they appreciated his generous offer to increase the amount of his loan but they could not bring themselves to accept it; while their assets, mostly frozen, far exceeded their liabilities, they believed that with Mr. Harvey in full control the company would soon make interest payments, both on Morgan's prior lien and on unsecured loans amounting to $2,000,000; they were prepared to initiate proceedings leading to the appointment of the State Trust Company, trustee under the mortgage, as receiver of the corporation, with Mr. Harvey named as agent for the receiver; thus the interests of their creditors and the honor and dignity of the House would be preserved. Mr. Morgan replied on November 27:

> We beg to acknowledge the receipt of your communication of this date, and to express our commendation of the spirit which animates it. The downfall of the House of Harper would be a national calamity. Everything that can be done lawfully to prevent it, should be done.
>
> Under the circumstances, we think your plan will prove in the end to have been the best for all your creditors, and it will receive our hearty co-operation.

On December 4, 1899, Harper & Brothers went into receivership.

William Dean Howells was returning home from a lecture tour when he read in the New York *Herald* of the failure of the House. "It was as if I had read that the government of the United States had failed," he wrote. "Apart from the anxiety I felt for my own imaginable share in the ruin, there was a genuine grief for those whom it necessarily involved; they had been my friends so long that I could not help appropriating their misfortune and making it personal to myself."

PUBLISHING
IN THE TWENTIETH CENTURY

After Harvey took control of Harper's he occupied the office formerly used by Joseph W. Harper. He placed a portrait of J. P. Morgan on the wall (left). The frescoes along the walls were the work of Harper artists, the one over the door depicting the four Harper brothers as young printers. This room later became known as the Board Room.

19

THE HARVEY REGIME (1900-1915)

"I suppose you are expecting me to tell you something of the Harper collapse," Howells wrote in January, 1900, to Mark Twain, who was then in England. "I know very little accurately, but though the business is now in the hands of a receiver, have a notion that the Harpers will sometime go on with it. As yet I have lost nothing by them, and I rather think I shall not lose."

Howells did not mention the thirty-six-year-old Harvey, who had been named agent for the receiver, although Harvey had his eye on Howells. But before he could give much attention to authors Harvey had to give his time to business concerns. Prior to the receivership he had effected reforms that would save $100,000 a year. He set up a reorganization committee to assist him in managing the business and, with its approval, sold the college textbooks and scholarly reference works to the American Book Company for $125,000. On February 17, 1900, the company was reorganized with Harvey as president, and authorization was given for an issue of capital stock with $2,000,000 par value, a large part of which was to go to Harvey over his contract period of five years; apparently this was never issued. However, the new corporation did not really get started until October 1st, at which time income bonds amounting to $2,000,000 were issued, some going to creditors as security.

At the end of his first year on Franklin Square, Harvey had whittled the firm's indebtedness, exclusive of the Morgan loan, down to nearly $1,000,000, and faced the necessity of saving enough out of the next year's income to pay authors' royalties, accrued interest and taxes, and reorganization expenses totaling $283,000. He also fired most of the compositors, many of them men grown old in the business, a task the Harpers had never had the heart to do. Linotype machines were leased with options to buy.

As president of the new company, Harvey himself took a considerable reduction in income. He was paid $25,000, which by his own admission was less than 10 per cent of what he had earned the previous year through his association with William C. Whitney and Thomas Fortune Ryan. He named J. Henry Harper and Clarence McIlvaine as vice-presidents, but reduced their salaries and talked Frederick A. Duneka, a former colleague on the New York *World,* into becoming the general manager and the secretary of the Board of Directors. Duneka was an able executive, made decisions promptly, and was especially considerate of the older employees, from Alden down. His competence was soon recognized outside the House as well, and he was offered a partnership with Doubleday, Page & Co., which he declined. Certain authors were drawn to him, particularly Mark Twain and Booth Tarkington. Harvey succeeded in getting Frederick T. Leigh, who had represented the State Trust Company on the reorganization committee, to stay on as treasurer. Major Leigh, as he was called, was a big man, erect and dignified, who met people easily. Harvey also hired Jerome B. Latour to head up the bookkeeping department and A. D. Chandler to manage the circulation of the periodicals.

With these men named to key positions, Harvey gave them desks centrally located in the counting room and ordered the desks of the Harper cousins, except J. Henry Harper's, placed on the top floor, where typesetters had long worked. They were literally kicked upstairs, and most of them soon resigned. The only one who was continued on the payroll for any length of time was another Joseph W. Harper ("Madison Joe") who retired in 1927 as head of the purchasing department. His cousin Sleeper Harper later joined the Board of Directors, where he served until his death in 1944.

Colonel Harvey took over the big private office as his own and placed a framed photograph of Mr. Morgan prominently on one of the mahogany-paneled walls. Except for the men he had named as business associates and the editors of the periodicals, few of the Harper personnel dared to venture into Harvey's sanctum. Those who did, like W. G. van Tassell Sutphen, who worked in the literary department, soon found that they not only respected Harvey but also, and surprisingly, developed an affection for him. Sutphen, who married into the Harper family, used a long string of adjectives to describe Harvey: gay, sardonic, autocratic, inscrutable, lovable, fascinating, prodigal.

Such was George Brinton McClellan Harvey's instinct for publicity that as soon as he had put the House back on a secure financial footing, he dressed up the eminent old lady with lipstick, a new hairdo, and fashionable clothes and began to present her properly in a long succession of luncheons and dinners. The first affair was a House dinner at Delmonico's, a gathering of one hundred and fifty men from the executive, editorial, business, and manufacturing departments, all in tails and white ties and top hats. It was a splendid affair and succeeded in getting columns of newspaper space and inspiring co-workers with new confidence and pride of association. In June, 1902, he entertained the American Booksellers' Association at Franklin Square and printed a picture of the event in the *Weekly*. While Harvey was thus recognizing the importance of booksellers in his new kingdom, his ambassador to the trade was Henry Hoyns, whom he had made sales manager in 1900. At that same time, Harvey advanced another young man from the old regime, making Edward J. Cullen an assistant to Latour in the bookkeeping department, and employed a young Yale graduate, Thomas B. Wells, to do promotion work on books and periodicals. These three men were to learn a great deal from Harvey about running a publishing house, including things not to do.

What Harvey had to do even before the business was completely reorganized was to pay royalties and otherwise reassure authors, without whom he would not survive even five years, and to give time to the periodicals, all of which were losing money. Harvey considered the *Weekly* to be the rustiest link in the whole Harper chain. In December,

1899, he discontinued *Literature* and asked Bangs to switch editorial chairs and see what he could do with the *Weekly*. Bangs said this order was comparable only to the inhuman act of a parent who yanks his small son out of a warm bed in midwinter and sends him out into the snow to saw wood. He continued sawing on Harvey's woodpile until September, 1901, when Harvey took the saw into his own hands and made Edward S. Martin his associate editor. Differences between Harvey and Bangs had arisen after Bangs came back from Havana in the early part of the year and wrote a series of articles extolling General Wood's administration in Cuba. These articles, as well as the friendship Bangs enjoyed with Theodore Roosevelt, did not please Harvey, who from then on began insinuating his own editorial ideas. After several months the unhappy but always outwardly cheerful Bangs saw that the *Weekly* represented neither his own nor his chief's ideals and asked Harvey what he thought should be done. "If I were you," Harvey replied, "I'd tell me to go to Hell and get fired." This Bangs did, with considerable relish.

When Colonel Harvey moved into Franklin Square, he took David Munro with him as nominal editor of the *North American Review*. Munro, a genial Scotsman, had worked with the Harper literary department for nearly twenty years, so his return was a sort of homecoming. It seems likely that Munro had been so impressed by Harvey that he was the one who suggested to J. Henry and Sleeper Harper that the Colonel might be just the man to put their business back on its feet; at least, he introduced them. Munro got along well with Harvey, probably because he did as he was told. The *North American Review,* ever since its founding in Boston in 1815, had been a magazine of prestige rather than profit, and so it continued under Harvey. He used it to serialize important authors and admitted in 1914 that during the preceding ten years it had lost $150,000. A sixth of this amount went down the drain in 1904, when he paid Mark Twain $30,000 for serial rights to his *Autobiography* and could show only $5,000 as additional revenue.

Mark Twain was one of the first authors Harvey gave his attention to. He saw Clemens during a trip to London in the summer of 1900 and got a promise that Harper's should have exclusive rights to all future Mark Twain works. When Clemens returned to New York that Novem-

New York, N.Y. Nov 26, 1900

G.B.M. Harvey Esq.
President of Harper & Bros.

Dear Sir—

The terms proposed in
your letter of recent date
~~~~~ are satisfactory; also
your proposal regarding
the publication of my
memoirs 100 years hence
contained in your previous
communication. I accept
both.

Very truly yours

SL. Clemens

Letter from Mark Twain to Colonel Harvey written at the time Mark Twain contracted to have all his books published by Harper's. His agreement to the publication of his memoirs followed an unusual proposal set forth in a letter Harvey wrote to H. H. Rogers on October 17, 1900. Harvey proposed that Mark Twain's memoirs, along with one hundred autographed sheets, be kept under seal by a trust company until the year 2000, when Harper's would issue them "in whatever modes should then be prevalent, that is by printing as at present, or by use of phonographic cylinders, or by electrical methods, or by any other method which may then be in use." Harvey suggested further that he give Mark Twain a dinner at which a contract would be signed before distinguished guests, all of whom would witness the contract and be given the privilege of subscribing for autographed copies at $50 each. Their descendants would pay like amounts when presenting the certificates to Harper's, who would divide the gross revenue from sales with Mark Twain's heirs. This grandiose scheme never materialized.

ber, the promise was made binding in a contract stipulating twenty cents a word for serial publication. This rate was raised to thirty cents in October, 1903, by a contract that included book rights as well, and Clemens wrote in his notebook that the contract "concentrates all my books in Harper's hands and now at last they are valuable: in fact they are a fortune. They [Harper's] *guarantee* me $25,000 a year for 5 years, and they will yield twice as much . . . if properly handled." By November, 1914, according to Harvey, $314,300 had been paid to Mark Twain and his heirs. Four new Mark Twain books were issued through 1909, including *Captain Stormfield's Visit to Heaven.* Money earned from this short extravaganza helped to build his new home in Redding, Connecticut, and inspired its name, "Stormfield."

William Dean Howells was equally important to Harvey, although by the summer of 1900 Harvey had done nothing more than send Howells a reassuring letter with his royalty check. Harvey did some hurrying the day he learned that Howells had started a new novel, to be called *The Kentons,* and had promised it to Dodd, Mead & Co. Harvey saw Howells and invited him to his New Jersey home over the following night so that they could talk business. Whereupon Howells asked Frank H. Dodd if he might be released should his Franklin Square association be revived, and Dodd complied, saying that no doubt Harvey would want him. Howells recalled the arrangement when, in 1911, he dictated a long memorandum to Miss Virginia Watson, a new employee who was helping J. Henry Harper with his House history. He said, "I was to give them [Harper's] so many thousand words for so much a year, and I was to be their literary adviser, however much or little that meant; only, as at a later time [Harvey] expressed it, he wished me to belong to the shop. . . . I had a room there for some months like other editors, and for a while I dealt with manuscripts."

Howells also agreed to take on "The Editor's Easy Chair," the *Magazine* assignment he had refused in 1885, and his monthly essays covering twenty years mark him as the giant of all the writers who have occupied that post. Again on a regular salary of $10,000 a year for contributions to the periodicals and with additional royalty income (from 1909 on, a straight 20 per cent), Howells was freed of financial worries.

On a warm December day in 1907, Colonel Harvey entertained for W. D. Howells, who was soon to leave for a winter's stay in Italy. More than fifty guests were brought in two chartered drawing-room cars from New York to Harvey's Lakewood, New Jersey, home. As indicated by the signatures, from left to right, are W. D. Howells, Mark Twain, Colonel Harvey, H. M. Alden, David A. Munro, and M. W. Hazeltine, literary editor, New York Sun.

He probably took a 10 per cent cut along with others in the panic year of 1907, and his salary may have been upped to $12,000 in 1910. *The Kentons* was published in April, 1902, and Howells noted with sardonic humor that the novel in its agreeable popularity narrowly escaped becoming a best seller. However, most of his books after 1900 were collections of essays and travel pieces. Two outstanding titles were *Literary Friends and Acquaintances* (1900) and *My Mark Twain* (1910). All

that Howells wrote in his lifetime was annotated in a bibliography of
143 two-column pages, and Henry Steele Commager, in his volume of
Howells' *Selected Writings,* wrote, "No other American ever comman-
ded such wide and prolonged literary influence in his own lifetime. . . .
Except Mark Twain, he was the most representative of American writers
in the long period between the Civil War and the First World War."

Colonel Harvey later took credit for obtaining most of the authors
published by the House during his presidency—wrongly including
Bangs, Henry James, Sir Gilbert Parker, and others. However, he did
give J. Henry Harper credit for holding on to old authors and developing new ones, and said that only one author withdrew his books because
of the firm's failure—the historian James Ford Rhodes. What Harvey
did not admit was that he lost Owen Wister and *The Virginian* to
Macmillan and Ellen Glasgow to Doubleday-Page. Wister, along with
other Harper authors, was solicited by other publishers as soon as the
bankruptcy was known, and such conduct made Wister all the more determined to stay on. In 1900 he gave them a book of stories, *The Jimmy-
john Boss,* but was unhappy that it received little advertising, with letters
urging more promotion going unanswered. Only when Harvey and
Harper realized that the author they had taken for granted was placing
The Virginian elsewhere did they try to wheedle him back. Then it was
too late. Ellen Glasgow had been pleased with what Harper's did to
launch her first two novels, but was won over to his new firm by Thomas
Nelson Page, who wrote to her as soon as the Harper calamity became
known.

Instead of getting James on the Harper list, Harvey actually lost him
to Scribner's. Most of what James wrote prior to 1900 had been issued in
Harper periodicals before coming out in book form. Except for *Daisy
Miller,* which had to be issued in cheap format because of an unfortunate
loss of copyright, most of his books were handsomely produced, especially *Washington Square* with illustrations by Du Maurier; *Picture and
Text* is a jewel of a book. However, James had little warmth of feeling
for any of the Harpers and looked upon them as purveyors of periodicals
who could pay good money for what he wrote. Thus, late in 1900, he
mailed Alden a long synopsis of a new novel, *The Ambassadors.* Alden

did not think that it promised to be a popular novel, and handed the synopsis to Harvey, who apparently shelved it, for two years later the expatriate novelist assumed it had been destroyed. Such ignoring of an author could hardly inspire good will, and James also probably knew that the House had in 1899 printed his *The Awkward Age* in a first edition of only 1,000 copies.

In August, 1901, James wrote to Howells saying that he had lately finished the manuscript of *The Ambassadors,* which was in Harper's hands, and that his inspiration for writing the novel had come from a casual remark that, years before, Howells had made and likely forgotten about. Howells could not have done otherwise than speak to Harvey, for he was still acting as literary adviser. But it was not until January, 1903, that Harvey began serializing the novel in the *North American Review* and James wrote to Howells to thank him profusely for his help in the negotiations. It was published in book form on November 6th. The serial did not contain the complete book, and James was reading final serial proofs at the same time that he was checking book proofs of both the English and the American editions. He was especially concerned about inserting into the American galley proofs material not in the serial. Somehow, in this process, one of the chapters was misplaced. The discrepancy was not discovered until 1950 and has inspired several scholarly articles since. The Harper's Modern Classics edition corrects the ancient error, and underscores the importance of an author's seeing page proof.

The Ambassadors was not the last book that Harper's published for James. He welcomed Harvey in 1904 to his home in Rye, England, and permitted Harvey to give a luncheon for him later that year in New York; moreover he gave Harvey, both for the *North American Review* and for book publication, a series of articles giving his impressions of the United States after an absence of twenty years; it was called *The American Scene.* During this visit, however, James arranged with Scribner's, who treated him with more promptness and courtesy, to publish his next two novels and to issue the "New York" edition of his works. Even so, he did not burn his Harper bridges, for as late as 1909 he gave the firm his short tale of *Julia Bride,* which appeared with illustrations as a novella of eighty-four pages, in large type with wide margins.

Even though neither Howells nor James made the best-seller lists, the House, during Harvey's tenure, did have a good share of such titles to keep it going, along with a healthy backlist. Early in the century Mrs. Humphry Ward, whom Tolstoy considered the greatest living writer, and Sir Gilbert Parker, the British Parliamentarian, turned out books the public clamored for. For an extended period Mrs. Ward's *Eleanor* sold over one thousand copies a day. Of Parker's three fiction titles, *The Weavers* climbed highest on the best-seller lists, as did Katherine Cecil Thurston's three leading novels, two issued anonymously, *The Masquerader* and *The Gambler*. In 1909, the first year of the Model T Ford, Harper's had the top three best-selling novels: *The Inner Shrine*, by Basil King (published anonymously); *Katrine*, by Elinor Macartney Lane; and *The Silver Horde*, by Rex Beach. Rex Beach's earlier book, *The Spoilers*, was the most famous of his two-fisted fiction and was the first six-reel movie produced. Several other movies were made from the ten Rex Beach novels published during this period, and he was the first author to insist on movie rights in his book contract.

Two best-selling authors gained that status elsewhere after Harvey had tried as well as he could to satisfy them—John Fox, Jr., and Robert W. Chambers. Both had started with Harper's before Harvey's time, and Chambers gave him six novels before going to Appleton, who in 1906 issued *The Fighting Chance* in a first printing of 50,000, which sales soon quadrupled. Two years later Fox's *The Trail of the Lonesome Pine* was doing even better for Scribner's. But such are the fortunes of books and authors; that the Harpers lost so many during the first two decades of the century made them value those who, like Margaret Deland, remained faithful. She had best sellers in 1906 and 1911, *The Awakening of Helena Richie* and *The Iron Woman*, issued after serialization in the *Magazine*. Few authors were as beloved as Mrs. Deland, both by the literary and the sales departments, and this affection of the publisher and, indeed, the public is still remembered by a few. Mary E. Wilkins Freeman ran Mrs. Deland a close second. Her total Harper output ran to nearly twenty volumes of novels and collected short stories, about equally divided between the two centuries. A father-son authorship also bridged the centuries in the English McCarthys. Justin McCarthy wrote, among other books, the popular *A History of Our Own Times,* and his son Justin H. McCarthy gave Harper's an average of a novel a year during the Harvey period.

Among the greatest English novelists then writing, although the Harpers did not seem to recognize the fact, was Joseph Conrad. He and his four novels and the autobiographical *A Personal Record* were apparently given only routine attention. Harper's continued giving considerable attention, however, to H. G. Wells, whose books had done so well in the nineties. They plugged two new novels of his and four nonfiction titles, including *The Future in America,* which he wrote following an American visit in 1906. Arnold Bennett came over six years later and the inevitable book followed, *Your United States.* He also published one novel from Franklin Square, *The Price of Love.* The most impressive Harper import from England, both in size and prestige, was Swinburne's collection of poems and dramatic works.

An even bigger project on the American side was the twenty-seven-volume historical series, the American Nation. It was edited by Albert Bushnell Hart, of Harvard, who wrote two of the volumes.

Two authors of short stories and novels added more distinction than publishing profit: James Branch Cabell, with three volumes of short stories, and Theodore Dreiser, with two novels, *Jennie Gerhardt* and *The Financier,* and a reissue of *Sister Carrie,* his first novel and the one that made him world famous. Charles Rann Kennedy gave the House five dramatic works and two of them sold exceedingly well, *The Terrible Meek* and *The Servant in the House;* the latter was one of Broadway's most successful plays of that time, and the book was illustrated with photographs of the stage production. The Philadelphia Baptist clergyman Russell H. Conwell was also attracting large audiences for his lecture "Acres of Diamonds," which he delivered some six thousand times. Income from this and fat royalty checks on sales of the lecture in book form enabled him to make his dream of Temple University come true. Other best sellers were two juvenile books by Albert Bigelow Paine and his three-volume biography of Mark Twain, published two years after Clemens died.

Forty Modern Fables was the best of four books by George Ade that came to Harper's with the purchase of the R. H. Russell publications in 1903; two more were issued later. The Russell purchase of more than one hundred titles was made up largely of art books and portfolios of prints. Especially important were several classical children's books richly illustrated by Louis Rhead. (These titles sold wonderfully well and were released in the nineteen-thirties to Eugene Reynal, after he left Harper's to start his own firm. Reissued with laminated covers, they found another generation of readers.) There were eight "Editions de-luxe" folios of illustrations by Charles Dana Gibson containing more than five hundred drawings. Some work of the Harper artists Abbey, Remington, Rogers, and Penfield was included, and the Remington work alone, if held long enough, would have cut an ample slice off the Morgan debt. But in order to stay liquid, a publisher must keep inventory moving into accounts receivable and cannot give hostages to the future except by happy accident.

An author whose books never presented an inventory problem did, however, have some difficulty in getting Harper's acceptance. His name was Zane Grey and, beginning with *Betty Zane,* he hopefully climbed the old iron stairs only, he said, to stumble down again with dim eyes and a rejected manuscript. That first book (published elsewhere), written while he was a young New York dentist, told the story of his Indian-fighting ancestors, after whom he and his home town of Zanesville, Ohio, had been named. The book that finally brought a contract in 1910 was called *The Heritage of the Desert,* and it was soon followed by *Riders of the Purple Sage* and *The Light of the Western Stars.* These three have been the best sellers of Zane Grey's seventy-eight novels of cactus and horses, of cowboys and bandits. When he died in 1939, he left stacks of manuscripts which were gradually readied for publication, and the last one, *Boulder Dam,* came out in 1963. Forty million copies of Zane Grey's books have been sold in original and reprint editions, and no one knows how many more in translations. Assuming five readers for every copy printed produces a figure that is as difficult to comprehend as the dollars in a federal budget. Another book of Western interest, Cody's *Adventures of Buffalo Bill,* published in 1904, sold more modestly, although disposals ran well over 100,000 and the book is still in print.

There are but scant records of which editors worked with these authors. Apparently J. Henry Harper gradually withdrew from editorial responsibilities although he continued as vice-president. Ripley Hitchcock, who had discovered and helped create *David Harum,* joined the literary department in 1906 and served there for twelve years. In 1907 William H. Briggs, a handsome young drama critic for Hearst's New York *Journal,* was hired as a reader and was soon doing editorial chores well enough to be asked to go with Hearst as editor of the *Bazar.* Since he was expecting to be married, he decided such a move would be too risky and stayed on. Thomas B. Wells, who was made assistant editor of the *Magazine* in 1906, often advised authors on book projects as well. Lee Foster Hartman, recently graduated from Wesleyan, joined the literary department in 1904 and was made associate editor of the *Magazine* four years later.

Robert Shackleton was for several years an editorial handyman. When Dr. Frederick Cook returned from the arctic and announced that he had discovered the North Pole, Harvey outbid all who clamored for his story by offering a rumored half million dollars for the rights, and gave Shackleton the job of ghosting the book. As he and Virginia Watson began copying details of the trip from old prescription blanks greasy with seal blubber, Major Leigh became suspicious, because Cook's account had no figures of latitude and longitude to show where he was at a given time. Shackleton's work was stopped and the contract remained unsigned until Cook could verify his account. This, of course, he could not do, and Harper's abandoned the Cook project shortly afterward when Admiral Peary returned with conclusive data to show that he, and not Cook, had reached the North Pole.

In a very real sense Harvey was general editor as well as president. Other authors he claimed as his own, in a letter he wrote to the Morgan Company in 1914, included many distinguished names—statesmen such as Senator Albert J. Beveridge, Woodrow Wilson, and William H. Taft; Beveridge wrote *The Russian Advance* and ex-President Taft's book was entitled *The Anti-Trust Act and the Supreme Court.* Wilson's work, of

course, was the five-volume *A History of the American People*. This he
might have brought to Harper's anyway, but it is captious to question
any credit for Wilson's writing that Harvey felt was due him. Harvey
also claimed writers such as Gertrude Atherton, May Sinclair, O. Henry,
and Booth Tarkington. Miss Atherton wrote four novels for Harper's,
none of them among her best, and a history of California. She did not
continue with the House and neither did the English novelist May Sinclair, who gave them but two novels. What O. Henry wrote for the
periodicals was brought together in two volumes. Harvey did admit
that Duneka had "cared for and guided" Tarkington, inducing him
against his will to write *The Turmoil*. While this story of a family's
greed in accumulating a fortune was being serialized in the *Magazine*,
Harvey declared it was the most powerful American novel published in
years. Until Duneka died Tarkington wavered between Harper's and
Doubleday, who took over his earlier books from S. S. McClure's short-
lived book-publishing venture. Thus, because of Duneka, Harper's had
the privilege of publishing seven books for Tarkington, from *The Conquest of Canaan* in 1905 to *Seventeen* in 1916. Tarkington never cared
much for the former book, a tale of contemporary Indiana, but booksellers disposed of 70,000 copies in six weeks. It was reissued in 1935
with an introduction by Tarkington.

Harvey's charming manners and cheerful ego and quick repartee did
inspire many authors to have confidence in him. But his forte was publicity, and both his Harper success and his ultimate downfall were
largely due to his spending large sums of money on luncheons and dinners and measuring his success in terms of the resulting linage in newspaper stories. He staged a seventieth-birthday dinner for Alden in 1906,
and two hundred guests came to Franklin Square, where the counting
room had been transformed into a garden of greenery and flowers and
potted plants. Nearly every important author in the United States and
Canada who could manage it was there, as well as a sprinkling of literati
from abroad, comprising, as one wit expressed it, "a living index to *Harper's Magazine*." The newspapers reported the speeches made, and
Harvey printed a supplement to the *Weekly* picturing the fashionably
dressed guests at their round tables. Everyone was identified except

Harvey, who may have assumed that naming himself was unnecessary, since his face was well known and because his horn-rimmed glasses, then a novelty, were always used by cartoonists as a convenient identification tag.

To honor Mark Twain on his seventieth birthday, Harvey in 1905 sent invitations to all the distinguished people he could think of for a banquet at Delmonico's. About two hundred showed up. This was the second birthday dinner Harvey had given for his most famous author. At the first one, a stag affair in 1902, Harvey, who presided, restrained Mark Twain from responding to those who proposed his health or read poems in his honor; after each tribute, as Mark Twain attempted to rise, Harvey pushed him gently back into his chair and spoke briefly as the great man's ambassador. Finally, after Henry van Dyke's poem, Harvey said, "And this, Mr. Clemens and Gentlemen, is the toast to the health of the guest of the evening," and removed his hand from the shoulder of Mark Twain, who by then was so charged with emotion and excitement that he gave one of the most eloquent speeches of his lifetime. Aware that such a tour de force could not be repeated at the seventieth-birthday dinner, Harvey presented Mark Twain immediately after Howells had read a double sonnet on the American joke, a creation of Mark Twain's, and everyone arose to cheer the world-famous author, knowing that it was one of the great occasions of his life as well as their own.

When Harvey figured up how much the banquet had cost Harper's, he must have decided that the return in publicity and good will was worth the expense. At any rate, he continued to give birthday parties and, in 1912, honored Howells on his seventy-fifth, this time at Sherry's. Again Harvey was master of ceremonies and welcomed the four hundred assembled guests, including another Ohio boy who, like Howells, had made good—President William Howard Taft. At least two parties were given for visiting English authors, Hall Caine and Arnold Bennett. The dinner for Bennett, in 1911, was also covered in a supplement to the *Weekly*. This time Harvey not only named his picture but put himself in the lead sentence of the full-page story. "A dinner in honor of Arnold Bennett was given by Mr. and Mrs. George Harvey at the St. Regis Hotel on the evening of November 27th. More than one hundred men

The dinner for Howells at Sherry's. At the speaker's table, President William Howard Taft sits at Harvey's left and the guest of honor at his right.

To the President's left are Margaret Deland and Basil King. Reprinted from
Harper's Weekly, *March 9, 1912.*

and women prominent in literature and otherwise joined in farewell to the eminent author."

Among the "otherwise" were Mrs. Nicholas Longworth, who sat at the left of the benign and bespectacled host, and Miss Anne Morgan and Mr. and Mrs. Thomas W. Lamont, at tables near the guest of honor. Harvey's faculty for protocol is indicated in other seating arrangements, including those of prominent politicians, and his placing of colleagues—in the order of Alden, Sutphen, Duneka, Leigh, Wells, Martin, Jordan, Chandler, Latour, Hartman, Hoyns, Phayre, Cullen, Joe Harper, and Briggs, the last five named being seated at the table farthest back.

One reason for Harvey's taking over the editorship of *Harper's Weekly* was an ambition to wield political influence. Curtis and Nast had helped to make Presidents—why shouldn't he? He launched the first of his two successful efforts to get men of his choice in the White House by giving a dinner in February, 1906, at the Lotos Club to honor Woodrow Wilson, president of Princeton. There he proposed Wilson as the next Democratic candidate for the Presidency of the United States. (What Harvey said was included in *The Power of Tolerance*, a book of his speeches issued in 1911.) But Harvey knew that Trenton, rather than Princeton, New Jersey, was the proper station from which to take off for Washington, and set about getting the Democratic politicians of his state to make Wilson the governor, which they did in 1910. With the Presidential campaign of 1912 looming ahead, Harvey began boosting Wilson editorially in the *Weekly* and running Wilson's name at the masthead. A few months before the Democratic Convention in Baltimore, Harvey asked Wilson whether he thought the *Weekly*'s endorsement was hurting his chances in the Middle West. Wilson gave a direct and honest answer, yes, for he knew that the public linked Harvey's name with Wall Street and Harper's name with Morgan. Whereupon Harvey said he would put on the soft pedal. The incident got into the newspapers, and the following issue of the *Weekly* appeared without Wilson's name in its featured position. Wilson tried desperately to make amends to Harvey and would have named him Ambassador to France had Harvey not blasted a tentative approach by permitting a *New York Times* reporter to interview him and to publish a highly critical appraisal of the new President. Later Harvey switched to the Republican Party and quickly found his place in its high councils. It was in his "smoke-filled room" at the Blackstone Hotel in Chicago in 1920 that the strategy was developed that got Warren G. Harding nominated for the Presidency. Harding repaid Harvey by making him Ambassador to Great Britain. Another President, Calvin Coolidge, paid Harvey posthumous tribute by writing an introduction to his biography.

Thomas W. Lamont, the Morgan partner responsible for the Harper account, became increasingly displeased with Harvey's penchant for publicity and expensive dinners and with the *Weekly*'s becoming less Harper's and more Harvey's. Furthermore the *Weekly* was losing money, partly because of the competition of the Sunday newspapers. In 1913 Lamont urged Harvey to sell it. The only buyer Harvey could find was the McClure Company, and Norman Hapgood became the *Weekly*'s editor. Harvey took perverse pleasure in saying later that "it was purchased by a man by whom, for the first time in nearly one hundred years, the name of Harper has been dragged in the mire. The almost complete loss of prestige, circulation and revenue which has ensued, however, constitutes a fairly adequate penalty." In 1916 *Harper's Weekly* was acquired by the *Independent,* and six years later the corporation that owned the *Independent* sold the name back to Harper & Brothers.

Colonel Harvey did not display as much expertise in finances as he did in publicity; for the first several years, by his own admission, the financial needs of the company were attended to by Laffan, who represented Morgan, and Alexander E. Orr, who represented creditor banks. Both men were on the Board of Directors and both had recommended in 1900 that the company authorize the issue of income bonds amounting to $2,000,000, some of which were delivered to creditors, the bonds to pay 1 per cent for two years, 2 per cent for three years, and 5 per cent thereafter. By 1905 these bonds were troublesome, since not even 1 per cent had been paid. Whereupon the Board of Directors met that September to accomplish a new financing of the company, the net result of which was to replace these bonds with $1,000,000 in noncumulative 6 per cent bonds, thus paying fifty cents on the dollar. At the same time the company was authorized to replace the old 6 per cent mortgage bonds, a $2,000,000 issue, with a like amount of 5 per cent mortgage bonds, of which bonds totaling $1,500,000 were to be sold, or used in exchange, to secure the firm's indebtedness and cancel the outstanding bonds and mortgage.

In nontechnical language this action revealed that the firm's total indebtedness now approximated $2,500,000. Messrs. Laffan, Orr, et al. apparently believed that out of the yearly business income it would not be difficult to pay interest on bonds and notes totaling $131,565. All went well until the panic of 1907, when, according to Harvey, he had to handle the fiscal problems alone. To secure bank loans, he pledged his own securities, which were liquidated at panic prices. Harvey estimated that the common stocks he had lost in 1907-1908 were worth $1,500,000 in 1914.

In 1909 Harvey endeavored to sell some or all of the 2,000 mortgage bonds which had been authorized in September, 1905, and issued the following February in denominations of $1,000. For each bond, Harvey promised the purchaser a twenty-five-year subscription to each of the four periodicals and twenty-four free books (average retail price, $1.75) each year for twenty-five years, or $1,075 in magazines and books along with each bond. He explained that, of course, this merchandise cost much less to produce and would offset, along with other savings, the usual cost of marketing securities through agents and commission men. The only cost to the House was printing and distributing the brochure.

It is not known how many bonds were sold or what was said to purchasers when three out of four of the periodicals ceased publication. Of special historic interest are figures given in the brochure summarizing the business operation for the eight years ending September 30, 1908:

Gross income	$16,911,374.34
Cost of goods sold, operating expenses and taxes	14,869,336.85
Trading profit	$ 2,042,037.49
Charged to depreciation	891,669.15
Net income	$ 1,150,368.34

What Harvey did not admit was that most, if not all, of the net income had gone for interest payments. It seems doubtful whether any of the indebtedness had been liquidated. In fact, the Morgan Company made further loans to Harper's, and the elder Mr. Morgan made several personal loans to Colonel Harvey amounting to $200,000. Thus, by 1914, the Morgan Company had become increasingly concerned about Harvey's administration, one of the partners saying that he was "dubious respecting the value of Colonel Harvey to Harper & Brothers." Harvey was requested to submit a written account of his stewardship. Harvey's reply was a thirty-two-page letter dated November 27th. He argued that he had increased the tangible assets to a level with the liabilities at the time he took control and that he had increased the value of "Copyrights and Goodwill" approximately $1,000,000. (This asset is now carried on Harper's books at $1, in accordance with current conservative accounting practice.) He also asserted that during the preceding four years assets had increased slightly and liabilities had decreased $250,000. He saw no possibility of paying off the loan other than by selling securities or liquidating the company. Most of his letter was an apologia for what he had done to keep the House going and to obtain and hold outstanding authors, the net profit on whose works he believed nearly equaled the interest paid during fourteen years. He admitted that he had done things in a semipublic way which did not relate to the business; however, he had virtually kept open house for authors, and what he had spent on entertainment "directly and wholly" in the interest of the business was more than he had received. With respect to the future he agreed to do anything that was best for Harper's, a name that had grown to be as precious to him as the name of Morgan could possibly be to any member of the Morgan firm.

What Harvey had to do was plain enough, and on May 17, 1915, the minutes of the Board of Directors recorded his resignation as president and director. Two months earlier J. Henry Harper, who never wavered in his loyalty and devotion to Harvey, had resigned from the Board. One of Harvey's last acts as president was to write Alden in appreciation of their years together. Alden replied that the brightest part of his Harper association had been during the Harvey presidency. Harvey walked out of Franklin Square with the eternal cigar cocked at a jaunty angle between his close-pursed lips. With the witty, sardonic, autocratic, inscrutable Colonel, something else left that made Harper's and the little world of book publishing less exciting and newsworthy. Few publishers have had the Harvey ability for doing most things exceedingly well— except the sticky and vexatious job of paying off a debt.

20

PUBLISHING BETWEEN TWO WORLD WARS (1916-44)

Even before Harvey left Harper's, there was speculation at Franklin Square about whom the Morgan Company would name as his successor. In December, 1914, two men were elected to the Board of Directors. C. T. Brainard replaced Major Leigh and was designated treasurer. Brainard had managed a subscription book business in Boston and was president of the McClure newspaper syndicate when he assumed his new duties. Willard D. Straight was chosen to replace Laffan. But since Laffan had been dead for five years and since the wealthy Straight and his wife had just founded the *New Republic,* Straight's election carried overtones that were too obvious to be overlooked. Duneka was also a possible choice and he was elected vice-president shortly after Harvey resigned.

By the summer of 1915, however, it was clear that the new treasurer was boss of the establishment, and in September Straight resigned on the pretext that he wanted to pursue legal studies at Columbia. Brainard had obviously been told to economize, and economize he did. He gave an object lesson by eating his lunch from a tin dinner pail as he sat in shirt sleeves where he could be seen, just inside the iron railing on the main floor. "There is no person here who can't be replaced by a ten-dollar-a-week clerk," he would say. He was a tall, somewhat heavy-set man and he suffered from chronic sinusitis. His uncouth manners and bluntness were offensive to Duneka, who was the epitome of graciousness, and to Wells, always a man of good taste. One of C. T. Brainard's early directives was that no book could be given away without his initials on the order. Such a ticket is still called a "C.T.B.," although the initials also stand for "charge to book."

The most tragic result of this financial retrenchment was the loss of important authors. Brainard's heavy hand not only held back favorable terms on new book contracts but also kept advertising and promotion expenditures to a minimum unless he could see assured results in sales. One of the best authors lost to Harper's—in terms of potential—was Sinclair Lewis. His second novel, *The Trail of the Hawk,* was issued about the same time as *The Turmoil,* and Lewis pleaded with Miss Jordan, his editor, to run a large ad which he wrote comparing himself with Tarkington. It was turned down, and Lewis was urged to write short stories for the big-circulation magazines and get his name established. This he did while he was writing another novel, *The Job,* which he subtitled *An American Novel.* But only a few thousand Americans bought the novel, and Lewis went for solace to his friend Alfred Harcourt, editor of trade books for Henry Holt & Co. Harcourt encouraged Lewis to come with Holt's as soon as his Harper options were satisfied, and when Harcourt and Brace left Holt in 1919 to start up their own business, they issued Lewis's *Free Air* as one of their first titles; *Main Street* came out the following year, and Sinclair Lewis achieved his ambition of becoming a famous American novelist. Harper's then sold the plates of the four Lewis novels to Harcourt at cost, $1,775. James Branch Cabell went to McBride with his three books, which he said Harper's had "misguidedly published," and Theodore Dreiser went to Boni & Liveright, taking *Sister Carrie* along with him. And there were others—all preceded by Joseph Conrad, the Harper author who, back in 1913, had been "discovered" by young Alfred Knopf, then working for Doubleday.

Furthermore the Harper editorial staff was far below par. Hitchcock was followed by a man named Marsh, of whom little is known, and Wells, aided by Hartman, was carrying the editorial load of *Harper's Magazine* with little available time to counsel on books. Briggs' literary stable contained such popular writers as Basil King, Zane Grey, Clarence Budington Kelland, and Homer Croy. Finally, Duneka, who of all the Harper staff had most to give authors in friendship and loyalty, died in 1919 after a long illness and forced retirement. Duneka had lost heart for the business after the departure of Harvey, whom he greatly admired (he named his only son Harvey), and after Brainard took over. And Duneka made miscalculations, as all editors do. He was Hamlin Garland's editor, after luring him from Macmillan, and saw a dozen Garland novels through the presses (later collected in a Border Edition), but he saw little hope for *A Son of the Middle Border,* and declined this, Garland's best book, which Macmillan promptly accepted. Curiously, Duneka discounted the book's autobiographical quality, which was what readers liked.

While Brainard evidenced little editorial ambition, he was a book merchandiser par excellence. His newspaper and syndicate experience (while with Harper's he was president of the Washington *Herald* and president of both the McClure and Wheeler syndicates) had given him considerable knowledge of popular authors and their works, and the handiest Harper tool he had to work with was the Franklin Square subscription books. Outstanding sets of subscription books included the ten-volume *Encyclopaedia of United States History;* the twelve-volume *Biblical Cyclopaedia,* by McClintock and Strong; the four-volume *Comedies of William Shakespeare,* illustrated by Abbey; the large, handsome illustrated editions of Thackeray and Dickens. Best of all was the twenty-five-dollar twenty-five-volume Hillcrest Edition of Mark Twain. In 1919 Brainard took a full-color page in the *Saturday Evening Post* listing the Mark Twain titles; the page pictured Huck Finn and was headed "He Walked with Kings." With this ad as a door opener, subscription agents swarmed all over the country writing up orders that within a year earned approximately $100,000 for the Mark Twain estate, more royalties than had been paid in any previous year.

The most exciting publishing enterprise of the Brainard period was a series called Bubble Books, the brain child of a Harper bookkeeper named Ralph Mayhew, who wrote them, with the help of Burges Johnson. The series grew to eighteen books, each containing nursery stories in rhyme, with illustrations by Rhoda Chase, and Columbia phonograph records containing the stories in song. Brainard employed a man from the Ingersoll Watch Company to merchandise the Bubble Books, and offices were set up in the field with high-salaried men to sell sets by the gross. In St. Louis, a hardware company employing three hundred salesmen bought fourteen hundred gross, typical of this nonbook enterprise. In Chicago, Marshall Field's piled them up in their book, toy, and phonograph departments. Millions of Bubble Books were sold, but like all bonanzas they were overpromoted, and suddenly Harper's had a quarter of a million copies that nobody wanted. To dispose of them required all the ingenuity that J. Ray Peck, the Harper sales manager, and his leading salesman, Adam Burger, possessed.

The first Bubble Book appeared in 1917, which was a memorable year because it marked the entry of the United States into the war and the firm's centennial. War books began showing up on publishers' lists by 1916, but that year only one Harper book reflected the public's concern, and none of the best-selling war books of 1917, like *Over the Top,* came out of Franklin Square, although a small volume of President Wilson's four messages to Congress, entitled *Why We Are at War,* was issued. In 1918, the year another house brought out Edward Streeter's *Dere Mable,* Harper's had a best seller in *Outwitting the Hun,* by Lieutenant Pat O'Brien. That year Zane Grey's *The U.P. Trail* was the book of fiction most in demand, and reports from the front named Zane Grey the most widely read author. Shortly after America's entry into the war, five hundred Harper employees bought Liberty Loan bonds amounting to $84,100, and twenty-eight of the staff enlisted in the armed forces. As did all publishers, Harper's found it difficult to buy printing supplies, and faced increased costs of labor and a trebling of the price of paper, all of which forced retail prices up, never to come down again.

The impact of the war naturally affected the Harper Centennial Year. The firm recognized its hundredth birthday by issuing *Seneca's Morals* with facsimiles of the original edition printed on left-hand pages and the same text set in a larger, modern type face printed on facing pages. The firm's major effort went into a mailing of gold-embossed cards announcing the Centennial Year to two hundred and fifty Ameri-

20 November, 1917

My dear Sirs:

May I not convey to you my warm
congratulations on your centennial anniversary
and an expression of my sincere hope that for
another hundred years the honorable traditions
of the house may be maintained, to the benefit
alike of those who read and of those who write?

Cordially and sincerely yours,

Woodrow Wilson

Messrs. Harper & Brothers,
Franklin Square,
New York City.

The President's letter of congratulations on the Harper centennial. Mr. Wilson lived to see his name on the title page of sixteen Harper works.

can and foreign publishers and to nearly three thousand authors. (Similar greetings had already been mailed to the American book trade.) A 118-page book, *The Harper Centennial 1817-1917*, was issued, containing a selection made from the letters of those who responded. Woodrow Wilson's letter led all the rest, and the book's foreword noted that the hundred years that began with Seneca closed with the President of the United States through the issue of a new Documentary Edition of *A History of the American People.*

During the years immediately following the war, only a few Harper books made the best-seller lists. *Now It Can Be Told,* by Sir Philip Gibbs, had first place in nonfiction in 1921, and *The Mind in the Making,* by James Harvey Robinson, ranked high both in 1922 and in 1923, as did *Mark Twain's Autobiography* in 1924. Other sturdy works of general interest included a four-volume *History of Art,* by Elie Faure, and *Life on a Medieval Barony,* by William Stearns Davis. This work, which continues to sell widely, was brought to Harper's by Fred Crofts, who was hired from the Century Company in 1919 with a five-year contract to establish a college textbook department. The book had both a trade and a college market as did several others, including a series called the Americanization Studies, with books by Robert E. Park, Sophonisba P. Breckenridge, and Bernard M. Baruch. The big bread-and-butter book—still in demand—was *Allen's Synonyms and Antonyms,* by F. Sturges Allen, editor of Webster's New International Dictionary. Three autobiographies found wide readership—Champ Clark's *My Quarter Century of American Politics, Raymond Robins' Own Story* (his account of life in Russia as an unofficial American representative to the Bolshevists), and *Ludendorff's Own Story.* Labor's leading spokesman, Samuel Gompers, wrote *Labor in Europe and America,* and Wall Street's Dwight W. Morrow, a Morgan partner, wrote *The Society of Free States.* Adding a bit of gaiety to the somber list were two books by the cowboy philosopher Will Rogers and one by Charlie Chaplin telling of his first trip back to his birthplace in England and of the famous Europeans he met. And to add excitement a 1919 novel entitled *Madeleine* upset Mr. John Sumner, who convinced a New York judge that the book was obscene. Harper's was fined a thousand dollars. The case was appealed, with Briggs producing six readers' reports to justify the book's publication; the appellate court reversed the decision and remitted the fine.

A thousand dollars was small potatoes compared with what was lost in *Harper's Wonder Book of the World War.* Harper's had done well with big books following the Civil War and the Spanish-American War, so this concept of a multivolume set of books was an obvious one, but by 1921 most readers had tired of reading about the war and Harper's wrote off $100,000 worth of sheet stock. That year the net profit was $5,536.15. Brainard took the rap for the book's abysmal failure. By that time he was president of the House and ready to spend big money on what he thought were big, meaty books.

When Brainard moved up, Wells and Hoyns were made vice-presidents. These two men were increasingly annoyed by Brainard's management of the business and began to discuss means of getting him out. The obvious method was to clear the firm of the Morgan indebtedness, which amounted to $1,230,000, and Brainard had done little to reduce it. Wells went to Thomas W. Lamont, the Morgan partner who handled the Harper account, and presented a plan to liquidate the debt. Wells proposed that the firm dispose of its subscription book business and sell its manufacturing equipment, turning over the proceeds to the Morgan Company. In addition he agreed to pay over all that Harper's should receive from the sale of the motion picture rights to *Ben-Hur* and suggested that the firm vacate the Franklin Square property and deed the land and buildings to Morgan as a further credit against the debt. In May, 1921, Wells set forth these proposals in a letter that Mr. Morgan approved.

By November, 1922, Wells was able to report to Lamont that more than $390,000 had been paid to Morgan: over $100,000 from P. F. Collier & Son Company, who took over the subscription book business; over $90,000 out of the $135,000 being paid for machinery by the International Textbook Company, of Scranton, Pennsylvania; and $200,000 from the motion picture rights to *Ben-Hur*. With nearly one-third of the indebtedness thus paid off, Wells was able to obtain the Morgan Company's agreement to give him until June 1, 1923, to reorganize the company and fund whatever balance was then due Morgan.

Hoyns managed the sale of the subscription book business (publicizing it as a transfer of agency) and negotiated the sale of machinery to the International Textbook Company, as well as the prompt erection of a manufacturing plant by the Scranton firm at Camden, New

In 1930 an annex was erected adjacent to the 49 East Thirty-third Street building.

Jersey. This plant began book production in June, 1922. That same year a contract was made with the owners of the Vanderbilt Hotel whereby they would erect a six-story building on land they owned at 49 East Thirty-third Street and rent it to Harper's on a twenty-six-year lease. (It soon proved to be too small, and its twin, called an annex, went up in 1930.) The disposition of the Franklin Square property was a more difficult matter, since the buildings were designed for a type of business that had long since moved uptown. The Morgan Company finally agreed to take the buildings and land at approximately $400,000, and the deed to the property was delivered to them on September 21, 1923.

Prior to that date, Mr. Morgan and Mr. Lamont had agreed to two issues of Harper preferred stock, the first to procure working capital and the second to cover the balance of the Morgan indebtedness. The first preferred called for 5,000 shares of 8 per cent cumulative stock with voting rights. The second preferred stock, all of which was turned over to Morgan, amounted to approximately $400,000; it was a 6 per cent noncumulative, nonvoting stock. Both issues carried a par value of $100 per share and were authorized by the Harper Board on June 1, 1923. There was also the important item of common stock to be dealt with, the 20,000 shares of $100 par value on which dividends had never been paid. By Board action a week later this stock was replaced by an authorized issue of 25,000 shares without par value.

The 8 per cent preferred was attractive as an investment not only because of the dividend rate but also because of voting rights. To this two-layer cake a thick coat of icing was added by the offer of one share of common stock free for each preferred that was purchased. J. P. Morgan insisted that at least $300,000 thus be raised for working capital before he would accept the second issue, although he agreed that promises by solvent people to subscribe would suffice. To help the cause along, Morgan promised Wells that he would take five hundred shares, if necessary, to make up the amount. When his stipulation had been satisfied, the second issue of preferred stock was handed to the Morgan Company in payment for the balance due on the old loans, and the 1900 issue of mortgage bonds, held as collateral, was destroyed.

While these financial arrangements were maturing, Lamont was aware

THE HOUSE OF HARPER

NEW YORK
One Door West of
Mr. Vanderbilt's Inn
Publishers of BOOKS and of
HARPER'S MAGAZINE
—
Established 1817

A book plate used after the move to Thirty-third Street.

that Wells and Hoyns were seeking to displace Brainard. In July Lamont wrote a long memorandum to Morgan summarizing what had happened since Lamont had requested Harvey's resignation. He praised Brainard for what he had done to put the business back on its feet, including making a personal loan of $50,000 to the firm when it was in a tight place. He sympathized with the feeling Morgan had expressed that Brainard was not the man to handle his money, but he did not share Morgan's confidence in Wells and said bluntly that Wells was not the man to manage the business.

To this comment Wells would have said a hearty "Amen," for his main concerns were editorial. In fact, he had been endeavoring to get his Yale classmate Harry Fisher to "come in and roll your sleeves up." Fisher was chairman of the Board of Directors of the McCall publications and had previously served as general manager of the McClure publications and as vice-president of the Crowell Publishing Company. Fisher was reluctant to do more than serve on the Harper Board, to which he was elected that April, and to act for a while as temporary chairman. He also purchased 2,000 shares of the first preferred stock, an act of faith which made it possible for Harper to meet Morgan's insistence that $300,000 of working capital be assured. It was also an act of prudence, since all the preferred stock was retired out of earnings by 1934 and Fisher owned 8 per cent of the common stock as well. Unwilling to participate in the firm's management on a day-to-day basis, he introduced Wells to Douglas Parmentier, a man he thought would be willing to join the firm as president. Parmentier was a young man of means associated with the industrial department of the New York Trust Company, and he took the Harper's presidency in 1924, following Brainard's resignation in May. For the first year of his separation Brainard was paid a third of his annual salary and expense account ($32,000) and for the following five years, the life of the voting trust set up for the 8 per cent preferred, he was paid $5,000 a year.

Dropping Brainard brought no regrets, but the move from Franklin Square the year before had brought much sadness. Some walked down the old iron stairs for the last time with tears in their eyes, and much was said and written about the famous men of letters who had come and gone there since 1855. But Hoyns indulged in no such nostalgia. The managerial concerns of the present and the bright prospects of the future were more exciting than memories of his forty years in and around the old buildings. He had found the new location on Thirty-third

Street, worked with the architects on plans, and managed details of the move. He had been so habituated to open floors, a tradition stemming from the time of the Harper brothers, that but few private offices were built. In later years he needed to take just a few steps from his office on the fifth floor to see his department heads at work at their desks, and he would only grudgingly permit partitions to be erected to give his subordinates the privacy they considered essential. The sixth floor was devoted to the trade-book editorial offices and those of the *Magazine.* The walls of the sixth-floor foyer, onto which the elevators opened, were faced with the mahogany paneling brought up from Franklin Square. The pride of the sixth floor was the directors' room. This was described in a full-page advertisement in the *New York Times* for July 18, 1923: "A Room that has welcomed the Great . . . has been moved bit by bit with every care—the walls, the doors, the old pictures of Abbey, Reinhart, and Church, the famous bookcases—all have been brought piece by piece to the new building. For it is the room richest with history in all the American business world." The advertisement reminded readers that their great-grandfathers were thrilled with the novels of Sir Walter Scott, their grandfathers rejoiced in Dickens and Thackeray, their fathers welcomed Mark Twain, they themselves owned Thomas Hardy, and their children played with Bubble Books, all published by Harper's. But a House that had been "closely bound up with the history of the American people" was now primarily concerned with the nation's future. "On with the new!" the advertisement read. "The old iron stairway is gone—the new door at 49 East 33rd Street stands wide open, leading to the elevators that rise to new ideas and new thoughts, daring youth and the future."

One such daring youth joined Harper's the following year. His name was Cass Canfield. After being graduated from Harvard and spending a year in graduate study at Oxford, he and a friend decided to follow Marco Polo's trek on foot from Burma across China. On his return he worked for a while for the New York *Evening Post,* helped to establish the magazine *Foreign Affairs,* and in 1924 was introduced by a friend to Wells. At that time Wells and Hoyns were concerned about a replacement for Frederick W. Slater, who, after McIlvaine's death in 1913, had managed the London office and was past retirement age.

Canfield's literary bent and his year in England made him the obvious choice, and after a few months' orientation on Thirty-third Street he was sent abroad.

Slater, who was retired on half salary, might well have been put out to pasture earlier, for he had done little to advance the firm's contacts with authors. In 1923 he declined a promising Alsatian author who, years earlier, had written an article on "Civilization and Ethics" for a German magazine which McIlvaine read. When McIlvaine wrote urging that the article be extended to book-length treatment, the author had replied that he planned to do so and would be pleased to submit the manuscript to Harper's. The war intervened and it was not until he had given his material as lectures at the University of Uppsala and then reworked it that the Alsatian author, Albert Schweitzer, was ready to publish. He wrote to Harper's, London, to say that he could now fulfill his promise, and Slater replied that they were not interested in seeing the manuscript. The work was issued in London by Messrs. A. & C. Black, to whom Schweitzer also entrusted the English-language rights of his later books.

One of Canfield's early calls in London was made on Thomas Hardy, then an old, shy, and retiring man. Learning that George Bernard Shaw was dissatisfied with Brentano's as his American publishers, Canfield went to see him. Shaw lectured him on the mistake that Harper's was making in not having a bookstore in their new building, and Canfield argued that publishing and retail selling were distinctive and separate functions. He was soon shown the door, and later a more seasoned competitor—Howard Lewis, of Dodd, Mead & Co.—signed Shaw up for a long-term contract. After hearing several people say that Richard Hughes was an extremely talented writer, Canfield looked him up. Soon his classic story of children, *A High Wind in Jamaica* (*The Innocent Voyage*), was on the Harper list. Other authors Canfield sought out, all of whom were soon publishing books from Thirty-third Street, included Sheila Kaye-Smith, E. M. Delafield, Susan Ertz, Philip Guedalla, Julian Green, J. B. S. Haldane, J. B. Priestley, H. M. Tomlinson, Harold Laski, and Julian Huxley. Of these Huxley was to become a special friend during the ensuing years.

In 1926 Canfield and his wife were giving a dinner party for the

Prince of Wales, later Edward VIII, with thirty or forty people invited. The day of the party, Harper's Paris agent, Mrs. W. A. Bradley, telephoned that Clemenceau had just finished a book on the struggle between Sparta and Athens to illustrate certain aspects of the First World War. "Business first," Canfield decided, and, leaving his wife to manage the dinner party, he took one of the uncertain planes then flying to Paris and went to Clemenceau's residence. When Clemenceau discovered that his American visitor would be glad to read the manuscript at once, he ushered Canfield to his library and left him to anything but an absorbing task. Canfield found the French original dull reading and finally told the formidable French leader that he was uncertain about its success in the United States. It did get published in the United States, but Canfield, who was then thirty years old, was proved right about the book's appeal to American readers.

The London assignment had never been considered a permanent one for Canfield, and in 1927 a young man named Hamish Hamilton was placed in charge of the London office, which was moved from Albemarle Street to Great Russell Street near the British Museum. To take the job, Hamilton left the publisher Jonathan Cape, who generously let this able young man go, perhaps because Mr. Cape owed his start in the book business to McIlvaine. In 1931 Hamilton began publishing books under his own name, and Harper's made it financially possible for him to start the firm. His firm continued for several years to act for Harper's in business transactions with other British publishers.

When Canfield returned to Thirty-third Street, he was already a director of the firm and was named assistant editor in the literary department, working alongside Eugene F. Saxton, who in 1925 had been made book editor. With prior experience at Doubleday, Saxton had for eight years been head of George H. Doran's editorial department before joining Harper's. Wells and Hoyns had sought the best man available because they were determined that the House should recover its former leadership in trade-book publishing. Few men had a stronger personal following among authors in both England and America than Saxton had. Even so, he was sensitive about trading on friendships, such as Conrad's and Frank Swinnerton's and William Rose Benét's. What he did bring in addition to experience was editorial expertness. He had sound instinct for a publishable book and keen appreciation of good writing. He was equally concerned about details of format and jacket that make a book readable and attractive. This concern was shared by Hoyns, but Saxton often had to battle with Hoyns, whose spirit of frugality, nurtured by the firm's lean years, would inspire him to question any manufacturing costs that might keep a book from showing a profit. While Saxton had a good knowledge of the public's taste in reading matter, he depended finally on his own reaction to a manuscript. Except for manuscripts of established authors, his reading was largely restricted to those that had survived the sifting process of first or second readers. After reading such a likely manuscript he would often leave it on his desk for a week or two. Then he would pick it up again, and if he found that he did not remember it well or if it no longer made an impression, he knew he had better reject it.

Saxton's editorial ideals were extremely high and he was always concerned that the Harper imprint stand for books of the highest quality. Shortly after I came to Harper's, a well-known clergyman stopped by to see how his recent book was selling. After noting that it was doing about as well as his earlier ones, he asked what I thought of his attempting a novel; he was sure he had something important to say to people who would never consider browsing in a religious bookstore. I made the obvious reply that there were plenty of precedents of preachers who had turned into successful novelists, and some months later he forwarded a manuscript entitled "Thirsty Fish" which was soon read and returned with a letter suggesting considerable revision. The second draft was sent to Saxton, who returned it to me with two readers' reports and his comment that while in his opinion it was second-rate fiction and not deserving of the Harper imprint, he would not want to stand in my way if I wished to undertake it. I rejected it, as did another New York house. Then the clergyman tried a small Chicago publisher, whose editor took great pains to get further revisions and changed the title to *Magnificent Obsession*. Lloyd Douglas, the author, soon gave up preaching to write novels that found an audience far beyond his fondest hopes in 1929.

THE
NEW YORKER
NO. 25 WEST 45TH STREET

EDITORIAL OFFICES
BRYANT 9-8200

Thursday this

Dear Mr. Saxton:
        The Whole dam
works will be in your hands
by Thursday next. Its been
harder 'n I thought. I
think it is a swell book,
but then I should.
                Thurber

Official
Seal

Letter from James Thurber to his editor promising delivery of the
manuscript of My Life and Hard Times, *published in 1933.*

However, Saxton was not unwilling to work with the author of a promising manuscript to make a book more publishable. This he often did, fully aware that the end result might satisify neither him nor the author. But the function of an editor, as he saw it, was to help young authors to achieve their potential. Because his standards were known to be high and the imprint respected, authors often sought him out. In 1928 two rather sad-looking young men came to see him and Canfield. One had a manuscript and the other a portfolio of drawings. The artist spread his drawings over the floor of Saxton's office and observed that nobody liked them very much; did Messrs. Saxton and Canfield think they were funny? They replied that they were interesting—and yes, quite funny. The drawings and the manuscript were the work of two quite unknown authors named James Thurber and E. B. White. Their book, *Is Sex Necessary?*, made an immediate hit and became a best seller. Thurber's droll drawings and White's felicitous writing produced further books for each of them, and antiquarian booksellers now feature first editions as collectors' items.

One of Saxton's editorial qualities was his ability to question non-fiction authors about the implications of their material, questions that often inspired them to go back to their sources, with results that surprised both author and editor. He also had an aptitude for titles. The Thurber-White title had at first been "After Sex, What?" When O. E. Rölvaag's first, unsolicited novel came in, it carried a cumbersome title. Everyone who read the manuscript thought it was a superb narrative of the struggle of pioneer Norwegian settlers in the Dakotas. (It was a combination of two novels that Rölvaag, of St. Olaf College, Northfield, Minnesota, had published in Norwegian and then translated into English with the help of the journalist Lincoln Colcord.) Saxton's eye detected just the right title, *Giants in the Earth,* from a Biblical quotation typed in the front matter, "In those days there were giants in the earth." Once he was asked to define a good title, and his laconic reply was "A good title is on a book that sells."

Saxton was at his best as an editor of fiction. Some considered him the outstanding fiction editor of his generation, although several of his contemporaries received more publicity. Publicity for himself he shunned. In March, 1932, he received a letter from Howard Vincent O'Brien, of the Chicago *Daily News,* saying that as he looked back over the books of the preceding year he was struck by the fact that the Harper imprint was on most of the good ones. He said he had no literary axe to grind but he could only conclude that the House of Harper had an editor blessed with a combination of genius and clairvoyance. Saxton replied, "Even the bronze hand of the St. Gaudens torchbearer on our bas-relief in the reception room would be apt to tremble and the light flicker in the warm draft of your praise. . . . Modesty alone would not deter me from appropriating the glory, but the plain truth is that the accomplishments in Harper's are to be set to the credit of at least a half dozen." One of the books that O'Brien admired (the credit for which Saxton shared with Canfield) was J. B. Priestley's *Angel Pavement.*

Saxton traveled little except to make annual scouting trips to London. Tomlinson's novel *All Our Yesterdays* was published early in 1930 with enthusiastic reviews, and autographing parties for him crowded bookshops. Saxton accompanied Tomlinson to Chicago, where he thoroughly enjoyed someone's quip that he was Tomlinson's godfather. For years a bust of Tomlinson graced Saxton's office.

The Harper Prize Novel Contest was launched before Saxton came to Harper's, but he supported it as enthusiastically as though it were his own idea. Some of the best of the novels in this biennial contest came during his period—such unforgettable books as Anne Parrish's *The Perennial Bachelor,* Glenway Wescott's *The Grandmothers,* Julian Green's *The Dark Journey,* H. L. Davis's *Honey in the Horn,* and Martin Flavin's *Journey in the Dark.* The last two were also awarded Pulitzer Prizes, as was the very first one, Margaret Wilson's *The Able McLaughlins,* published in 1923.

The characteristics of Saxton that most endeared him to authors and to his colleagues were his accessibility and his hatred of protocol and pretentiousness, qualities that so often interfere with free relationships among literary people or office personnel. Writers such as Robert Benchley and Gerald Johnson and Bernard DeVoto and Roark Bradford would drop into his office just for the pleasure of gossiping with him, and he would never deny them although such a visit might make him an hour late for another appointment. He was never hurried, never harassed, always calm, good-natured, friendly. Thus department editors, over whom he never assumed surveillance, often sought his advice when faced with a perplexing author or book problem. He spoke slowly and deliberately with an occasional pause as he lighted a cigar or turned to gaze out his window; what he said was succinctly phrased and often illuminated by a quiet humor. His work with and for Richard Wright, for example, helped to make *Native Son,* the story of a Negro murderer, the moving and popular book that it was. And if an author, however popular, failed to come up to his standards of literary excellence and good taste, Saxton would reject the book. He refused to publish the Dos Passos novel *Nineteen Nineteen* unless biased references to J. P. Morgan were removed. Neither could he be argued into making what seemed to him to be unreasonable demands for royalty terms or promotion expenditures even though it meant the loss of a talented writer.

Authors come and go in every publishing office when they fail to see eye-to-eye with their editors. One who thus came to Saxton was Aldous Huxley. Although they seldom met, a strong friendship and mutual respect drew them close together. And when Saxton died in the early summer of 1943 it was Huxley who wrote most movingly of an author's affection for his editor. In his letter to Mrs. Saxton he said, "In a curious, hardly analysable way Gene was, for me, a living proof of the firm triumph of character over matter—physically almost always absent, and yet firmly present in my mind as a trusted friend, to whom I could turn in any crisis without fear of disappointment."

In December, 1943, the Eugene F. Saxton Memorial Trust was set up by the House to assist talented writers who would otherwise be unable to complete book projects. An important stipulation of the Trust was that an author should be free to offer his completed work to any publisher he chose. Among the outstanding authors who have received Saxton fellowship grants are Rachel Carson, Eugenie Clark, John Brooks, and James Baldwin. The House discontinued the Trust in 1967, replacing it with "Harper-Saxton Awards" for books projected or completed. Decisions as to authors and books thus financed and honored will be made by trade-book editors.

Eugene F. Saxton and Aldous Huxley at Saxton's summer home in the Berkshires, May, 1933.

Other books that Saxton worked on included Anne Parrish's popular novels, such as *All Kneeling*, and George A. Dorsey's *Why We Behave like Human Beings*, a top best seller of 1926. Among the few books of poetry that achieved such status was Edna St. Vincent Millay's *Fatal Interview*, one of her many works of poetry, most of which are included in *Collected Poems*. Miss Millay wanted no editor to check her manuscripts, insisting that she knew exactly where the commas belonged. Her poems were set in type by Arthur Rushmore, who was head of the production department and, as an avocation, set type by hand at the Golden Hind Press in his Madison, New Jersey, home. Once, Miss Millay brought a set of proofs to his office desk to discuss alterations and, while there, lighted a cigarette. After she left, an enterprising office boy retrieved the cigarette butt and auctioned it off to the highest bidder. Her autographs were more salable. When limited autographed editions of her books were issued, orders had to be rationed among dealers, some of whom were smart enough to hold on to copies for a few years, when prices more than tripled.

Rushmore was given his position when the manufacturing operation was closed and its personnel of several hundred was reduced to eight or ten. He liked to tell the story of Jimmy White, a printer who, boy and man, had worked at Franklin Square for fifty-five years. When he came with his final goodbye, Rushmore said, "Well, Jimmy, now that you have picked up some experience with Harper's I suppose you'll go out and get a permanent job and settle down." "That's what I figger," Jimmy replied. "I don't like moving around. 'Course I knew when I took this job it was just temporary."

Rushmore could mix artistic excellence with business efficiency. Books that he designed were frequently included in the fifty best of the American Institute of Graphic Arts. He might have had even more awards had not Hoyns gone to his desk so often with new book estimates to ask if something could be saved on paper or binding costs. Rushmore may not have coined the aphorism "A penny shaved is a penny hoyned," but it was typical of his quick and lively humor. (He tagged the religious book department "the department of commercial theology.") It is doubtful that Hoyns ever heard his thrift thus parodied, but he would have enjoyed it for he took pride in the economies he could effect. In his later years, as the firm's prosperity was self-evident, he became less concerned about expenditures except for bound-stock inventories, which never ceased to worry him.

For Hoyns, Harper & Brothers was the most important institution on earth, and his loyalties ran so deep that it was often remarked about him that he would fire himself if he thought it would be for the good of the House. Actually he never paid himself much of a salary, and once he said to Adam Burger, who was named sales manager in 1927, "Did you see by the morning's paper, Adam, what Babe Ruth's salary is? Why, with all my responsibilities here I only make a small fraction of that." Burger, who was ever Hoyns' foil, replied, "Yes, Mr. Hoyns, but, you see, Babe Ruth does fill up the Yankee Stadium!" Hoyns and Cullen

were paid picayune salaries while they worked under Harvey, and later
parlayed many a financial deal to meet payrolls and make royalty payments. Those wounds never fully healed, and both men were resolved
that if they could help it the House must never again suffer such financial indignities. Thus, when Hoyns bargained unshamefacedly for lower
discounts to the trade, or urged lower royalty rates to keep a book in
print, or refused increases in salary to employees, he did so because he
had seen hard times.

Hoyns was also shrewd enough to know that the imprint he loved
had tremendous bargaining power. In 1932 he consummated the purchase of the religious book list of Richard R. Smith, who was being
forced into bankruptcy because of the depression. It was the best buy
Hoyns ever made; the House paid but a few thousand dollars in cash
over what Smith owed printers for long-overdue bills. The total purchase
price was amortized through sales within two years. To be sure, Smith
had already unloaded a lot of stock to dealers at fancy discounts
and he could have sold his list elsewhere at a much higher figure,
but Hoyns was smart enough to know that Smith's main concerns
were to get his bills paid and to place his authors where they could be
secure. Likewise Hoyns knew the bargaining power that a popular
new book placed in his hands. *Man the Unknown,* by Alexis Carrel, was
published at the time the *Reader's Digest* started its monthly book con-
densations. Its editors were sold on Dr. Carrel's book and felt that
they had to have it as an early feature. Hoyns held out against their
offers on the ground that the magazine's wide readership might satisfy
the reading public's interest and the book would stop selling. Of course,
he may have been sincere in this belief and not just bartering for the
best possible offer, which he did get; at any rate he could never use
that argument again, because it was the magazine digest that made the
book a best seller.

Even though Parmentier had been brought in as president, he knew
from the beginning that Hoyns was boss. For his part, Hoyns treated
Parmentier with cordiality and respect; he appreciated Parmentier's
financial ability. As Parmentier began to learn about the business, his
interest shifted from financial to editorial concerns. In 1928 he returned

from England and announced that he had signed up all the forthcoming works of Edith Sitwell and her two brothers by agreeing to pay them a large sum annually as advances on royalties. As soon as Saxton and Canfield learned of this trumpeted coup, they went at once to Hoyns to protest both that this was an unwarranted expenditure, in view of the limited output of these writers at the time, and that it was an un-warranted trespass on the literary grounds the two of them were care-fully tilling. Parmentier was unwilling to confine his activities to financial matters and shortly resigned from the firm.

Perhaps the greatest contribution that Hoyns made to the House was to initiate departmental publishing in specialized fields and to place competent men and women in charge without editorial restrictions. Thereafter department heads could say of Hoyns and his successors, as Curtis once said of Fletcher Harper, "Editorial success was im-possible without perfect freedom, and there could not be perfect free-dom if there were authoritative interference."

College textbooks were the first to be placed on a departmental foot-ing. When Fred Crofts was taken on, he was given a partnership deal whereby Crofts and the House would invest equal amounts in the expenses of the department and share profits equally. In the five years covered by the contract, Crofts brought in Woolbert's *Fundamentals of Speech,* Smart's *Handbook of English,* and other profitable books. In fact, he did so well that Hoyns would not renew the contract, offer-ing instead full House financing, a smaller share of the profits, and a place on the Board of Directors. Crofts spurned the offer and threatened to sue for profits he thought were due him for sales of general books he was responsible for. He soon furled that sail and ran up another one. He said he would be glad to review manuscripts that might be submitted to the young college traveler who had been hired from Henry Holt & Co. to replace him. This new man, Frank S. MacGregor. soon found that Crofts was starting up his own business and soliciting such Harper authors as F. Stuart Chapin and Guy Stanton Ford, of the University of Minnesota. Following the Hoyns dictum that the best way to make a sale was to talk directly with a prospect, MacGregor went at once to see the two men and got their promise to stay with the

House. Chapin agreed to edit a social science series, and Ford became general editor of a history series which is still going strong. Crofts also discovered Harold Underwood Faulkner, whose *American Economic History* has gone through several revisions, is still in print, and has had enormous sales.

MacGregor gradually added new salesmen to visit key professors in the leading colleges, seeking textbook adoptions and soliciting manuscripts. Edward J. Tyler, hired to cover large institutions on the East Coast, talked Harry Shaw, of New York University, into writing *A Complete Course in Freshman English;* published in 1940, it is now in its sixth edition, having passed the half-million mark years ago. Of the many books that MacGregor published through 1943, when he turned the management of the department over to Tyler, he particularly enjoyed developing *Art in the Western World* with David M. Robb, of Colgate University; this book filled a great need for an introductory course and has also been revised several times and has stayed continuously in print. During the MacGregor period, the annual sales of the department increased from $120,000 to over $1,000,000 and the number of salesmen from one to seven.

In 1925 the second department, social and economic books, was started under Ordway Tead, who had been editing such books for McGraw-Hill, including one on personnel administration of which he was co-author. With experience also in undergraduate teaching and industrial counseling, Tead soon became the leading publisher of books for the general reader and for specialists in the fields of the social sciences, education, and business and finance. Such definitive works as Lilienthal's *TVA—Democracy on the March,* Mooney's *The Principles of Organization,* Elliott Smith's *Psychology for Executives,* and Bingham and Moore's *How to Interview* went through many new and revised editions and were sold through bookstores as well as by direct mail.

Concerned to publish in the area of race relations, although profits would likely be minimal, Tead undertook a series of books about the Negro sponsored by the Carnegie Foundation and edited by the well-known Swedish political economist Gunnar Myrdal. Numerous scholars contributed to this Carnegie series of six books, which culminated in the summary volume, *An American Dilemma,* by Myrdal, published in 1944. When the manuscript, consisting of more than 2,000 pages, was submitted to Tead, he was alarmed at the risk entailed in bringing out such a large volume on a relatively specialized theme. He went to the Carnegie executive Mr. Frederick Keppel, explained the publishing problem it presented, and made the cautious proposal that he would print an edition of 2,500 copies of two volumes, boxed, at a retail price of $9.00 or $10.00, with the proviso that at the end of two years the Carnegie people would purchase any unsold copies at the actual manufacturing cost. Mr. Keppel and Tead shook hands on this agreement, which in retrospect is an amusing footnote to efforts made in advance to gauge the public's response to a new book. Within two months after publication the entire edition was disposed of, and over the years the book in both single- and two-volume format has sold well over 50,000 copies and is still active in a Twentieth Anniversary edition. The success of the Myrdal work brought other books on race relations and sparked the significant series Studies in Prejudice, developed by the American Jewish Committee a decade later.

The year following Tead's start with the House, Miss Virginia Kirkus was employed to organize a department of books for boys and girls, building on the strong backlist of titles that had been developing since the days of *Harper's Young People.* After familiarizing herself with these books, including such classic titles as *Greyfriars Bobby* and *The Hole Book,* and after studying the catalogues of a few other houses, which had also entered this specialized field, she talked with leading librarians regarding needs and trends. Learning of a forthcoming American Library Convention, she asked Hoyns who was covering it. "Oh, nobody does it—only a waste of time and money," he replied. She talked him into allowing her to go, and worked with Rushmore to build an exhibit around a new edition of *Toby Tyler,* with original illustrations and representation of steps in the book's manufacture. Her booth was thronged with librarians and, having tasted such success, she was ready to go on a trip to find out what booksellers had to say about children's books. When Burger backed her up and Hoyns reluctantly agreed, she went from Toronto through large cities in the

Middle West and returned with a notebook full of ideas. She filed an expense account that was meticulously exact, with no personal items included. Burger stormed when he saw it. "This has to be revised. I won't pass it." Miss Kirkus was aghast. "But there's nothing there that doesn't belong. I can't cut it!" "Cut it?" Burger howled. "No, expand it. I can't have you traveling on fourteen dollars a day and my men on twenty-eight!" So Miss Kirkus added a few items, though not monetary ones. She had not needed a sample room, or a raft of bellboys, or liquor; or entertainment expense, for she was entertained; or cabs, for she enjoyed walking.

Miss Kirkus did some exciting trail blazing in her seven years with the House when it was generally thought that only stories would sell for children. She started a City and Country series with illustrated books on bread, milk, printed pictures, and so on. Her most important discovery was Laura Ingalls Wilder, whose *Little House in the Big Woods* (1932) was the first of eight volumes of child life on the American prairies in frontier days, books that have won the affection of millions of readers. In 1953 the Wilder series was reset in a uniform edition with illustrations by Garth Williams.

When Miss Kirkus left to start her service of supplying librarians and booksellers with information about forthcoming books of all publishers, she was succeeded by Louise Raymond, who steered the department through the difficult years of the nineteen-thirties, and in 1941 by Ursula Nordstrom. Miss Raymond accepted Meindert DeJong's first manuscript, *The Big Goose and the Little White Duck,* after a librarian encouraged him to write down the stories he told her (he was then selling eggs to the Grand Rapids Public Library). In a few years his goose was laying golden eggs, winning for him the 1955 Newbery Medal for *The Wheel on the School* and the 1962 Hans Christian Andersen Medal, an international award based on the whole of his work, which Miss Nordstrom had helped him to shape. Miss Raymond also accepted the first of more than thirty books that Margaret Wise Brown was to write, most of which are still in print. Her book *Little Fur Family* (1951) was designed for the youngest of children and was appropriately bound in real fur. The binding caused some consternation among adults, but the book was loved by children, who slept with it, fed it, and kept asking to have the story reread. In 1942 Miss Nordstrom published *The Tall Book of Mother Goose,* which has sold more than a million copies and was the first of a series of "tall books" that are still in demand and have been copied by other houses. Two years later, Esther Averill wrote *The Cat Club,* the first of the delightful stories of the cat Jenny Linsky.

A religious book department was organized in 1926 under the direction of Walter Lewis, who for many years had been manager of the Presbyterian Book Store in Philadelphia and was known and respected by both Hoyns and Burger. Lewis died within two years of his employment but, even so, launched a significant English series, the Library of Constructive Theology, which still survives under the editorship of Dean Matthews, of St. Paul's Cathedral, London. Lewis's greatest contribution was one of organization, and his insistence that religious books should be sold by salesmen who know their books' content and market has been a main reason for the success of this department.

When I came from the University of Chicago Press as Lewis's successor, the three leading general houses with specialties in religious books were Macmillan, Scribner, and Doubleday, Doran & Co. In the early nineteen-thirties George Brett, of Macmillan, dismissed a long-time editor of religious books, and several of his authors gravitated to Harper's, as did the old George H. Doran titles, which Doubleday sold in 1929 to Richard R. Smith, who, in turn transferred them to Harper's in the depression year of 1932. One of the bright ideas of George Doran was an annual minister's manual containing sermons and other preaching aids, which he named for himself and not for the hard-working compiler. It has been published every year since, and Doran's name has been kept, although in small type and within brackets, for some clergymen still ask for "Dr. Doran's manual."

The best books included in the Smith purchase were staple titles from Messrs. Hodder & Stoughton, Ltd., especially a translation of the Bible by James Moffatt. Moffatt had undertaken the work partly because he wanted to augment his salary at the United Free Church College, Glasgow, where he taught Church History, in order to pay off an indebtedness incurred by his father. Furthermore he preferred to be paid a guinea a day rather than to risk royalty payments that, he modestly thought, would be meager. Many years after this translation had made his name known among church people the world around, Professor Moffatt would come to my desk once a year to ask how it was selling. He was then being well paid by Union Theological Seminary, was earning good royalties from other books, and was always grateful that Hodder's had enabled him to honor his father's memory. Moffatt was an ardent Yankee fan, knew batting averages, and never let scholarly studies interfere with home games.

The year 1932 was also notable in the religious book world for the publication of *Re-Thinking Missions.* This volume resulted from a study of mission fields financed by John D. Rockefeller, Jr. A group of research men visited Asia and Africa to gather facts which were used the following year by fifteen laymen, under the leadership of Harvard's William Ernest Hocking, who toured these same countries. Another philosopher, Rufus Jones, of Haverford, and Pearl Buck, the novelist, helped with the report, as did several leading businessmen, including Harper Sibley, Fletcher Harper's great-grandson. This book produced a radically revised approach to missions and was sharply criticized by conservative church groups; the disagreement helped its sale. But what helped most were the tons of publicity releases sent to newspapers over a period of months by Ivy Lee, Mr. Rockefeller's publicity expert.

Shortly thereafter, the outstanding authority on Christian missions, Kenneth Scott Latourette, of Yale, began publishing his scholarly six-volume *History of the Expansion of Christianity,* which brought him many honors, including the presidency of the American Historical Society. In the nineteen-forties, Anson Phelps Stokes, whose name is inseparable from that of Yale, was writing his three-volume *Church and State in the United States,* an authoritative history of this complicated relationship. It was recently issued in a single-volume condensation with updating by Leo Pfeffer.

More popular books were written by Harry Emerson Fosdick, whose sermons, published in nine volumes at intervals during the thirties and forties, were not only preached from his pulpit but also broadcast on

Sunday afternoons on N.B.C.'s "National Vespers." Never before had a preacher's voice been heard by so many millions, and the impact of the sermons as preached and published can never be fully measured. Dr. Fosdick recalled some of the experiences later in his autobiography, *The Living of These Days.* He always considered preaching a means of speaking to individual concerns and problems, and as a result a constant flow of troubled people passed through his office high in the tower of the Riverside Church in New York. Out of this counseling experience grew a book, *On Being a Real Person,* of which a half million copies have been sold.

Dean Willard L. Sperry, of the Harvard Divinity School, never had Fosdick's readership, but in urbanity and scholarship and style he was unequaled. For years he was my trusted adviser, reading manuscripts that had first passed the highly critical opinions of a long-time associate, Dudley Zuver. Sperry directed many important books and authors to Harper's, including those of his colleague Robert H. Pfeiffer, whose *Introduction to the Old Testament* for years was the most widely used text in that field. Sperry was indirectly responsible for Elton Trueblood's submitting his first book to Harper's, and it was followed by seventeen titles totaling in sales well over a million copies. The Quaker Trueblood's genius as an author is, in part as exemplified in *The Predicament of Modern Man* (1944), that of clarifying emergent religious and social ideas. The department's largest royalty checks have gone to Cynthia Pearl Maus for her several giant anthologies, especially *Christ and the Fine Arts.* For years her book sales placed her among the top three or four highest income-producing authors for the House. However, few books have been surpassed in sales by those of Emmett Fox, whose *Sermon on the Mount* has averaged better than 25,000 copies a year since publication in 1935. Devotional titles have always been catalogued by Harper's, and for several years a series of gold-jacketed books brought classic spiritual works to American readers. A prime example is Thomas Kelly's *A Testament of Devotion,* which was published posthumously in 1941 with an introduction by his Haverford colleague and fellow Harper author, Douglas Steere.

A medical book department was started in 1935 with the purchase of the Paul B. Hoeber Company, largely known for publications in the cultural-historical field of medicine and for important scientific works. Hoeber books were also distinguished for their typography, supervised by the famous type designer Frederick W. Goudy. The firm faced insurmountable financial difficulties in 1935 and was brought into the Harper fold through Hoeber's friendship with Saxton and was operated as a wholly owned subsidiary. Hoeber came to Harper's with a small stock of books, including Walter C. Alvarez's *Nervous Indigestion,* one of the largest-selling medical books of its time, and Tilney's *The Brain from Ape to Man,* a classic two-volume work in the field of evolution, and also the periodical *Annals of Medical History,* a distinguished scholarly journal which was issued until the paper shortage forced its discontinuance during the war. In its first full year the department had gross sales of about $25,000.

Hoeber brought with him plans for *Handbook of Hematology,* to be edited by Hal Downey, of the University of Minnesota. This was projected as the most elaborate scientific work yet published in the United States. With Harper financing, it was published in 1938 in four volumes with many color plates. The edition was 1,250 copies at the then unheard-of price of $85.00. It proved successful and has become such a well-known classic that an offset reprint was published by Hafner in 1965. Hoeber died in 1937, just as he was getting well established in his new Harper venture, and his son Paul B. Hoeber, Jr., was asked to carry on in his stead.

One of the first books published by Paul B. Hoeber, Jr., was *Culture of Organs,* by Alexis Carrel and Charles A. Lindbergh. Carrel's only previous medical book had been issued by the old Hoeber firm, and his *Man the Unknown* had made his name widely known to the public. The more famous Lindbergh name gave this book, a technical report of the "artificial heart," tremendous publicity, much to the annoyance of Lindbergh. Carrel introduced young Hoeber to a protégé, Raymond C. Parker, whose *Methods of Tissue Culture* was welcomed by laboratory investigators and will soon be issued in a fourth edition.

Walter C. Alvarez, of the Mayo Clinic, revised two of his earlier works for Hoeber, and they were published as *Nervousness, Indigestion and Pain* and *Introduction to Gastroenterology.* Another major work before the war was *Treatment of Cancer and Allied Diseases* by 147 authors, edited by George T. Pack and Edward M. Livingston; published in three volumes, it was the first detailed guide to the subject in the modern era of medicine. It was highly successful, as was the 1941 issue of Nielsen's *Textbook of Clinical Neurology.* Many projects planned in the period 1938-41 were delayed by the war and published in the late forties and fifties. One of the most important was *Biomicroscopy of the Eye,* by Milton Berliner, which reported significant knowledge of eye diseases stemming from new techniques for seeing inside the eye. It required 100 pages of color plates and was published in two volumes. In spite of wartime difficulties the first volume came out in 1944, but the second did not appear until 1949.

Hoeber added several popular books to his list, including a reprint of Sir William Osler's *Way of Life* and two books by the eminent anatomist George W. Corner, *Attaining Manhood* and *Attaining Womanhood.* These books have since attained their majority and are still catalogued. Hoeber was also instrumental in introducing two authors to the House whose books became important trade books. One was Arthur M. Hertzler, whose *Horse and Buggy Doctor* was a Book-of-the-Month Club selection and a top best seller in 1938. Another was Arnold Gesell, of Yale. Hoeber published *Developmental Diagnosis* (still in print) but turned over another, *The First Five Years of Life,* to Canfield. An outside reader reported favorably but the sales prospects did not seem encouraging, and a letter of publishing perplexity was posted to Dr. Gesell, who countered by offering to invest a small sum of money of his own. This partially subsidized book was followed by the very successful *Infant and Child in the Culture of Today.* When the fourth book in the Gesell series, *The Child from Five to Ten,* was published, it had an advance sale to booksellers of 30,000 copies. In all, more than a million copies of his books have been sold. After Dr. Gesell's death his work was continued by his associates Drs. Ilg and Ames, who established the Gesell Institute of Child Development in New Haven, in part with book royalties. The House has also contributed financially to this work, including a return of the money Dr. Gesell invested in the first book.

Some of the editorial work on the Gesell books was handled by Mac-Gregor, who carried on a holding operation for the medical book department while Hoeber served as a Navy officer in the Second World War. By that time Hoeber had the satisfaction of knowing that his annual sales had gone over $100,000 and the department was out of the red.

A separate department was set up in 1940 to publish staple books, works of nonfiction that are practical and informative and have a long-term sales potential. The best example of a Harper staple book is *Engineers' and Mechanics' Pocket-book,* by Charles H. Haswell. It was first published in 1844, as a small volume of some 300 pages, and stayed in print until 1935. In the meantime, the book became known as *Haswell's Engineering,* went through seventy-three editions, and grew in length to over 1,000 pages. To head up this new department, the House employed George W. Jones, who had been editing this type of basic book for Funk & Wagnalls, the firm whose business had suffered through the failure of the *Literary Digest.* When Jones came to Thirty-third Street, many of his authors followed, including Charles Earle Funk, a nephew of one of the founders, whose three lively and colorful books about word origins are in constant demand.

During World War II and the Korean War, Jones was on leave as an officer in the U.S. Army Air Force. Before 1941 he had obtained two semitechnical books on aviation by Generals "Hap" Arnold and Ira C. Eaker. General Arnold became a five-star general in World War II and later brought his memoirs to Jones, refusing to consider offers from other publishers. It was published under the title of *Global Mission.* One of the staple department's first books was *The Army Wife,* by Nancy Shea, which developed into a timely series including *The Navy Wife* and *The Air Force Wife.* These were popular and useful during World War II, and with repeated revisions the series is still selling.

During Jones' first absence, his editorial responsibilities were carried by Elizabeth Lawrence, a senior editor of trade books. It was also during this period that Miss Lawrence devoted considerable time to a manuscript that had been submitted in the firm's 125th Anniversary Contest for nonfiction. It was the story of a Brooklyn family; its author was Betty Smith. Enthusiastic about the book's possibilities, and with Sax-

ton's approval, Miss Lawrence convinced Betty Smith that the book
would sell much better if it was recast in fictional form. Together they
revamped the book and issued it as a "Harper Find," a designation
calling for special promotion of a new author's work, and soon *A Tree
Grows in Brooklyn* was off to the races. Its popularity was, in a sense, an
embarrassment because of the difficulty of procuring paper under wartime paper quotas. In hard-bound editions and in reprints it has sold
more than three million copies and is one of the best-selling titles ever
issued by the House.

The success of *A Tree Grows in Brooklyn* made publishing history.
Two quite different books by women authors also did well, Susan Ertz's
Anger in the Sky, a chronicle of English life against the background of
total war, and E. M. Delafield's *The Provincial Lady in Wartime.* Miss
Delafield's charming *Provincial Lady* books were widely read during the
thirties and forties, partly because they revealed the life of a cultivated
and seemingly unsophisticated English gentlewoman who was striving
gallantly to meet the demands made upon her by her family, her friends,
her lecture audiences—and her publishers. Harper people figured prominently in *The Provincial Lady in America,* from the Canfields, who
entertained her, to the salesmen, who steered her through the ordeals of
autographing parties. Miss Ramona Herdman, for many years in charge
of the Harper publicity department, received much praise from Miss
Delafield for her tactful guidance through the unfamiliar territory of
newspaper reporters and radio interviewers.

In the thirties Canfield signed up three young American authors whose
knowledge and wit and cultivated writing added much luster to literature and life both here and abroad. The first was Thornton Wilder. Canfield sent an announcement of a forthcoming Harper Prize Novel
Contest to Wilder, which was received at a propitious time, because the
author of *The Bridge of San Luis Rey* was unhappy with his publisher
and ready to talk about another association. Canfield urged that nothing
be put in writing just then, but assured Wilder that Harper's would
take his next novel not covered by an option. Thus *Heaven's My Destina-
tion* came to Harper's in 1935, and was followed by two Pulitzer Prize
plays, *Our Town* and *The Skin of Our Teeth.*

"Isn't it about time another one of John Gunther's 'Insides' came out?"

A cartoon from The New Yorker *of October 7, 1944.*

The second author was Louis Bromfield, all of whose books beginning with his novel *The Farm* in 1933 were published from Thirty-third Street. Bromfield had returned to his farm, "Malabar," near Mansfield, Ohio, after living in England, France, and India, and there he wrote books as zestfully as he pursued agricultural hobbies. Two novels with Indian settings—*The Rains Came* and *Night in Bombay*—were best sellers, as was *Pleasant Valley,* a delightful account of Bromfield's passion for the land.

John Gunther, foreign correspondent for the Chicago *Daily News,* was the third author. Canfield was convinced of the need for a lively, colorful book interpreting modern-day Europe and was sure that Gunther was the man to write it. But he could not convince Gunther that writing a book was worth the sacrifice of a well-paying newspaper job. Clearly the Wilder technique would not work with this author, so Canfield tried a desperate expedient. The morning on which Gunther was to sail for Europe, Canfield called to see him at his room in a New York hotel. Gunther had had a late night and had not finished his packing, and was hardly prepared for Canfield's quiet comment that he planned to sit there until he got Gunther's promise to undertake the book. Finally Gunther burst out, "I'll do anything you ask if you will just get out of this room and give me a chance to pack and get on that boat." Canfield said that fortunately he had a contract in his pocket providing for advance royalty payments and that if it could be signed he would leave immediately. Published a little over a year later—1936—*Inside Europe* has sold nearly 200,000 copies. More *Inside* books followed, among them *Inside Asia* in 1939 and *Inside Latin America* in 1941.

A writer who shared Gunther's gift of productivity came to Harper's in the thirties. And he was nearly missed. He was Thomas Wolfe. "I understand that Thomas Wolfe has been calling Harper's," Bernard DeVoto remarked to Canfield one day in 1937. "Not to my knowledge," Canfield replied, and immediately made inquiries of the trade department editors, including Edward C. Aswell, a recent addition to the staff. No one had been called. Finally he asked Hartman, then editor of *Harper's Magazine*, who replied, "No, I haven't been talking with Thomas Wolfe. Well, come to think of it, a few days ago a man did call me from somewhere in the South and *said* he was Thomas Wolfe. But he wasn't making sense and I thought he was intoxicated and couldn't be Wolfe, so I rang off."

Canfield immediately got in touch with Wolfe's agent and found out that Wolfe had absolutely decided to leave Scribner's. A publishing contract was soon drawn and signed, and shortly thereafter Saxton and Canfield had Wolfe to dinner in Saxton's Gramercy Park apartment. After dinner Wolfe started telling the story of his life to give them a sense of the kind of man he was, why he wrote as he did, and why he chose certain subjects for his novels. He fascinated the two men with his intelligence and his power of expression, and the talk continued throughout the night. Aswell was designated Wolfe's editor and did so well helping him that Wolfe named Aswell his literary executor. Wolfe died in 1938 before either of his Harper books—*The Web and the Rock* and *You Can't Go Home Again*—was published.

To walk through the portrait gallery of this period of Harper's literary expansion bestowing blue ribbons is as difficult a job as judging winners in a beauty contest. Even so, there are a dozen more Harper authors who deserve mention. Louis Adamic, the handsome Yugoslavian immigrant, is one, not only for his emotion-packed *From Many Lands* and his charming *The House in Antigua* but for his explosive *Dinner at the White House*. This last book was an account of a dinner to which Mrs. Roosevelt had invited Adamic, with Winston Churchill as the guest of honor. It was in 1945, when Churchill was the hero of everyone there except Adamic, whose Socialistic leanings made him highly critical of the great man. The manuscript was cleared for libel, as were the proofs, but no one thought to look at the final page proof that Adamic returned. Thus the book carried a footnote misquoting the columnist Drew Pearson and implying that Churchill's policy in Greece was dictated by Churchill's indebtedness to Hambro's Bank. It was clearly libelous, and as soon as Churchill saw the book he brought suit against Harper's. The case was settled out of court in return for a written apology from Adamic, a change in the footnote in future printings, and a payment of $25,000.

At an earlier and less dramatic dinner party, Canfield happened to sit next to the author Margaret Leech, with whom he talked of the problem of compressing vast historical detail into manageable size. The outcome of that talk was *Reveille in Washington,* an account of Civil War events in the nation's capital, a book that was awarded the Pulitzer Prize. In fact, Harper editors were often in Washington seeing such authors as W. M. Kiplinger (*Washington Is Like That*) and Sumner Welles (*The Time for Decision*), whose books were timely, readable, and informative. And in nearby Baltimore both book and *Magazine* editors were seeing Gerald W. Johnson, editorial writer for the *Sun,* who turned out an average of a book a year; important among them was *American Heroes and Hero-Worship.*

One of the most distinguished authors of the period was the director of the Oriental Institute of the University of Chicago, James Henry Breasted, who wrote *The Conquest of Civilization,* a book that had a companion volume, *The Ordeal of Civilization,* by James Harvey Robinson. Robinson is also remembered at Harper's for his reader's report on *The Decline of the West.* He thought that Oswald Spengler's book was too erudite to have much popular appeal. Such gambles with literary fortune require a sense of humor, and there were always Robert Benchley's books to turn to on gloomy days. *Benchley Beside Himself* is one of several titles of the humorist that remain in print, helped along by the hilarious drawings of Gluyas Williams.

In addition to Edna St. Vincent Millay in the poetry corner, there was Countee Cullen, with his own books and his anthology of Negro poetry entitled *Caroling Dusk,* and in addition to Bromfield at the fiction table there were Fannie Hurst, with many best sellers to her credit, including *Five and Ten;* Eric Knight, with his war novel *This Above All;* and the Italian novelist Ignazio Silone, whose *Bread and Wine* is such a fine book. Silone had once been a revolutionist, but the most famous of the revolutionists who got his picture in the Harper gallery was Leon Trotsky, and thereby hangs a tale indeed.

Trotsky was assassinated in the study of his home in the outskirts of Mexico City. In the struggle with his assailant he was pushed up against large hooks on which hung Harper galley proofs of the first part of his biography of Stalin, and his blood was spattered over the proofs. The book was completed by Charles Malamuth, who worked from copious notes that Trotsky had left. It was finished, and bound stock was delivered on Friday, December 5, 1941. Two days later came Pearl Harbor, and Canfield, who was editing the book, realized that within a very few days Stalin would be America's ally. Faced with the question of the effect of publishing a biography of Stalin by his archenemy, Canfield telephoned friends in government in Washington on Monday morning seeking advice. Two of those who were questioned gave evasive answers, but one said bluntly that he could consider nothing worse from the point of view of relations with the Soviet Union than to have the book published.

The basic issue was whether or not a publisher has the right to withhold the publication of a book which he believes to be against the public interest. Canfield decided that in this case he was obligated to withhold the book, and he wrote reviewers asking that they return their copies

THE WHITE HOUSE
WASHINGTON

March 6, 1942·

Dear Mr. Canfield:

   The one hundred and twenty-fifth anniversary of the distinguished publishing house of
Harper & Brothers is indeed an occasion worthy of
celebration. The activities of your house have
been contemporary with a long and notable period
in our national life. There are few businesses
that are so intimately interwoven with the national
fabric as a publishing house.

   I congratulate you and all your associates
on a fine job in keeping your institution so valiantly
on the side of civilization -- and always under the
same flag, the Stars and Stripes, and the house
pennant of Harper's. You have survived three wars
and are about to survive a fourth. May I venture
the hope that you will have many more scores of
years of service to your countrymen.

      Very sincerely yours,

      Franklin D. Roosevelt

Cass Canfield, Esq.,
President,
Harper & Brothers,
49 East 33d Street,
New York, N. Y.

A Presidential letter on the occasion of the 125th anniversary of the House.

Edward J. Cullen being given a medal in 1930 in recognition of his many years of service. Left to right, Henry Hoyns, Mr. Cullen, Thomas B. Wells, Cass Canfield, and Eugene F. Saxton.

(all but two did so) and sealed up the first printing of 10,000 copies in the warehouse. Mrs. Trotsky's attorneys expostulated and many of Trotsky's friends wrote angry letters of protest, but to no avail. The book was not published till about four years later, when the Cold War had started.

The period between the two world wars was thus marked by a notable recovery in the House's editorial activity. After the stock market crash in 1929 the sale of books continued surprisingly well. As the depression deepened, however, book sales fell off, some booksellers became insolvent, and credit risks increased. The ills of the book industry called for a study, and the so-called "Cheney Report," by O. H. Cheney, was sponsored by the National Association of Book Publishers, of which Canfield was president in 1932-34. By 1933 Harper's income from sales of books and the *Magazine* had dropped nearly 60 per cent. But as sales went down so did the cost of doing business. Salary cuts of 10 per cent were made twice and other economies were introduced by Hoyns, Canfield, and Cullen. No dividends were passed; in fact, the remaining preferred stock was retired. By 1937, when the business cycle reached another peak, the House was sharing fully in the general recovery of the book business.

In 1931 Hoyns replaced Wells as chairman of the Board and Canfield became president. When Canfield took a leave of absence in 1942 to join the Board of Economic Warfare, MacGregor was made executive vice-president. At the same time, on Cullen's retirement after more than fifty years with the firm, Raymond C. Harwood was advanced from assistant treasurer and organization manager to treasurer and general manager.

When Hoyns reached his fiftieth anniversary of Harper employment, he had no notion of retirement, but he did thoroughly enjoy a dinner given in his honor in January, 1934, by his close associates and publishing friends from other houses. Hoyns had the good executive's respect for detail and always carried a sharp pencil for figuring costs, although he was often surprisingly generous in financial matters affecting personnel. He asked for reports of progress on agreed-on projects, carried an amazing number of things in his head, and kept records of important agreements in memorandum books. His tall, slim, agile figure was often on the move, since he was more likely to go to a colleague than to summon a man to his office, and he was alert to the need of bringing together all who by position or special knowledge should share in making decisions. He was modest, disliked egotistical display, was not above admitting his own mistakes, and respected candor on the part of others. He worked with people easily and was gracious and friendly to those who met him as head of the House. While he cherished his friendships with other publishers, he would take a strong position if he felt a competitor was challenging Harper's rights or prestige. To work for Harper & Brothers was for him both an obligation and a privilege. He died on January 23, 1945, in his seventy-seventh year, and during his last, short illness he struggled to get out of bed insisting he had important things to see about at Harper's.

21

HARPER'S MAGAZINE (1900-1967)

The fiftieth birthday of *Harper's Magazine* was not a happy one. In the issue of May, 1900, Alden closed his genial article of historical reminiscence with the hope that the boys on the cover would continue to blow their bubbles forever. But winds of change were threatening to blow them out. McClure and Munsey were taking both advertising and subscribers from *Harper's* and the other quality magazines by printing less literary and more popular pieces in lower-priced periodicals. In Philadelphia, Lorimer, of the *Saturday Evening Post,* and Bok, of the *Ladies' Home Journal,* had discovered readers Alden had ignored, that growing group of middle-class Americans who were unintellectual but eager to spend money for good reading matter. Thus *Harper's* was losing money when Harvey moved in, and one of the jobs he gave to Duneka was that of applying new promotion ideas to win back subscribers and advertisers. Apparently Harvey urged Alden to seek more popular stories, as illustrated by Alden's declining *The Ambassadors* as too highbrow. In the nineties Alden would have accepted any new Henry James work without question. Harvey also revived "The Editor's Study" and told Alden that he was the man to write it, which he did until a few months before his death.

Paradoxically the London edition of *Harper's,* under Andrew Lang, was at this time enjoying its greatest acceptance. It led all competitors with a circulation of 100,000, and most of its readers considered it as originating in Britain. English novelists also helped lift the American edition out of its doldrums. Among these were the gay Mary Cholmondeley, whose *Red Pottage,* after serialization, pushed toward the top of the best-seller list in 1900, and Gilbert Parker, soon to be knighted, whose *Right of Way* repeated this performance a year later. Best of them all was Mrs. Humphry Ward, a niece of Matthew Arnold and an aunt of Aldous Huxley, who wrote *Lady Rose's Daughter.* It began as a *Harper's* serial in May, 1902, and during the next twelve months it brought more letters from readers than any other feature had theretofore inspired. It was the top fiction best seller in 1903. Compton Mackenzie, G. K. Chesterton, and Israel Zangwill were among other novelists whose *Magazine* serials later made Harper books.

Several serials of nonfiction also stepped up reader interest, and Harvey was willing to pay competitive prices to get the best writers. In fact, he paid the expenses of Henry W. Nevinson to Africa to investigate the shocking conditions of the slave trade that still secretly flourished there; the articles, later published in book form, astonished Americans and were quoted around the world. In another field, that of politics, John Bassett Moore wrote a remarkable series on the spirit and achievements of American diplomacy. John Fiske and Henry Cabot Lodge continued writing articles, as did Woodrow Wilson; two other Presidents, Roosevelt and Taft, added prestige and reader interest. Scientific articles, from the beginning an important feature, included "Cathode Rays"— one of the first articles to inform readers of a general magazine about the radioactive properties of uranium—and articles in 1904-1905 on what is now known as atomic physics by Sir Ernest Rutherford.

Illustrations, all halftones, brightened the pages. Circulation was also built up by a new Harper department, the Franklin Square Agency, which handled magazine subscriptions. This soon became a leading wholesale operation which brought in new business for all Harper periodicals from newsstands, booksellers, and individual agents. It continued under Harper ownership until 1961. So successful was *Harper's* revival that in 1914 an outside offer for its purchase at $500,000 was quickly turned down. By that time it was showing a profit of $5,000 a month and carried 797 pages of advertising. Harvey noted with satisfaction that all the cheap magazines were losing money.

Henry Mills Alden lived long enough to round out a full fifty years as editor. He died on October 7, 1919, just short of his eighty-third birthday, and Howells devoted an "Easy Chair" to his memory, saying that Alden was the greatest editor of his time and the one who held in his control more hopes and fears of authors than any other editor. Among the many tributes printed, one of the most appealing was written by an editorial associate of the nineties, John Corbin. In his *New York Times Book Review* article, he told of once bringing the proof of a contents page to Alden for an O.K. Alden asked Corbin if he thought the selection was a good one. Corbin answered that Alden was the best judge of that. Alden smiled and shook his head. "Did you ever reflect," he said, "that the only creature who can never know what the finished cocoon is like is the silkworm that spun it?" Corbin said that Alden had two basic editorial principles, an avoidance of sensationalism and a search for what he called "vital" in articles and stories. He was eager for novelty but not melodrama, and argued that a magazine that dealt wisely and cogently with human concerns had no need of "features."

Alden was succeeded by Thomas Bucklin Wells, who had long been his associate editor. He had carried most of the editorial load during the last years of Alden's tenure and was ably assisted by Lee Foster Hartman. It is to the credit of Wells that *Harper's Magazine* has survived to the present day, for the years following the First World War were trying ones for the quality magazines. Many of them eventually ceased publication—the *Century*, the *World's Work*, *Scribner's*, the *Forum*, the *Review of Reviews*. By 1925 Wells had seen that *Harper's* could not long survive unless it extended its appeal beyond genteel literary-minded readers to those who were concerned about public affairs as well. A few years earlier, Meredith Nicholson had praised *Harper's* for having kept faith with its own high standards through all the changes of public taste and feeling that had marked its long history. In the twenties public taste preferred realism to sentiment, was often cynical of moral, religious, social, political, and economic standards. Mencken's *American Mercury* and Ross's *New Yorker* were new magazines attractive to the modern reader.

Wells had only to read his own mind to see that the shifting values of the intelligent, concerned citizen were also true of himself. Whereupon he began soliciting and accepting articles that reflected the current disillusionment with conformity and sought to establish new values in art, morality, and politics. With such a concept in mind Wells was faced with the risk and the necessity of changing the seventy-five-year-old cover. Obviously Lossing's bubble-blowing cherubs would have to go. An advertising friend said that orange was a more attention-getting color than the green used on Mencken's magazine, so Wells adopted a brick-orange cover. Parmentier helped with these plans, and W. A. Dwiggins designed a new format. Except for a frontispiece in color, illustrations were dropped. The "new" *Harper's* appeared in September, 1925, with the lead article by Harry Emerson Fosdick. Its concern for intellectual honesty and distinguished writing and its emphasis on controversial issues and disinterested public service appealed to thoughtful and discriminating people. Its circulation soon doubled.

Wells was a man of middle height, with a bald head, a strong face, and a deep, resonant voice. He could speak his mind with devastating frankness when he encountered pretense, intolerance, shabby dealing, or complacency. In 1931, at the age of fifty-six, he decided to retire. Under his leadership the House had paid off its long-standing indebtedness and had reasserted its editorial leadership. Wells told his colleagues that he believed they could now anticipate a prosperous future and that he merited a release from editorial chores and business problems. Despite their protests that he could not be spared, Wells cleared off his desk, locked the door to his New York apartment, and with his wife went to Paris, where, as one of his authors, James Truslow Adams, had said, a man of moderate means who preferred simple living, simple pleasures, and the things of the mind could live contentedly. He was seriously ill during the war and had to remain in occupied Paris under a tyrannical rule he detested. There he died a month before the city was freed.

The editorial mantle was placed on the strong shoulders of Hartman, who was thoroughly in accord with his predecessor's editorial policies. It was his immediate task to guide the magazine through the difficulties of the depression. Once, an important advertiser brought pressure on Harper management because of Hartman's liberal editorial policy. Saxton came to his colleague's aid with a memorandum which is a classic statement of editorial freedom. He said, in part, "If you destroy the sense of editorial freedom in the conduct of *Harper's Magazine* you destroy the magazine itself. . . . The morale and the tradition of *Harper's Magazine* have been editorial responsibility and editorial freedom. . . . There is no more destructive idea (destructive in dollars and cents) than the fear of business office dictation once it gets loose in an editorial room. . . . It doesn't worry me that the magazine irritates certain people; when it ceases to do that it will be dead. . . . Unless the Editor is upheld by a generous view on his Employer's part and a willingness to endure some bruises for the cause of freedom, then the Editor's sense of personal integrity is lost and he can be replaced only by a Yes-man or a stuffed shirt."

The Saxton memorandum was a statement that Harper management could show to Hartman's critics because it represented a House policy of noninterference with all editors who were working as specialists in various fields. During the depressed thirties, advertising and circulation revenues slimmed down for economic rather than ideological reasons, and sometimes the *Magazine* showed a loss. Even so, the prestige of the *Magazine* helped book editors, and Fletcher Harper's 1850 dictum of its being a tender to the business of the House was also true in 1940, as it is in the House's sesquicentennial year. Hartman's own editorial ideals were always higher than he could attain, and the best he could ever say was "We got out a pretty good magazine this month." Significantly he said "we," for, as the *New York Times* editorialized at the time of his death, teamwork was paramount for him, and he was always eager to share credit with Frederick Lewis Allen and other associates. His major contribution as an editor was threefold: he sought out experts who could write articles of general interest out of their specialties; he made the *Magazine* a forum for trusted authors; he worked closely with authors until potentially significant articles could be brought up to his exacting standards. He carried on Wells' policy of publishing topnotch fiction, some of which—as always—was issued in book form by other houses, exemplified by Christopher Morley's *Thunder on the Left* and Clarence Day's *Life with Father.*

Among Hartman's trusted authors, Elmer Davis was chief. He could write on any subject he chose—on cats or a hurricane, on Hitler, Herbert Hoover, or Wagner. In 1933 Hartman signed up America's leading essayist, E. B. White, to write a monthly department, "One Man's Meat." For five years it was for many readers the magazine's leading feature, and the best of these pieces were later collected into a book by the same title. Hartman's greatest contribution was made through his patient labor with authors who had something important to say but didn't quite make the grade. Once, Hartman returned an article to Bernard DeVoto, one of his most esteemed contributors, saying that the firm's insurance would have been canceled if the underwriters had known the article was in the safe overnight. Years later DeVoto reread the piece and realized that it was not inflammable but only pretentious, which was Hartman's point. In 1935 he asked DeVoto to take over "The Editor's Easy Chair," which had been written after Howells' death by Edward S. Martin, on the basis of his writing about anything that interested him. Another time, Hartman turned down a piece saying it was trivial; sometimes he asked DeVoto to comment on something that had appeared in the *Magazine* or to commemorate some anniversary; otherwise he let DeVoto alone. After Hartman's death in September, 1941, DeVoto commemorated his long-time friend and editor in his seventy-fourth "Easy Chair." He said that during Hartman's editorship *Harper's* had given "an honest, trustworthy presentation of the time, its colors and rhythms and accents, its aspirations and experiments, its hopes and its dreads, its achievements and failures—and a constant endeavor of honest minds to work with these things and to pass judgment on them."

Frederick Lewis Allen, who had served as associate editor for ten years, became the sixth editor of *Harper's.* To the reading public he was better known than Hartman because of his articles and several popular books, the first of which, *Only Yesterday,* a brightly written informal history of the nineteen-twenties, was a Book-of-the-Month selection and sold over a half million copies. Others included three books of pictures and text written with his wife, Agnes Rogers; *The American Procession* was the one most widely read.

It fell to Allen to direct editorial policy during the Second World

War, when it was difficult to give objective appraisal to fast-moving events in a world lost in the jungle of almost total warfare. Then came the years of unquiet peace, the emergence of the United Nations, and the Korean War. Roosevelt and Truman and Eisenhower were Presidents. Their governments and policies and advisers were proper subjects for articles, and one who began in 1954 to write about them for *Harper's* was himself a Presidential aspirant, Adlai Stevenson. Henry L. Stimson chose *Harper's* as the medium for what the *Magazine* called perhaps the most important historical article it had ever published: "The Decision to Use the Atomic Bomb."

It was Allen's agreeable duty in 1950 to edit the centennial issue of *Harper's* although he delayed it from June until October, a better month for both subscribers and advertisers. It was a giant issue of 296 pages jammed with gay pictures pulled out of the preceding two hundred volumes and with pleasant, though not sentimental, articles written in the long reflection that the *Magazine* had made of American life and letters. John A. Kouwenhoven, for many years a contributing editor, wrote "America on the Move," and DeVoto compressed one hundred years of the nation's political, social, and economic history into nine pages at the front of the issue. Editor Allen wrote about the coming and the disciplining of industrialism (1850-1950). It was his seventy-seventh article in nineteen years, and the title of this one, "The Big Change," also named his book published subsequently. During the *Magazine's* centennial year Allen gave an address before the Newcomen Society in North America. "We deliberately edit," he said, "for a minority of educated—though not necessarily formally educated—people, intelligent people, responsible people, whom our promotion department, not without reason, refers to as *the real leaders of America*." He saw the functions of *Harper's* to be interesting, to provide news in the widest sense, to provide interpretation and discussion of important public issues, to provide a platform for original and inventive thinkers, and to provide a vehicle for the artist in literature.

Allen was never cloistered, as Alden had been, in a private office. He was often out on lecture trips, attending meetings—for several years—of the Bennington College trustees and the Harvard Board of Overseers, of the directors of the Foreign Policy Association and the trustees of the Ford Foundation. He also concerned himself about inner-office relationships, was a close friend of many Harper associates, and was sensitive to the individual concerns of all who worked for the House. He retired as editor of *Harper's* in 1953 and died the following year. In his memory the Ford Foundation fitted up and endowed the Frederick Lewis Allen Reading Room at the New York Public Library, the need of which Allen had often felt as he used the library's rich resources for his own writing but had no desk where he could work quietly and leave his books and notes until a writing job was completed.

On Allen's retirement John Fischer was named editor. He had joined the staff in 1944, but shortly thereafter interrupted his publishing career to go with a group named by the United Nations Relief and Rehabilitation Administration to check on the distribution of relief supplies in the Ukraine. After he returned to his job in New York, he wrote a book, *Why They Behave Like Russians,* which was a Book-of-the-Month Club selection. For six years he was chief editor of Harper's general books before moving into the editorial office of *Harper's Magazine.* Russell Lynes also came to the *Magazine* in 1944 and later became managing editor. Among his books are *Snobs,* which sold 25,000 copies, *Confessions of a Dilettante,* and *The Tastemakers,* which contains his well-known essay "Highbrow, Lowbrow and Middlebrow." (He categorizes *Harper's* as "Upper Middlebrow.") Currently the editorial staff is larger than ever before, a necessity because of an increasing number of manuscript submissions, a wider coverage of subject matter, and more intensive work on manuscripts accepted. From time to time a Supplement of forty or more pages is published on a special subject. The first Supplement, *Writing in America,* appeared in 1960, and others were *The Crisis in American Medicine, The College Scene, The American Female.* Some of them, including one full-length novel, *A Long and Happy Life,* by Reynolds Price, were later published as books.

While *Harper's Magazine* has the longest record of any quality magazine for serializing fiction, the publication of Price's novel in a single issue reflects the declining public interest in serials. Since its hundredth birthday, single works of only three novelists have been serialized in the *Magazine:* W. Somerset Maugham, Aldous Huxley, and Graham Greene. Now it prints, on the average, only one short story a month.

In today's world the trend of the *Magazine* is toward nonfiction, with such featured writers as Arthur Schlesinger, Jr., Anthony Eden, Paul Goodman, Jim Brosnan, Barbara Tuchman, and General James Gavin. America's leading management consultant, Peter F. Drucker, has written dozens of articles, most of which have become Harper books.

Several collections of articles and short stories from the *Magazine* have been published in book form, the most ambitious anthology being *Gentlemen, Scholars and Scoundrels,* a selection of articles, poems, and stories taken from issues up to 1959. The *Magazine* has won many awards in recent years, including two for nonmedical science writing from the American Association for the Advancement of Science, and three National School Bell awards in five years "for distinguished interpretive reporting on education." In 1962 Fischer received the second annual Richard L. Neuberger award of the Society of Magazine Writers as "The editor or publisher who in the preceding twelve months has done the most to raise the standards of magazines as a medium of democratic communication."

Through the decades, the *Magazine*'s special departments have come and gone. The "Editor's Drawer" was finally emptied of its stereotyped humor by Wells, but Fletcher Harper's desk has been kept as an honored link to that editorial past. A section of book reviews is the only department that has continued uninterrupted from Volume I, Number 1. Then it was called "Literary Notices"; now it is "The New Books" and "Books in Brief." Begun in 1851, "The Editor's Easy Chair" is still continued. This traditional monthly essay is now written by John Fischer or an invited guest, and a recent volume of his "Easy Chair" pieces was called *The Stupidity Problem*. New departments have been added to accommodate changing times and editorial tastes; one of the best is "After Hours," written mostly by Lynes. Illustrations—drawings and cartoons and photographs—are now used copiously, although they hardly resemble the form of art that Wells discarded and Lynes reinstated twenty years ago.

Changing times have affected the business department as well. In 1965 ownership of *Harper's Magazine* was transferred to a separate corporation, Harper's Magazine, Inc., jointly owned by Harper & Row and by the Minneapolis Star & Tribune Co., of Minneapolis, Minnesota.

Cass Canfield is chairman of the Board of Directors of the new corporation, and John Cowles, Jr., editor of the Minneapolis *Star & Tribune* and a director of Harper & Row, is its president; Cowles is related to Canfield, having married his stepdaughter. The *Magazine* continues to maintain a close relationship with the book publishing company, and the new corporate arrangement did not involve any changes in editorial direction. The Cowles company now holds a majority stock interest.

The circulation of the *Magazine* is now about 285,000 copies, twice what it was ten years ago. Several other "doubles" might be listed. Both the type page and the type size are nearly twice what they were one hundred and seventeen years ago. Twice as many pages of advertising were carried in 1966 as Harvey could boast of in 1914. And manuscript submissions have more than quadrupled since 1865, when editor Guernsey added up 4,600. One hundred years later, his successor came up with nearly 20,000. Out of these manuscripts, some solicited, the editorial staff chooses about two hundred. These are accepted after the editors have read and discussed them; generally they agree but sometimes (often a good omen of reader interest) there is a strong disagreement. The final decision is made by John Fischer, who recently described his editorial quest: "The best material for us is something utterly unlike anything we ever published before. What we seek is the germinal idea, the unexpected talent, the fresh mind on the growing edge of American culture; the manuscript which will surprise and delight us just as much as our readers. It is true that we don't often find it, because such treasures are rare. Nevertheless, it is this search, this perpetual treasure hunt, that makes the editor's job, for me at least, the most interesting job in the world."

EDITORS OF *Harper's Magazine*	WRITERS OF "The Editor's Easy Chair"
Henry J. Raymond—1850-56	Donald G. Mitchell—1851-53
Alfred H. Guernsey—1856-69	George W. Curtis—1853-92
Henry Mills Alden—1869-1919	William Dean Howells—1900-20
Thomas B. Wells—1919-31	Edward S. Martin—1920-35
Lee Foster Hartman—1931-41	Bernard DeVoto—1935-55
Frederick Lewis Allen—1941-53	John Fischer—1955
John Fischer—1953	

(22)

YEARS OF EXPANSION (1945-67)

The revival of the House which followed the move uptown from Franklin Square continued unabated in the decades following the Second World War. Each Harper department, with one exception, continued to extend and deepen its growth, new ones were added, and their work was undergirded by sound financing and expert management. The trade department, issuing books for the general reader, epitomized this expansion of literary activity.

Thornton Wilder's novel of the time of Caesar, *The Ides of March*, was published after World War II and his *The Eighth Day* was one of the highlights of Harper's sesquicentennial year. In the intervening years he wrote three one-act plays and *The Matchmaker*, on which the popular musical *Hello, Dolly!* was based. Wilder has received a number of literary honors, among them the Gold Medal for Fiction awarded in 1952 by the American Academy of Arts and Letters, the Presidential Medal of Freedom in 1963, and, in 1965, the first National Medal for Literature. Aldous Huxley also received the Academy's Gold Medal in recognition of his work as a novelist. His most recent novels were *Time Must Have a Stop, The Genius and the Goddess,* and *Island.* Many of his novels, including one of his earliest successes, *Brave New World* ("revisited" in 1958), are still in print, either in hard-bound or paperback editions. *The Gallery*, a book about Italy after the war, by John

Horne Burns, has been continuously catalogued since 1947.

Ranking high among recently published novelists is John Cheever, who has written three volumes of short stories and two novels chronicling the remarkable Wapshot family's exuberant activities. The first one received a National Book Award. Simon Michael Bessie was Cheever's editor until he resigned to help launch the Atheneum Press. His Harper editorial contribution was outstanding. In 1959 Leo Rosten wrote his first book for Harper's, *The Return of H*Y*M*A*N K*A*P*L*A*N*, which was followed by *Captain Newman, M.D.*, another novel. Other newcomers were Richard McKenna, whose *The Sand Pebbles* was the 1963 Harper Prize Novel, and John Ehle, whose regional novels *The Land Breakers* and *The Road* have found a national audience. *Seven Days in May* by Fletcher Knebel and Charles W. Bailey was a best seller in 1962-63.

English novelists continued to add luster to Harper's output of fiction; *The Early Life of Stephen Hind* is Storm Jameson's latest. Howard Spring's *Winds of the Day* is at this end of a shelf of best-selling novels, and John Dickson Carr's Dr. Fell books rank high in booksellers' re-orders. *Herself Surprised, To Be a Pilgrim,* and *The Horse's Mouth* are among the best of Joyce Cary's novels, and *The Fox in the Attic,* by Richard Hughes, is a fascinating story, the first of a modern-day trilogy.

Other established writers who turned out novels during this period are Margaret Culkin Banning and Edward Streeter. Mrs. Banning has been a perennial favorite, sometimes with a problem novel, and her recent one, *The Vine and the Olive,* has followed a well-blazed trail of sales. Streeter, whose vocation was banking and whose avocation is authorship, amused readers with a number of books, among them, *Chairman of the Bored* for those retired from business cares, vicariously or actually. And the Texan Fred Gipson wrote unforgettable stories called *Hound-Dog Man* and *Old Yeller.*

For twenty years, under the editorship of Joan Kahn, some of the best current fiction has been published as Harper Novels of Suspense. This distinctive label was chosen by Miss Kahn in order that her books would be noticed in the mystery field, and it proved to be a name of such aptness

*Mrs. Lyndon B. Johnson with Thornton Wilder on May 4, 1965, when
Mr. Wilder became the first recipient of the National Book Committee's
National Medal for Literature.*

and prestige that most mysteries have begun to be called suspense novels. More than half of the Harper Novels of Suspense are by English authors, which is in the Harper tradition of having published *The Moonstone,* by Wilkie Collins, in 1868 and the Sherlock Holmes stories, by A. Conan Doyle, in the early eighteen-nineties. Among the first novels of suspense were *Come and Be Killed!,* by Shelley Smith, and *Disposing of Henry,* by Roger Bax (the pen name for Andrew Garve, which is a pen name, too). These authors were pleased then and now—for they are still being published—that their mysteries are treated like all regular novels in format, binding, and jackets, and in marketing. Harper Novels of Suspense have won six Edgar Allan Poe Awards given annually by the Mystery Writers of America for the Best First Mystery by an American Author, and four awards for the Best Mystery of the Year. Helen Eustis was the first Best First in 1946, with *The Horizontal Man,* and John Ball the latest, in 1965, with *In the Heat of the Night.* The four Best were *Beat Not the Bones,* by Charlotte Jay (1953); *Room to Swing,* by Ed Lacy (1957); *The Color of Murder,* by Julian Symons (1960); and *Gideon's Fire,* by J. J. Marric (1961). Marric turns out a book a year and has seven *Gideon* books currently catalogued.

Over the years, Harper's has been known for its distinguished nonfiction, such as the work that won the Presidential Medal of Freedom for E. B. White and Genevieve Caulfield. Miss Caulfield's book, *The Kingdom Within,* was an autobiography edited by Ed Fitzgerald. The subtlety, wit, and style of White's books, including *The Second Tree from the Corner* and *The Points of My Compass,* have given him preeminence in the essay. In 1960 White became the third recent Harper author to receive the Gold Medal Award (for essays and criticism) of the American Academy of Arts and Letters, an institution that is for Harper people a kind of lengthened shadow of William Dean Howells, who was a founder and its first president. Some of medal-winner Aldous Huxley's best works were essays, such as those included in *On Art and Artists. Collected Essays,* published in 1959, contains a preface that is a graceful essay on the essay itself. In 1964 Sir Julian Huxley wrote *Essays of a Humanist,* which he dedicated to his brother Aldous, and two years later he edited a memorial volume, *Aldous Huxley 1894-1963.* Two vol-

A limited edition of The Love Letters of Mark Twain, *published in 1949, contained recently discovered autographs of Mark Twain. A drawing of names in the Harper Board Room allocated copies to booksellers. Pictured from left to right are: Frank S. MacGregor, William Briggs, Gilbert Good-kind, of the American Booksellers' Association, Adam W. Burger, Arthur W. Rushmore, and Louis Greene, of the* Publishers' Weekly.

umes giving Sir Julian's scientific and philosophical ideas about evolution are still in print.

Jacques Barzun, Dean of the Faculties and Provost of Columbia, took the authoritarian role of science in our society as the theme of his recent book, calling it *Science: The Glorious Entertainment*. The breadth of his mind and the brilliance of his style were earlier evidenced in *The House of Intellect*. J. B. Priestley's *Literature and Western Man* is in the best tradition of good writers who can themselves illuminate good writing. Also speaking for the intelligentsia, John W. Gardner, formerly president of the Carnegie Corporation and now Secretary of Health, Education, and Welfare, has written two books concerned with the position of the individual in society: *Excellence* and *Self-Renewal.* In the field of economics, Robert L. Heilbroner ranks high with such books as *The Great Ascent* and *The Limits of American Capitalism.* Cleveland Amory detailed American social doings from the early days to the present in *Who Killed Society?* Looking at the problem of the individual in an increasingly collectivist society, the longshoreman-philosopher Eric Hoffer recently wrote *The Temper of Our Time,* which was welcomed by many who knew his first and much-acclaimed *The True Believer.* Hoffer has been widely quoted in academic circles and was the subject of a *New Yorker* Profile in January, 1967. *The Silent World,* by Jacques-Yves Cousteau, grew out of a magazine article about this pioneer underwater explorer. Evan Thomas was Cousteau's editor and visited him and did some below-surface exploration too, aided by Cousteau's chief diver. The book was an immediate best seller; two subsequent volumes, *The Living Sea* and *World Without Sun,* also reached wide audiences.

In this same period Mark Twain had the last word, as so often he did. From thousands of pages of his unpublished writing Bernard DeVoto selected for publication essays on the human condition called *Letters from the Earth.* And Charles Neider edited *The Autobiography of Mark Twain,* which appeared in 1959—not in the year 2000, which Clemens and Harvey had thought the proper time for such a book's publication.

Of the books of poetry published after World War II, the latest are *Lupercal,* by Ted Hughes, *Selected Poems,* by Gwendolyn Brooks, whose *Annie Allen* won the Pulitzer Prize in 1950, and *The Rescued Year,* by William Stafford, whose *Traveling through the Dark,* published in 1962, won the National Book Award for Poetry. With a few notable exceptions poets are little read today, and their works are categorized by publishers as books of prestige rather than of profit, though in 1966 *Ariel,* by Sylvia Plath, provided both.

In the past two decades an impressive number of meritorious books in the field of history have been published from 49 East Thirty-third

Columbia University

On behalf of the Trustees of the University,
this citation is presented by the Friends of
the Columbia Libraries to

Harper & Row

in recognition of its service in publishing in 1965

The Peacemakers:
The Great Powers and American Independence
by
Richard B. Morris

which this year received one of the two
Bancroft Prizes of equal rank awarded
each year for the most distinguished works
in American history in its broadest sense,
American diplomacy, and the international
relations of the United States. Presented
at a dinner sponsored by the Friends of
the Columbia Libraries.

April 21, 1966

Hugh J. Kelly
Chairman
Friends of the Columbia Libraries

George Kirk
President of the University

Street. Historical writing has been featured since the years of Fletcher Harper, who in 1855 published the miscellaneous writings of George Bancroft, known now as the "father of American history." Bancroft's name is memorialized in Columbia's annual Bancroft Prizes, five of which have been given to these Harper authors: Robert E. Sherwood for *Roosevelt and Hopkins;* William L. Langer and S. Everett Gleason for *The Undeclared War;* Margaret Leech for *In the Days of McKinley;*

Award for one of the "Ten Best Adult Books of 1967 for the Pre-College Reader"—an honor previously awarded to other Harper books including Eleanor Roosevelt's Tomorrow Is Now.

William E. Leuchtenburg for *Franklin D. Roosevelt and the New Deal;* and Richard B. Morris for *The Peacemakers.* Miss Leech's book also received the Pulitzer Prize in history, as did Merle Curti's *The Growth of American Thought.*

The Leuchtenburg work was one of the volumes in the forty-volume New American Nation Series, edited by Henry Steele Commager and Richard B. Morris. Morris himself prepared a most valuable reference book entitled *Encyclopedia of American History,* and Commager edited an anthology of documents entitled *Living Ideas in America,* available in a recently revised edition. Professor Langer, of Harvard, is editor of the Rise of Modern Europe, a series of twenty volumes, now in process. Other historical works for the general public are John Chamberlain's business history, *The Enterprising Americans,* and John Brooks' *The Great Leap,* a lively history of the past twenty-five years in America. (John Brooks' other books include a novel, *The Big Wheel.*) Cecil Woodham-Smith, the British biographer-historian, is most recently

known for her moving book on the Irish famine, *The Great Hunger,*
and D. W. Brogan, the leading British authority on America and France,
has achieved recognition for such books as *Politics in America* and *The
French Nation.* Alan Moorehead, a remarkable storyteller and an outstanding interpreter of history, is particularly well known for *The White
Nile* and *The Blue Nile,* but his many books include *The Fatal Impact,
Gallipoli* and works on the exploration of central Australia and the
Pacific. Henry A. Kissinger's *Nuclear Weapons and Foreign Policy* was
a milestone in its field, and Herbert J. Muller's historical works, including *The Loom of History* and three volumes evaluating freedom in
different historical periods, were equally significant.

Closely allied with history is the field of biography and autobiography.
Aldous Huxley once observed that most people devote their reveries to
revising their own autobiographies; even so, when men and women with
unusual experiences are prevailed upon to publish, they often find that a
wise editor is a helpful rod and staff to lean on. Thus Miss Elizabeth
Lawrence worked closely with Santha Rama Rau on her several books
of autobiography and travel, with Lois Crisler on her book *Arctic Wild,*
about adventures in Alaska and her pet wolves, and with George and
Helen Papashvily on their humorous memories, best known of which
is *Anything Can Happen.* Similarly Miss Marguerite Hoyle, who helped
Sumner Welles to translate diplomatic language into simpler English,
was guide and prompter to Mrs. Eleanor Roosevelt for her autobiographical books. Once, Miss Hoyle asked Mrs. Roosevelt what she did
with her spare time. Instead of getting several paragraphs of good copy,
she had Mrs. Roosevelt's offhand comment that probably most of her
spare time was spent rearranging closets and desk drawers.

A Choice of Weapons described Gordon Parks' vicissitudes as a young
Negro. The *Life* photographer's first novel, *The Learning Tree,* was also
autobiographical, and both books were widely acclaimed. One of the
most extensive autobiographies currently being published is that of the
dynamic David E. Lilienthal. Three volumes of his *Journals* have so far
appeared covering his public life from 1939 to 1955. Scheduled for
October, 1967, publication is a memoir by Mme. Svetlana Alliluyeva,
Stalin's daughter.

The journal has been the form of several interesting and successful ventures during this period, notably major league baseball pitcher Jim Brosnan's account of a year in the big leagues, *The Long Season,* and its sequel, *Pennant Race,* and the even more successful best seller *Intern,* the journal kept by a young intern during his year of hospital training, published under the pseudonym of Doctor X.

Of recent notable biographies, a goodly number have been written by English authors. Hesketh Pearson was most prolific; when he died in 1964, he had published at least fourteen full-length biographies including such distinguished volumes as *G.B.S., Dizzy* (Benjamin Disraeli), and *The Man Whistler.* Virginia Cowles chose Winston Churchill and Edward VII, among others, for subjects of her biographies, and Desmond Young wrote the stirring account of the German General Rommel, which he subtitled "The Desert Fox." Elizabeth Longford wrote a major biography of Queen Victoria which was a Book-of-the-Month Club selection, as was A. L. Rowse's *William Shakespeare.* Rowse also has written a number of books on the Elizabethan period, which is his specialty. His scholarly lucid works have won for him a wide readership. Perhaps none of the English biographers can equal the output of the Frenchman André Maurois (although he writes elegantly in other fields as well), whose lives of George Sand, Victor Hugo, and Balzac are outstanding.

American writers of biography include Louis Fischer, who wrote on Gandhi and Lenin; Frances Winwar, who wrote on the Brownings and Poe; and Ishbel Ross, who wrote a life of Clara Barton as well as biographies of other famous American women. John Mason Brown, critic, author, and lecturer, came to Harper's for the publication of his book *The Worlds of Robert E. Sherwood,* as did William S. White for his Pulitzer Prize-winning biography of Robert A. Taft. This coveted prize was also won by Senator John F. Kennedy in 1957 for his *Profiles in Courage.*

While Senator Kennedy was writing *Profiles in Courage,* he forwarded two chapters to the House commenting that he was unsure whether what he had written would make a book or possible articles for the *Magazine.* Evan Thomas read the manuscript and went at once to see

Kennedy at the Hospital for Special Surgery in New York. The Senator was flat on his back, writing on a board propped up in front of him. He read a portion of new material to Thomas and told of the research work being done for him by Theodore C. Sorensen and others. Thomas urged Kennedy to consider his material as a book project, though some of it did appear in *Harper's Magazine.* When the book was completed Kennedy wrote in his preface, "The editorial suggestions, understanding cooperation and initial encouragement which I received from Evan Thomas of Harper & Brothers made this book possible." Published in January, 1956, *Profiles in Courage* was an immediate success. There were later editions—Inaugural, Memorial, Young Readers, and Perennial paperback. In all editions, including book clubs, paperbacks and translations, the book has sold millions of copies. When the Memorial Edition of *Profiles in Courage* was published in 1964, it was decided that all publisher's profits from this edition would be used to establish a John F. Kennedy Memorial Award in biography and history.

Thomas was also Kennedy's editor for *The Strategy of Peace* (Allan Nevins advised on the Senator's behalf) and consulted with Theodore Sorensen in the White House while *To Turn the Tide* was being published. This book, which contains President Kennedy's statements and addresses from his election through the 1961 adjournment of Congress, was edited for publication by John W. Gardner. A third volume of President Kennedy's speeches, *The Burden and the Glory,* edited by Nevins, came out in 1964. In the meantime Thomas had become Robert F. Kennedy's editor, seeing *The Enemy Within,* a report on the Senate's investigation of labor and management, through the press; it was followed by *Just Friends and Brave Enemies* and *The Pursuit of Justice.*

Shortly after the death of President Kennedy Thomas learned from Pierre Salinger, who was still in the White House, that a book on the assassination was to be written by William Manchester; but Thomas made no effort to get it, feeling that Harper's did not want to commercialize a national tragedy. Thomas was shortly invited to Robert Kennedy's office. There Thomas agreed to publish Manchester's book with the understanding that the bulk of the profits from the Harper publication would go directly to the Kennedy Library. The resulting manuscript, *The Death of a President,* was submitted in March, 1966.

It was not the first time that manuscript cards had been duly entered under Manchester's name. In 1949, he submitted through his agent, Harold Matson, a manuscript on H. L. Mencken which Harper's published as *Disturber of the Peace.* Subsequently Little, Brown became his publisher, but they kindly consented to release Manchester so that *The Death of a President* could be issued by Harper, in accordance with Robert Kennedy's request.

Manchester's bulky manuscript was read with mounting enthusiasm by Thomas and two associate editors, each of whom, as a normal course of editorial procedure, queried a number of passages. Thomas prepared two edited copies of the manuscript for John Seigenthaler and Edwin Guthman, both close friends and associates of Senator Kennedy, whom the Senator had requested to review the manuscript. During the ensuing weeks Thomas saw these men in New York and Washington, in Nashville and Los Angeles, to collate their revisions with his own, many of which had been accepted by Manchester. In the meantime Manchester had given a reading copy of the manuscript to Richard Goodwin, a friend and neighbor of his as well as a friend of the Kennedys. At Senator Kennedy's request Thomas sent the edited manuscript to Arthur Schlesinger, Jr., author of *A Thousand Days,* a definitive work on the Kennedy presidency. Schlesinger sent his comments and suggestions to Thomas, Manchester, and Senator Kennedy. Subsequently, Thomas and Manchester reviewed all corrections and deletions suggested by the outside readers.

Long before, it had become evident that at least one other book covering the assassination of the President might be published in 1966. Accordingly, it had been agreed that the date of the Manchester book should be advanced, and Senator Kennedy had indicated approval of the forthcoming serialization in *Look* (Harper was not involved in the *Look* agreement or serialization).

On July 29 Senator Kennedy telegraphed Manchester (and confirmed to Harper's):

Should any inquiries arise re the manuscript of your book I would like to state the following:
While I have not read William Manchester's account of the death of President Kennedy I know of the President's respect for Mr. Manchester

as an historian and a reporter. I understand others have plans to publish books regarding the events of November 22, 1963. As this is going to be the subject matter of a book and since Mr. Manchester in his research had access to more information and sources than any other writer members of the Kennedy family will place no obstacle in the way of publication of his work.

However if Mr. Manchester's account is published in segments or excerpts I would expect that incidents would not be taken out of context or summarized in any way which might distort the facts of or the events relating to President Kennedy's death.

On the basis of their understanding that book publication and magazine serialization had been authorized for 1966, Harper's sent an edited manuscript to the printer and galley proof was soon ready.

The first problem began in connection with the projected *Look* serialization. Mrs. Kennedy feared that widely publicized serial use would be harmful, partly because sections might be printed out of context, and she attempted to persuade Manchester and *Look* to cancel the serialization.

With galley proof now at hand, Thomas asked four Harper editors to read them and to mark any passages that they thought as a matter of editorial judgment might be discussed further with Seigenthaler and Miss Pamela Turnure, Mrs. Kennedy's press secretary. He urged Miss Turnure to have Mrs. Kennedy communicate directly with the author regarding any passages Mrs. Kennedy herself found troublesome.

Thomas continued to devote practically all his time to the book. In order that finally corrected proof could be sent to the printer, he sought Manchester's approval of further changes, including some advised by Harper's counsel and further suggestions which were continuing to be made by Kennedy representatives.

In the meantime arrangements were made for a "final" reading on behalf of the Kennedy family by Richard Goodwin, who, as it turned out, did not then read proof because he was on a trip to Italy. Galley proof went into page proof and Manchester, as earlier planned, took off for England. Both book and magazine publication were postponed until after January 1.

The imminence of the serialization caused the Kennedy representatives to press for further changes. As a result, on November 21, Canfield and Thomas called on Mrs. Kennedy at her request; she asked them to carry to Manchester in London a letter she would write and a report to be written by Goodwin on certain passages. They took this letter and this report to London and met with Manchester in the office of his English literary agent, A. D. Peters. As a consequence, Manchester agreed to a number of changes.

Harper, *Look,* and Don Congdon, Manchester's literary representative in New York, worked intensively to achieve a text that would meet the Kennedy wishes, and Senator Kennedy, Mrs. Kennedy, and their counsel were advised of this activity. Canfield and Gardner Cowles of *Look* wrote Mrs. Kennedy that changes had been made, and Thomas invited Goodwin to meet with him on December 12 to discuss the scope and substance of the alterations. But on that date Mrs. Kennedy's counsel served summonses on Harper and *Look,* and Harper and *Look* were advised that there was no basis for further discussion since the matter was in the hands of Mrs. Kennedy's attorneys. The summonses were followed four days later by Mrs. Kennedy's moving in the Supreme Court of the State of New York for an injunction against the publication of the book by Harper, *Look,* and Manchester.

By this time newspapers, television and radio broadcasts had been filled with stories and editorials about the controversy, with claims and counterclaims. Some felt that history was being emasculated, an author's privileges curtailed, and the public's right to know abridged. Others sympathized with Mrs. Kennedy's claim that she had been denied the right to disapprove material which had been made available by agreement with the Kennedy family. The controversy over these issues raged from the beginning of the case until the end, the Kennedy family claiming a breach of the original agreement, the author and publisher claiming that the manuscript had been released for early publication by the family. In reality, the problem was one of a breakdown in communications among intelligent and well-meaning persons.

The case was settled out of court on January 16, 1967. Mrs. Kennedy, Harper, and Manchester issued a joint statement saying that all differences had been resolved and that the historical record had in no way been censored.

Final proofs of the 728-page book were passed to the printer, and the production of a 500,000-copy edition was begun (booksellers' orders soon upped the printing by 100,000 copies). Several printers and binders worked overtime to produce the separate Harper and Book-of-the-Month Club editions. The publication date was set for April 7, and a week earlier bulk shipments began to fan out across the country. Soon the most publicized book of the century was being eagerly read, and the controversy over the writing and publishing of this important historical work had itself become history.

Theodore C. Sorensen was often with Thomas during the publication of J. F. Kennedy's first two books. In the early pages of Sorensen's biography *Kennedy,* he tells an anecdote involving Thomas, although Thomas is not identified. "Once, lunching with a noted radical's son who was involved in a complicated altercation with the senior Kennedy, he [J.F.K.] asked, 'Do you always agree with your father [Norman Thomas]? No? But you love him?' Smiling with pleasure at his companion's affirmative answer, he leaned back and said simply, 'Same here.' " Sorensen's book of nearly eight hundred tightly packed pages was written in a little more than a year's time, and in it he portrays Kennedy, the man and the statesman, as no one else could. Sorensen was privileged to be Kennedy's most trusted friend and confidant for nearly ten years and kept full notes of shared experiences. Once, Kennedy said to Sorensen, "I just wanted to make sure you got that down for the book we're going to write." Sorensen replied, as he had on other occasions, "You mean the book *you're* going to write, Mr. President." But it did turn out to be Sorensen's book, and its writing revealed that Sorensen was also a literary craftsman in his own right. The book has sold 150,000 copies in the trade and was also a Book-of-the-Month Club selection.

Over the years, books dealing with national and international problems have been an important part of the Harper list. Many of these were written by people who had held important positions in government. Henry L. Stimson's *On Active Service* was an autobiographical volume; Sumner Welles wrote *Time for Decision,* among other books; one of James F. Byrnes' books was *Speaking Frankly*; Justice William O. Douglas made a unique contribution with such books as *Of Men and Mountains* and *Strange Lands and Friendly People*; Chester Bowles' *Ambassador's Report* grew out of his first tour of duty in India. An ambassador of a somewhat younger generation, William Attwood, Ambassador to Guinea and later to Kenya, wrote *The Reds and the Blacks* for publication in 1967; Allen Dulles wrote from his experience in the Central Intelligence Agency and the OSS in *The Craft of Intelligence* and *The Secret Surrender*; and General Maxwell Taylor spoke out in *The Uncertain Trumpet,* as did General Leslie R. Groves in *Now It Can Be Told* and General James M. Gavin in *War and Peace in the Space Age.* Outstanding, too, were books by Adlai Stevenson, among them *Call to Greatness, Friends and Enemies,* and *Looking Outward,* the last a book of addresses concerned with the United Nations. As a human being, a statesman, a thinker, and a stylist, Stevenson ranked high in the affection and esteem of his publishers, particularly of Cass Canfield, whose close friend he was. The firm also has the honor of publishing the American edition of the memoirs of publisher–Prime Minister the Honorable Harold Macmillan, the first volume of which was entitled *Winds of Change.*

Presidents and Prime Ministers help to make history and there are authors competent to write of history in the making—Harrison E. Salisbury, for one. As a correspondent for the *New York Times,* Salisbury spent much time in Russia. He is the author of a number of successful Harper books including *American in Russia* and, early in 1967, *Behind the Lines—Hanoi.* His *Times* colleague Hanson W. Baldwin drew upon his vast knowledge of military tactics to write several volumes, the most recent of which are *World War I: An Outline History* and *Battles Lost and Won: Great Campaigns of World War II.* While Stuart Chase writes for magazines, rather than newspapers, what he has to say is often background material for current news; for example, *The Proper Study of Mankind* and his recent book on the rate of economic growth in the United States, *Money to Grow On.* Jim Bishop was a pioneer in minute-by-minute, fact-by-fact history in such books as *The Day Lincoln Was Shot.* Similarly Walter Lord has a reporter's passion for facts and what he digs up of America's past makes his books, such as *The Good Years* (1900-1914), *A Time to Stand,* and *The Past That Would Not Die,* seem as timely as the morning paper. David Douglas Duncan blended photography and journalism into a unique report on Korea, *This Is War!,* and into two distinctive studies of Picasso and his work. Charles

W. Thayer is both family chronicler (*Muzzy*) and serious writer (*Diplomat* and *Guerrilla*).

The most famous of the reportorial group is, of course, John Gunther. Since the war he has added further *Inside* books on the U.S.A., Africa, Russia, and South America, and revised several of them as changing events and personalities called for updating. The remarkably productive Gunther has also found time to write books on, among others, General MacArthur and Franklin D. Roosevelt, and edited *Procession,* a book of profiles of world leaders taken from his *Inside* books. Once, in recent years, he turned to fiction, writing of Vienna between the wars in his novel *The Lost City.* Twelve of Mr. Gunther's books have been distributed by the Book-of-the-Month Club. His work has also been successful in England and has been translated into over thirty different languages. Excluding the book club distribution, Harper's has sold nearly one and a half million clothbound copies of books by Gunther. Readers everywhere have benefited from his gift for blending factual detail, humorous anecdote, and telling characterization with apt phrasing and colorful style. In 1949, two years after the death of his son John, he wrote a moving memoir entitled *Death Be Not Proud.* The beautifully written story of human frailty in the face of inexorable fate may outlive everything else he has written.

Life has its humor as well as its tragedy and those who have added gaiety to the daily round should begin—alphabetically, at least—with Bennett Cerf, who edited *Out on a Limerick,* a book that those who knew Cerf as a TV personality and columnist went out on a limb to buy. Not wishing to surfeit readers with humor, he also edited *Reading for Pleasure,* an anthology of writings he particularly liked. Emily Kimbrough's felicitously written volumes of travel and personal reminiscences, among them *Forever Old, Forever New* and *Water, Water Everywhere,* are highly informative as well as humorous. Two books of cartoons by Bill Mauldin (his latest is *I've Decided I Want My Seat Back*) are a joy to leaf through; James Thurber, whose name is identified with *The New Yorker,* has a number of books on the Harper list, including such favorites as *Alarms and Diversions, Lanterns and Lances,* and *The Thurber Carnival.* His latest, published posthumously, is called

Thurber & Company. A newcomer to the humorous corner is George Plimpton, editor of the *Paris Review,* who writes with distinction about his experiences as an amateur playing with professionals in baseball and football. His books are *Out of My League* and *Paper Lion,* a recent best seller.

One of the fastest-growing groups of Harper books in recent years comprises those published for boys and girls. This growth is due not only to the exploding birth rate but also to the increasing emphasis on children's reading that has come from parents, teachers, and librarians. Even those pressures would not have stimulated reading had there not also been book editors who insisted on quality and who inspired authors and artists to do their best. It takes a good book to engender a taste for reading and to compete successfully with other interests for an hour in the life of a child—always much longer than any hour in the life of an adult. Chief among such editors is Ursula Nordstrom, a vice-president of the company, whose enterprise and skill have developed the largest list of quality hard-cover books for children published annually and the greatest number of books kept regularly in print. Her staff has grown from three to more than twenty-five as the annual sales of juveniles have grown from a few hundred thousand dollars in the early forties to about ten million in the year ending April 30, 1967. One of Miss Nordstrom's editors, Charlotte Zolotow, has fourteen books on the Harper list for younger children, including *Mr. Rabbit and the Lovely Present,* a runner-up for the Caldecott Medal. Miss Nordstrom is an author too—in 1960 *The Secret Language* was published, a story book about boarding school life for ages seven to nine.

There are two kinds of authors who get little encouragement from Miss Nordstrom—the one who asks what type of book she is looking for and the one who outlines an idea for a book he will write if she is interested. What she and her editors are looking for is the author who is fired with an idea; then their job is to stimulate him to use his imagination and to guide him, if necessary, to bring his idea to fruition. Miss Nordstrom's main concern is that author and artist be honest in dealing with whatever aspect of the child's world they are describing and illustrating.

Sometimes this concern for integrity gets author, illustrator, and publisher into difficulties with adults. Once, a librarian told Miss Nordstrom that she did not like Emily Cheney Neville's *It's Like This, Cat,* which won the Newbery Medal in 1964. Miss Nordstrom expressed regret and asked why. The librarian replied that the boy did not show his father sufficient respect and that she thought young people should respect their parents. Miss Nordstrom agreed but pointed out that in real life young people did not always do so, and that Mrs. Neville's book was about a boy who, at least at the beginning of the story, did not have a good relationship with his father. One of the most popular books of a number by Ruth Krauss is *A Hole Is To Dig,* yet it, too, was criticized by one librarian who was appalled by one of its definitions: "A face is so you can make faces"—for she did not want *her* children making faces.

In 1945 Miss Nordstrom published *Call Me Charley,* by Jesse Jackson, who had aroused her interest when he told of his boyhood in Columbus, Ohio, where he was the only Negro boy in the neighborhood. The intensity of his experience was later conveyed in text and pictures and its success brought further books. Such creative talent is what Miss Nordstrom and her associates are constantly seeking, although she admits that talent is sometimes difficult to recognize, especially if only part of a manuscript is in hand at its first reading. Often an author must be asked to work harder on a certain episode, or to go deeper, or to be utterly honest. One author, Mary Stolz, revised her manuscript *In a Mirror* eight times—and it was her sixth book. It received the Child Study Association's Children's Book Award in 1953. Some years later two of her books, *The Noonday Friends* and *Belling the Tiger,* were runners-up for the Newbery Medal.

Occasionally a manuscript comes in that is letter-perfect, as was E. B. White's *Stuart Little.* Here the major problem was in finding the right artist. After eight had submitted sketches, Miss Nordstrom asked Garth Williams to try his hand. He was able to create the deft, droll characters that helped make Stuart's world believable. Thus when the doctor wanted to listen to Stuart's heart, Stuart was drawn standing up; other artists had drawn him lying down, looking like a little dead

Garth Williams' drawing of Stuart Little.

mouse. A few years later came *Charlotte's Webb,* also illustrated by Garth Williams; it is one of the classics of our time.

Among other authors and artists who have contributed to the success of Harper children's books in the past twenty-five years are, for younger readers, Crosby Bonsall, Syd Hoff, Crockett Johnson, Anita and Arnold Lobel, Karla Kuskin, Ezra Jack Keats, Russell and Lillian Hoban, Tomi Ungerer, Gene Zion and Margaret Bloy Graham, and Maurice Sendak. Such authors as Annabel and Edgar Johnson, Louise Fitzhugh, Nan Gilbert, Betty Baker, and Jennie Lindquist have written books for the enjoyment of older children. Authors such as Millicent E. Selsam have equal facility in writing for the younger and older reader.

In 1950 Maurice Sendak was a twenty-two-year-old artist, helping create window displays for the F. A. O. Schwarz toy store in New York, when he was introduced to Miss Nordstrom by Frances Chrystie, the store's book buyer, who said he was an artist who should be illustrating books. Sendak was soon given a manuscript to illustrate, and by 1952, when he collaborated with Ruth Krauss on *A Hole Is To Dig,* he was

From Where the Wild Things Are *by Maurice Sendak.*

earning enough to leave his job at the store and become a free-lance artist. He wrote and illustrated the first *Nutshell Library*, a tiny boxed set of four books, which became the outstanding success of the 1962 season. He was a five-time runner-up for the coveted Caldecott Medal before he won it in 1964 for *Where the Wild Things Are*. Sendak once received a letter from a boy. "How much does it cost to get to where the wild things are?" he asked. "If it is not too expensive my sister and I want to spend the summer there. Please answer soon." *Time* magazine

has called Sendak "the Picasso of children's books" and *The New Yorker* published a Profile of him in its issue of January 22, 1966.

The Caldecott Medal was won by Marc Simont in 1957 for *A Tree Is Nice,* a story written by Janice May Udry. Two further Child Study Association awards were won by Meindert DeJong for *The House of Sixty Fathers* and Natalie Savage Carlson for *The Empty Schoolhouse.* Other awards in children's books have been won by Harper authors and artists, but what pleases them and Miss Nordstrom almost as much are selections made each year by the American Library Association as Notable Books for Children. In the last five years Harper juveniles have twice outnumbered those of any other publisher, and they almost consistently take first place in the annual *New York Times Book Review*'s list of the best books of the preceding year. Librarians and reviewers have taken special note of the best-selling I Can Read books, begun in 1957 with publication of *Little Bear* by Else Holmelund Minarik. There are now sixty-seven titles in the series. Also highly regarded by librarians and critics are the American Heritage Junior Library Books (now numbering thirty-five titles) and the Horizon Caravel Books (twenty-three titles) which Harper distributes.

Frequently Miss Nordstrom brings out books that were published originally for adults but have been adapted for younger readers, such as the scientific works of Arthur C. Clarke, issued originally in the staple books department. Clarke's *The Exploration of Space* was published in 1952 by George Jones, in the department of staple books; this brilliant book became a dual selection of the Book-of-the-Month Club and has since sold, both in hard-cover and paperback editions, in the millions of copies. It has often been called the "Bible of the space age" and has been followed by *Interplanetary Flight, Profiles of the Future,* and *Voices from the Sky.*

Other scientific authors published by Jones include Sir Bernard Lovell, D. S. Halacy, Jr., and Fred Hoyle. Hoyle, probably the world's outstanding cosmologist, is also a sort of Renaissance man. His associates frequently refer to him as "Lorenzo the Hoyle." He has produced, in addition to his astronomical works, six science-fiction novels, two plays, one produced by the Mermaid Theatre in London, and an opera, for which Leo Smith of the University of Chicago wrote the score.

Science in Everyday Things was the first in a series of four question-and-answer books by William C. Vergara. All have sold widely in America and in England and have been translated not only into European languages but also into Arabic, Urdu, and Japanese. Sharing honors with Vergara in number of translations is Dr. Grantly Dick-Read, whose *Childbirth Without Fear* came out in 1944. Dr. Dick-Read gave comfort and guidance to untold mothers who wanted to bear their children naturally. He was a pioneer in natural childbirth and, like most pioneers, he was almost fanatical in his devotion to it. Despite Harper's efforts to publicize and sell the book, the author felt that not enough was being done. When 100,000 copies had been sold, Jones did the usual thing of sending a leather-bound copy inscribed to the author, and then sat back expecting the usual expression of delight. Dr. Dick-Read wrote: "Thank you very much for the handsomely bound book. However, I wish to point out that there are 3½ million babies born every year in the U.S., and I think you have merely scratched the surface." *Childbirth Without Fear* sold over 275,000 hard-bound copies in this country and a million throughout the world.

Two other best-selling staple authors are Frank N. Magill and Rudolf Flesch. Magill's great series of reference books, beginning with *Masterpieces of World Literature in Digest Form,* has been published over the last twelve or more years. These books are among the most popular of all reference books in the fields of literature and philosophy. Rudolf Flesch was an Austrian refugee from the 1938 *Anschluss.* In a few years he had so mastered the English language that he was appointed consultant to the Associated Press on writing style. His early books, such as *The Art of Readable Writing,* made an enormous contribution in simplifying journalistic and business writing. His later best seller *Why Johnny Can't Read* created a nation-wide controversy, helped along by postpublication serialization in a hundred and twenty-five daily newspapers and by the publication of paperback editions. Irate educators wrote letters to Harper's protesting that an honored imprint should not be sullied by such a book, and academic pressure on the college department's editors and salesmen proved embarrassing. However, many educators took the position that this book contributed to a healthy discussion of the problem of how to teach children to read.

Sometimes even editors are easy marks for books advertised as aids to their craftsmanship. Such a book is *Brewer's Dictionary of Phrase and Fable.* It has had a very long history, having originally been published ninety-five years ago by Cassell. In 1952 Jones became publisher of the American edition, which has since sold over 50,000 copies. John B. Opdycke has contributed several English usage books and his *Harper's*

English Grammar, originally published in 1941, is still in print in a revised version available in both paper and hard-bound editions.

The staple department's books of games are outstanding. Margaret Mulac contributed ten books, all of which have been widely used by schools, libraries, and the general public. In the field of travel, Jones wanted a book about England written by an American who shared his warmth for that country. He commissioned Ruth McKenney to take on this project, and with her husband, Richard Bransten, "A Highly Informal Guide" was produced called *Here's England,* published in 1950. This book is still selling actively. One of its delightful features is the illustrations contributed by Osbert Lancaster. Currently a series of beautifully illustrated travel books entitled the *Companion Guides* is being issued in collaboration with Messrs. Collins of London.

A vocational series, started ten years ago, has also proved its popularity. About seventeen titles have been published, with more to come. The books are entitled *So You Want to Be a Doctor, So You Want to Be a Lawyer,* and so on, the vocations being limited to those requiring graduate study. Thus *So You Want to Be a Publisher* will not be included, although Jones might try his hand at such a book anyway; since he retired in 1966, he now has time for his own writing. He took with him a book that he had advertised as the leading book in its field. It was Buckley's *The Retirement Handbook.*

Departmental publishing permits a wider circulation for many books whose subject matter covers more than one field; often two departments share in the costs of the same book and double its potential sale through promotion to distinct markets. Thus Magill's *Masterpieces of Christian Literature* was a joint publication of the staple and the religious departments. Such an arrangement has the advantage of two groups of salesmen who call on booksellers. All books published in what is called "trade complex" are sold by trade salesmen, yet many of these titles can also be marketed to religious bookstores covered by the religious department's salesmen. Examples are the juvenile *The Tall Book of Bible Stories* and Aldous Huxley's *The Perennial Philosophy* published by the trade department. Similarly, religious books can often reach more booksellers by being catalogued with general books of nonfiction and sold as well by trade salesmen. Examples of this cooperative venture are the best sellers of Fosdick and the books of Teilhard de Chardin.

Père Teilhard was one of the most creative minds of this century and it is one of life's ironies that this devout French priest and scholarly anthropologist did not live to see the world-wide influence of his thought. He died, relatively unknown, in New York City on Easter Sunday of 1955. Teilhard was a loyal member of the Society of Jesus and when his order denied him the privilege of publishing his religious and scientific works he was obedient to his authorities. However, such restrictions did not bind his literary executor, Mlle. Jeanne Mortier, to whom he bequeathed his manuscripts with instructions that a committee be named to decide whether or not to publish. The decision to publish resulted in English-language rights being entrusted to Messrs. Collins, of London, who generously turned American rights over to Harper's.

The first of Père Teilhard's works to be issued was his basic scientific book *The Phenomenon of Man.* Its publication called for restraint and good taste. To publicize the prohibition to publish during Teilhard's lifetime would have placed the liberal—and generally younger— members of the Jesuit order in a more difficult position, and while news- paper publicity might have increased book sales initially, it might also have boomeranged into a Vatican order to place his books on the Index. In order that the book could be presented as of the greatest scientific and philosophical interest, Sir Julian Huxley wrote an intro- duction for the English and American editions. Then came difficulties of obtaining a satisfactory translation from the French, owing in part to the fact that Teilhard was blazing new trails of thought and had resorted to neologisms and coined phrases that were difficult to translate. By 1959 the English translation by Bernard Wall was approved by the French committee and published. The public response, both in England and in America, was more immediate and generous than any of the editors had dared to hope. The book was accepted on its own merits, which was right, and leading Catholic writers reviewed it with praise, as did such authorities as Arnold Toynbee, who called it "The #1 book of the year," and Loren Eiseley, a leading American anthropologist. Seven books of this great thinker have followed, including the deeply spiritual *The Divine Milieu* and *The Future of Man,* which received the Thomas More Association Medal in 1965.

Dr. Albert Schweitzer is an equally towering figure of our time, and Harper's has published several anthologies of his writing and two important biographies. Erica Anderson, whose "Albert Schweitzer" received an Oscar as the best documentary film of the year, wrote a moving book, *Albert Schweitzer's Gift of Friendship,* and her own photographs, some of which illustrated this work, also made possible two other volumes of text and pictures depicting Schweitzer's life and work. *Dr. Schweitzer of Lambaréné,* by Norman Cousins, published in 1960, remains one of the best introductions to the man and his impact on today's world.

Schweitzer, the most famous of modern missionaries, is, however, not a hero to many theologically conservative Protestants. And they, too, know how to write books that attract wide readership. Witness Elisabeth Elliot, who wrote the story of the missionaries, including her husband, who were murdered by the Auca Indians. That book, *Through Gates of Splendor,* featured by the *Reader's Digest,* sold 100,000 copies in ten months and has been followed by a novel, *No Graven Image,* which gives compassionate insight into the problems faced by missionaries.

The religious book department also issues books of social concern. Dorothy Day, of the *Catholic Worker,* is a valued author, as is Martin Luther King, Jr., who was awarded the Nobel Peace Prize in 1964. I went to Montgomery, Alabama, to convince Dr. King that he should undertake a book on the Montgomery bus strike and to offer what aid we could to enable him to write it. *Stride Toward Freedom* was the result, and it has been followed by *Why We Can't Wait,* and *Where Do We Go from Here?,* books written during his personal involvement in work for social equality. Theological books have been equally stressed with such featured authors as H. Richard Niebuhr, Paul Tillich, Dietrich Bonhoeffer, Karl Barth, Rudolf Bultmann, Nels Ferré, Walter Horton, Daniel Williams, and Jaroslav Pelikan. The Harper list of theologians is almost endless, as is the list of clergymen, such as Samuel Shoemaker, R. J. McCracken, Howard Thurman, Gerald Kennedy, Harold Bosley, John Sutherland Bonnell, Helmut

Thielicke, Dean Samuel H. Miller, and Bishop James Pike, who have attempted to make theological ideas relevant to laymen. For years two of the department's most productive authors have been Margaret Applegarth and the Swiss physician Paul Tournier, whose books, such as *The Meaning of Persons,* speak to the needs of the "whole man." Another physician, Franz Winkler, wrote *Man: The Bridge Between Two Worlds,* now in a paperback edition. A current best seller is an anthology edited by Charles L. Wallis. It is called *The Treasure Chest,* a name inspired by an early-nineteenth-century iron trunk that survived the perils of Harper fires and moves.

For thirty years the greatest of religious books, the King James Bible, was carried in many editions and several translations and was only recently sold to another house. The Bible operation was managed by David H. Scott and later by Fred C. Becker. Scott was also responsible for the painstaking work that resulted in *Harper's Bible Dictionary,* of which nearly a half million copies have been sold. Becker joined Harper's in 1935 and has directed the sales of religious books with the help of an expanding corps of loyal salesmen, who, since 1931, have helped the department to show a profit and to increase its business, decade by decade, in geometric progression.

John B. Chambers was associate director of the religious book department until his death in 1955, and he was succeeded by M. L. Arnold, of the Beacon Press, who was a pioneer in publishing quality paperbacks. Shortly after joining Harper's, Arnold launched such a series in Torchbooks, named for the House colophon. He was made manager of the religious department in July, 1965, but was advanced later to senior vice-president in charge of the elementary and high school division ("El-Hi"). The religious book department is now directed by Erik A. Langkjaer. Selling and promoting religious books to specialized markets is a difficult job, and the Harper salesmen have been aided by a sort of credo that is regularly printed on the back of religious book catalogues: "It is the policy of the Religious Book Department of Harper & Row to publish books that represent important religious groupings, express well-articulated thought, combine intellectual competence and felicitous style, add to the wealth of religious literature irrespective of creedal origin, and aid the cause of religion without proselyting for any particular sect."

This department has sponsored a Religious Perspectives series under the general direction of Ruth Nanda Anshen; *Unity in Freedom,* by Augustin Cardinal Bea, is one of the recent titles published. For the trade department, she is editing a series called World Perspectives, in which Erich Fromm's *The Art of Loving* has been a best seller.

Dr. Anshen was introduced to Harper's by Ordway Tead, whose *extra-liber* activities acquainted him with many potential writers for his department of social and economic books. For fifteen years, beginning in 1938, he was chairman of the Board of Higher Education of New York City and, as such, he was administrative head of the four large municipal colleges. This concern for higher education was reflected in many books that he sponsored, including *The Conflict in Education,* by Robert M. Hutchins, and several important ones in educational philosophy by Abraham Maslow, Theodore A. Brameld, and others. Professor Huston Smith, of the Massachusetts Institute of Technology, wrote *The Purposes of Higher Education* and *Condemned to Meaning.* College presidents and college trustees bought *Higher Education in Transition,* by Brubacher and Rudy, and *Goals for American Education* by the President's Commission of which Tead was himself a member.

Since managerial and labor relations was an area of Tead's special interest (he was one-time president of the Society for the Advancement of Management), it was natural that many leading writers came with this type of book to him: Philip Taft, of Brown University, with a labor history; Florence Peterson with a popular *American Labor Unions;* Jack Barbash with *The Practice of Unionism;* and Donald E. Super and J. O. Crites with their authoritative *Appraising Vocational Fitness.* Outstanding works in the field of political science include the definitive volume of William Mosher on public personnel administration, the several books of Marshall Dimock, papers of Miss Mary P. Follett edited by Henry C. Metcalf, and Lewis Mayers' *The American Legal System* (revised 1964). Outstanding in the field of finance and banking are *The Reserve Banks and the Money Market,* by W. Randolph Burgess, and *The Interpretation of Financial Statements,* by Benjamin Graham and Charles McGolrick. This book went into its second revised edition in 1965, the year that Graham's now classic *The Intelligent Investor* came out in its third revision. Herbert V. Prochnow, president of the First National Bank of Chicago, edited a book on the Federal Reserve System, but his name is perhaps better known for his several books, including *The Public Speaker's Treasure Chest,* that give public speakers all they can possibly use of wit and wisdom, epigrams and satire, humor and quotations—"Source material to make your speech sparkle."

Series of books published by this department include the Annual Lectureship of the John Dewey Society, the books of the Industrial Relations Research Association, and a series for the National Council of Churches centered upon the theme of Christianity and modern ethical problems. Under the guidance of Dr. Louis Finkelstein, chancellor of the Jewish Theological Seminary, Tead published for a number of years the proceedings of the Conference on Science, Philosophy and Religion, to which a variety of notable speakers contributed.

Tead also introduced the work of several general authors, such as Rudolf Flesch with *The Art of Plain Talk* and *The Art of Readable Writing,* which, along with books like Bonaro Overstreet's *Understanding Fear* and Huston Smith's *The Religions of Man,* were widely sold through bookstores.

On Tead's retirement in 1961, the direction of the department was given to his assistant, Richard B. McAdoo, who had also been developing a specialty in nature and outdoor books. One of the first was *Familiar Animals of America,* by Will Barker, with illustrations by Carl Burger. Its popularity started a series including *Familiar Insects of America, Familiar Reptiles and Amphibians,* and *Familiar Garden Birds.* Under the later editorship of John Macrae this program of nature and outdoor books has grown to a list of ten to twelve titles a year, the majority of which are proving to be long-term books with a steady sale. Representative titles are *The Complete Field Guide to American Wildlife,* by Collins, *The Face of North America,* by Farb, *Downstream: A Natural History of the River,* by Bardach, and an Outdoor Life series with books on guns, hunting, and camping. Tying in with the growing public interest in conservation are several recent books, such as *Wildflowers in Color*.

The department continued also to develop the editorial lines laid down earlier. It published perhaps the foremost author writing in the field of management, Peter F. Drucker, widely known for *The Practice of Management* and *Managing for Results*. In the field of social problems there are such books as *Dark Ghetto,* by Kenneth Clark, *The Wasted Americans,* by Edgar May, and *The City Is the Frontier,* by Charles Abrams, another Harper author who has been profiled in *The New Yorker.* In addition the department has brought out *The Culturally Deprived Child,* by Frank Riessman, and *Comparative Guide to American Colleges,* by Cass and Birnbaum. While all these books are sold in bookstores and in colleges, they have also been marketed extensively by direct mail to special audiences.

Between 1945 and 1960 the sales volume of social and economic books rose from about $350,000 per year to over $600,000. By 1965 the total for these and the nature and outdoor books had climbed to $1,200,000, reflecting both a strong back list and a quality selection of new books.

Several other departments in the House were making increasing use of direct-mail selling to extend the market for their books, and in 1945 the mail-order department was born. Its function was nothing less than to reach out for new book buyers, lovers of books who, for one reason or another, were not normally exposed to Harper's books. The idea worked. Thousands of books poured out of Harper's warehouses bound for homes all over the country. Joseph R. Vergara, who was given the direction of this department, soon began to call on the editorial departments for new books tailored for mail-order buyers. In the end, Vergara was encouraged to edit his own books for direct-by-mail sales. Among his several ventures were *Look Better, Feel Better,* by Dr. Bess Mensendieck, and a series of books done jointly with *Esquire, Golf, Ski,* and *Bride's* magazines. Books by Julius Boros, Candy Jones, Bonnie Prudden, Gene Leone, and Dorothy Hayden were successful. Then one day a brilliant diplomat at the United Nations, Ben Cohen,

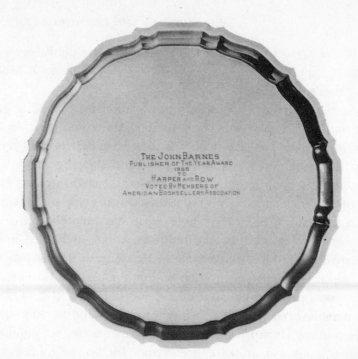

The silver tray presented by the American Booksellers' Association in 1966; a similar one was received in 1964.

and an equally brilliant young Israeli journalist, Moshe Sachs, approached Harper's with a dream. They wanted to capture the whole world in one volume—all the basic political, geographic, and historical information about all the nations, conveniently arranged in one huge reference book. This dream became the *Worldmark Encyclopedia of the Nations,* now in its third, revised edition.

In 1966 the *New York Times Book Review* published its nineteenth selection of the best books of the preceding year, and for the fourteenth time Harper's topped the list with the largest number of adult titles of any one publisher, this time with 15 out of 203 titles of some 58 publishers. Shortly thereafter the American Library Association announced its selection of Notable Books of 1965; for the sixth time in eight years Harper's titles (of books from adult departments) totaled more than those of any other house. The House did not do so well in another selection—American books for the White House reference library; of the 1,780 titles chosen in 1963 the top five publishers were Macmillan (124), Harvard University Press (109), Houghton Mifflin (93), Scribner's (89), Harper's (88).

In 1964 the American Booksellers' Association established a Publisher of the Year Award, with the 2,100 bookstores and book departments voting for the publisher who was considered best in sales representation, advertising and promotion campaigns, shipping and billing policies, handling book returns, and expressing general interest in the welfare of the trade. Harper's won the award in 1964 and again in 1966. Since World War II, the whole world has been clamoring for books—primarily for scientific and technical works—published in the English language. To meet the demand the House set up an international division which is under the direction of Emile Dubrule. The international division operates from four main centers: Harper & Row, Ltd., London, is a sales agency responsible for the warehousing, promotion, and distribution in the United Kingdom of all Harper books not published in British editions and of the entire Harper list on the continent of Europe and in the Middle East, subject to territorial rights. Harper & Row, Ltd. is managed by Godfrey Golzen from 69 Great Russell Street, London W.C. 1. Here also is the office of Michael Canfield, who, as Harper liaison with British authors and publishers, can trace a heritage all the way back to Obadiah Rich.

In 1965 Harper & Row set up a distribution and promotion center in Australia—Publishers Service Centre Pty Ltd. in Sydney, N.S.W.— to handle sales in Australia and New Zealand. Special salesmen cover the Philippines, India, and other parts of Southeast Asia. In 1962 an affiliated company, John Weatherhill, Inc., was established in Tokyo to handle sales promotion in Japan and Korea. This affiliate also manufactures an English-language International Series that features inexpensive editions of Harper books that are most in demand in the overseas market. Currently about 200 titles are thus sold in areas where the U.S. edition would be prohibitively expensive. John Weatherhill, Inc. has also started a program of publishing Japanese-language translations of some of the best-selling juvenile titles.

The most recent addition to the international division is a depository in Mexico City, under the direction of Louis A. Nistal, who promotes and distributes the international editions and a selected list of the regular U.S. editions throughout Latin America. In 1966 the annual income from sales in the international division almost doubled that of the preceding year.

Working side by side with Dubrule and his colleagues is the foreign-rights department, under the direction of Miss Lillian Hansen. This department arranges for the sale of publishing rights on American books to British publishers and disposes of translation rights. Books are generally offered through commission agents on the Continent.

From early in the twentieth century until a few years ago, Harper books were sold in Canada by the Musson Book Company, of Toronto. In 1966, Robert I. Fitzhenry resigned as director of sales of the trade department to organize his own Canadian company, with some financial backing from the House, to distribute Harper books in Canada, a market that has grown in importance steadily since Canada became a Common-wealth nation one hundred years ago. Fitzhenry's predecessor was the able William H. Rose, who cut short his Harper career by an early retirement. Fitzhenry's position, in turn, was taken by William Ash-worth, who now supervises the work of twenty salesmen who have as friends, as well as customers, more than two thousand American book-sellers who funnel books to the American reading public. Three times a year, Ashworth—as does Becker—corrals his salesmen for conferences in New York, where the editors do the job of selling forthcoming books to the salesmen.

The trade advertising department is now under the direction of Mrs. Frances Lindley, whose advertising knowledge and skill as a copy writer are exceeded only by her literary competence. While her budgeted expenditure is nearly half a million dollars, it must cover a wide assort-ment of titles. Fortunately authors and books often make good copy; hence the publicity department, directed by Stuart Harris, helps to spread the news of books in the press and by radio and TV.

The production department is under the direction of Daniel F. Bradley, who is also a vice-president of the company. He came to Harper's in 1942 from the Haddon Craftsmen as assistant to Rushmore, and when Rushmore retired in 1950 Bradley took charge. Since 1950, as the volume of business (excluding elementary and high school books) has multiplied by approximately six to one, the pressures and personnel of book production have increased also. His staff now numbers nearly sixty, including book designers and copy editors, whose work is vital in the early life of any book. With hundreds of titles in production each year, each of which must be manufactured in a salable and attractive format that is at the same time appropriate to the book's content and character, this department is extremely important in the firm's operations.

Some books involve complicated production procedures; others require an accelerated schedule to meet an early publication date. At such times the problems that beset Bradley and his colleagues are multiplied. An illustration of this kind of problem was Gunther's *Inside U.S.A.* (1947), on which the production schedule became more complicated as the manuscript grew in size, and the book's timeliness compelled early publication. Before the author had written the last chapter of the book, he was already reading galleys, arguing with libel lawyers, and considering suggestions from experts on the first part of the book. Further complications resulted from the fact that the manuscript could not be turned in in sequence, because elections and the resulting political changes were bound to affect some parts of the book more than others. When the Book-of-the-Month Club chose the volume as a selection, this necessitated exact timing, extra paper, and an increase in the Harper run to 125,000 copies. Nevertheless, finished copies of the thousand-page book started coming from the printer three weeks and two days after the last bit of proof was O.K.'d, though the entire process had taken several months. While this was a production *tour de force* by present-day standards, Bradley took little comfort in the knowledge that after only five years in business Harper had manufactured a volume of one of Walter Scott's novels in twenty-one hours.

The production department serves all the editorial departments, as do the accounting, billing, and shipping departments. Supervision of these operations was largely the responsibility of Harwood even before the death of Hoyns. In 1945 Harwood was made executive vice-

President Johnson greets Raymond C. Harwood, president of the American Book Publishers' Council, at a White House reception, April 11, 1965, honoring those who contributed to the passage of the Elementary and Secondary Education Act of 1965.

president, at which time Canfield became chairman of the Board and
MacGregor president. Ten years later, Harwood was made president
and chief executive officer. Thus recognition was given to his managerial
abilities, his intimate knowledge of all the details of the business, and
his wisdom and tact in dealing both with individuals and with matters
involving broad publishing policy. Harwood's competence was also
recognized by his fellow publishers when he was elected in 1964 to
a two-year term as president of the American Book Publishers' Council.
With Harwood's becoming the president of Harper's in 1955, Mac-
Gregor was advanced to Board chairmanship with further opportunities
to develop his editorial concerns. Canfield, eager to give more time to
authors and to properly direct the expanding editorial program, became
chairman of the Editorial Board in 1955; he did, however, continue as
chairman of the executive committee of the Board of Directors. To assist
Harwood in a managerial capacity, Evan Thomas was made director of
trade books, and in 1958 he was named executive vice-president.

Of all Harper departments, the medical and college textbooks are the
most specialized and self-contained. The Paul B. Hoeber subsidiary was
discontinued as a separate corporation in 1961, when it became a co-
ordinated department. During the last two decades it has expanded its
publication of medical journals, of which it now publishes seven. *Psycho-
somatic Medicine* was the first one to be published, and others include
Fertility and Sterility, Obstetrics and Gynecology, and *Clinical Chemistry.*
Major book undertakings of the fifties were a three-volume *Clinical
Neurology,* by A. B. Baker, M.D. (revised and enlarged in 1962), and
a three-volume *Anatomy for Surgeons,* by W. Henry Hollinshead, of
the Mayo Clinic. In 1962 Dr. Hollinshead wrote *Textbook of Anatomy*
for freshman medical students, a book that spearheaded a program of
basic medical textbooks. Perhaps the most distinguished aspect of
Hoeber's medical program has been roentgenology, and pioneer books
were issued just as the X-ray was coming into use. Building on this
foundation, Hoeber has published, among other titles, *Physical Founda-
tions of Radiology,* now in its third edition, and *Roentgen Diagnosis
of the Heart,* the first comprehensive book on the subject. In 1959 he
published *Essentials of Roentgen Interpretation,* by Paul and Juhl,

which has become the standard general text in the field. Recently this department has absorbed the W. F. Prior Co. and will continue distributing the five sets of loose-leaf medical references for practitioners established more than fifty years ago by Prior, who had once been with Harper's.

When Hoeber started in 1937, he and two others carried on the work. Now the department numbers thirty-five and a three-and-a-half-million-dollar volume is projected for the sesquicentennial year.

The expansion of the college department has more than paralleled the growth of the college population. When Tyler retired in 1958, he was replaced briefly by Kenneth Demaree; for several years now James M. Cron has been director of the department. Cron started with Harper's in 1947 as a salesman in the upper Midwest. He was so successful in attracting important authors from Minnesota and Wisconsin to the Harper fold that he was named a regional editor responsible for author contacts in the ten big schools of the Midwest. In 1958 he was brought to the New York office.

To list important authors and titles that the college department has issued since 1945 would take numerous pages. Some books begun in the twenties, thirties, and forties are still available in revised editions; for example, Oliver P. Chitwood's *A History of Colonial America* (Third Edition), William E. Lunt's *History of England* (Fourth), Carl Stephenson's *Mediaeval History* (Fourth, as revised by Bryce Lyon), and Michael F. Guyer's *Animal Biology* (Fifth, as revised by Charles E. Lane).

Currently the department's best sellers are: Leonard Broom and Philip Selznick's *Sociology* (Third Edition)—initially a Row, Peterson title; John A. Garraty's *The American Nation* (published jointly with *American Heritage*); Charles W. Keenan and Jesse H. Wood's *General College Chemistry* (Third); Paul H. Mussen, John J. Conger, and Jerome Kagan's *Child Development and Personality* (Second); Richard G. Lipsey and Peter O. Steiner's *Economics*; Yvone Lenard's *Parole et Pensée*; Herbert J. Klausmeier and William Goodwin's *Learning and Human Abilities* (Second); Zenia Sacks Da Silva's *Beginning Spanish;* and W. Gordon Whaley *et al.*'s *Principles of Biology* (Third).

Cron has an outstanding roster of advisory editors from leading universities who help to develop important books in their respective disciplines. In addition, many other authorities are called upon to advise and review titles and specific courses. Eleven staff editors, four field editors, eight rewrite editors, and fifteen production editors are required to obtain manuscripts and get them ready for production. Roy Arnold is director of marketing to colleges and, with his associate, supervises the work of five regional sales managers and forty-four salesmen. A staff of seven handle research and ten do advertising and promotion. In all, more than one hundred and fifty men and women are required to carry on a publishing program that will pass the ten-million-dollar mark at the end of the 1967 fiscal year.

In addition to the general increased production of textbooks, both hard-bound and paperback, this department is alert to new educational developments affecting future publishing programs. Cron foresees that in ten years or so he will not be a publisher of textbooks *per se* but a producer of educational materials, in which the book will still be central but will be surrounded by tape recordings, filmstrips, motion pictures, and computer programs, either for instruction or testing. Definite steps have been taken in this direction, as witness the success of the tape recordings produced to accompany basic language texts, and an introductory-biology project, recently undertaken, which will integrate text, laboratory experiments, tape recordings, and motion pictures.

In the field of supplementary or assigned reading in the universities, paperbacks have made and continue to make an important contribution. Material of this sort is supplied by Torchbooks and Colophon Books, the two quality paperback lines, with presently almost 700 titles available, the bulk of which are reprints of established scholarly works in various fields. Perennial Library, the latest paperback line, is lower-priced and aimed at school and college students with the emphasis on literature. Cass Canfield, Jr., is the publisher of these three paperback lines, which for the next fiscal year should produce net sales of nearly three million dollars.

An effort to publish high-school books in the nineteen-thirties and forties proved unsuccessful, although Richard M. Pearson, who was placed in charge of this department, brought in some books of good quality. Sales were never sufficient to maintain a large sales force adequate to meet the competition. Pearson resigned to become editorial head of Macmillan's schoolbook operation, and the department was discontinued in 1951. Shortly thereafter, the rapidly growing school population demonstrated to Harper's management that this challenging field could not be overlooked by a House that prided itself on publishing significant books in nearly every area of human interest. To regain its enviable nineteenth-century position as a schoolbook publisher, Harper's resorted to a twentieth-century method, the merger. On April 30, 1962, Harper & Brothers merged with Row, Peterson & Company, of Evanston, Illinois, and the firm name was changed to Harper & Row, Publishers, Incorporated.

Row, Peterson & Company was established by R. K. Row and Isaac Peterson in 1906. Their resources were $5,000 in cash, a tiny office in downtown Chicago, and a manuscript with a great potential. It was *Essential Studies in English,* written by Mr. Row in association with Miss Carolyn Robbins, a fellow graduate student of the University of Chicago. Mr. Peterson had been a salesman for D. C. Heath & Company and in the new firm assumed responsibility for sales. Row handled the office and editorial work. With his book selling at the rate of 100,000 a year, there were profits to put into editorial projects. From the beginning the Row emphasis was to edit meticulously and test widely, and some text programs were worked over for ten years before publication. In 1932 Row died (his partner had predeceased him) and so did not live to see the 1936 issue of the Alice and Jerry readers, the firm's most successful program.

These readers, created by Mabel O'Donnell, brought a new editorial idea: original continuous story material with assured appeal to children, backed up by supplementary materials and teaching aids and presented in the most lavishly printed form heretofore seen in schoolbooks—four-color offset. The combination was an immense success. The *Alice and Jerry* series swept competition aside and has sold almost one hundred million copies. A British adaptation of the series has captured an estimated 70 per cent of the total market for basic reading texts in Britain. Science "Unitexts," each dealing with a special theme, grew to 87, from grades 1 through 9, and were aided, beginning

in 1946, by filmstrips. A rich assortment of textbooks in English, mathematics, history, and social studies was gradually developed, so that in
1962 the business had branch offices in New York and California and
employed sixty-eight salesmen and eight women consultants to visit
schools and school systems. Jack E. Witmer is now director of marketing, with an expanding sales staff. Joseph F. Littell is editor-in-chief; the
editorial department is developing programs in "language arts"—
grammar, composition, literature, and spelling—and new programs in
mathematics and social studies. These will round out an elementary and
junior high school program consisting of the highly successful Today's
Basic Science series and the Harper & Row Basic Reading Program
(successor to Alice and Jerry).

With the merger of Harper & Brothers and Row, Peterson & Company, the elementary and high school division (El-Hi) remained in
Evanston under the direction of Gordon M. Jones, who since the merger
has been chairman of the Board of the new company. Soon afterward,
Maynard B. Hites, previously sales manager, took over operation of the
El-Hi division. In 1965, Walter Brackman was named executive vice-
president. Early in 1966, Brackman became chairman of the El-Hi Advisory Board, and M. L. Arnold was transferred from the General
Division to Evanston as executive vice-president.

Harwood, continuing as president of Harper & Row and chief executive officer, assumed the responsibility of directing and coordinating this
large publishing enterprise—a task he has ably fulfilled. He turned over
the direction of fiscal policies to T. J. Ahlberg, who was named senior
vice-president and treasurer. Louis F. Haynie was named secretary.
Thomas is Arnold's New York counterpart, and he shares executive
and operating responsibilities with Richard B. McAdoo, recently named
general manager of the General Division and made a vice-president.
McAdoo's former editorial responsibilities have been assumed by John
Macrae, who is now in charge of Special Trade books, publishing the
nonfiction issued by the social and economic, the nature, and the staple
books departments. The managing editor of General Trade books is
M. S. Wyeth, Jr.

The merger of Harper & Brothers and Row, Peterson & Company

50 DEEPWOOD DRIVE
HAMDEN 17, CONNECTICUT

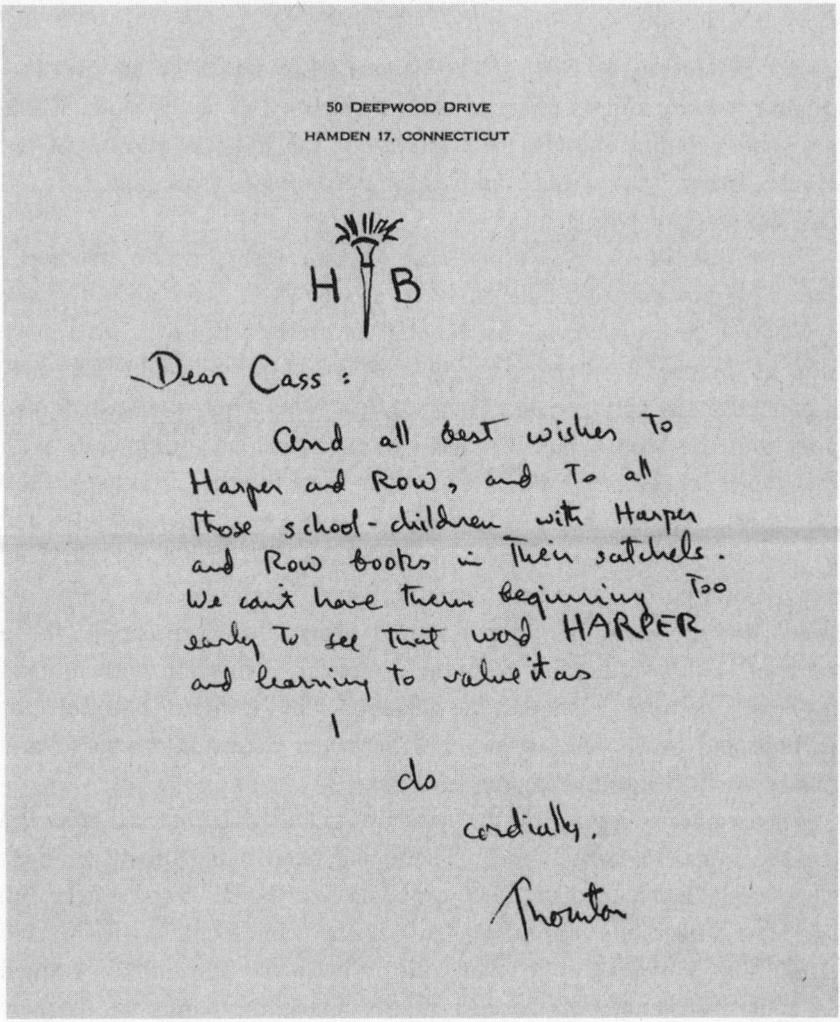

H B

Dear Cass:

And all best wishes to Harper and Row, and to all those school-children with Harper and Row books in their satchels. We can't have them beginning too early to see that word HARPER and learning to value it as I do

Cordially,

Thornton

A letter from Thornton Wilder to Cass Canfield referring to the merger.

strengthened the total outreach to colleges through combined titles and salesmen; it broadened the distribution of trade titles, particularly of juvenile books, through the El-Hi division's work with school libraries. But, most of all, the merger rounded out the Harper publishing program to include nearly every interest that books may serve. Because Harper & Brothers merged with a publicly owned company, its stock, when reissued as Harper & Row stock, became marketable as an over-the-counter security and its financial record was open to public view. While the general public showed little interest in the financial records of the House, many were vitally and volubly concerned that the old and familiar imprint was gone.

"Any one of us is Harper and all the rest are the brothers," James Harper had said back in 1833. In 1876 the New York *Tribune* apologized in an editorial for having referred to the firm in a news story as "Harper Brothers & Company" and said that the word "Cousins" might be more appropriate. Then came a time when the cousins had gone and the House was directed by other men, including men with the names of Harvey and Hoyns, who were neither "Harpers" nor "Brothers." But the name remained the same, for it was deeply rooted in tradition. What Dr. Francis had called a Cliff Street oak survived a consuming fire and a persistent financial blight and an uprooting when it was more than one hundred years old. Surprisingly for a commercial house, it grew to be an American institution with its own mystique, because it shared the affection that millions had felt for authors and books and periodicals that were read and treasured and passed on to children and grandchildren.

Then came the spring of the year 1962, and onto the old tree was grafted a strong, new branch. There had been many other graftings since 1837, when George Dearborn's classical books were spliced on, but none so capable of bearing fruit as the schoolbook branch named Row. Was it necessary to change a 129-year-old imprint? It seemed so at the time, not only because of the financial strength of the new partner but also because it dramatized the importance of textbooks in the nation's economy. Furthermore there was historical precedent, for in 1833 the imprint was changed from J. & J. Harper to Harper & Brothers in order to recognize new partnership strength.

The flaming torch that Plato described and the Harper brothers claimed for their own has passed on to many hands, but it never burned brighter or promised more light for the future than in 1967, the Harper sesquicentennial year.

ACKNOWLEDGMENTS AND CREDITS

This book could not have been written without the help and cooperation of my Harper colleagues who have given generously of their time to provide material of current interest and historical value. Mrs. Beulah Hagen's editorial expertise helped greatly to smooth the way from early drafts of the manuscript to printed book; her special knowledge of Harper historical records was invaluable. Mrs. Marguerite Hoyle also contributed valued editorial assistance to shorten and clarify this account, as did Mr. Wallace Exman in reading proof. Miss Rose Daly, secretary to four editors of *Harper's Magazine,* made available resource material on this periodical, and I am especially indebted to Mrs. Ruth Hill for her perceptive and critical research covering the years that followed the firm's new beginning on Franklin Square. I am also grateful to three others who went beyond the call of duty to help with this book: to Mrs. Mildred Maynard for a superb job of copyediting, to Mrs. Nancy Etheredge for the book's design and picture layout, and to Mrs. Julia Stair for her loyalty in undertaking still another index to Harper history.

Since this book has been written for the general reader I have made minimal use of quoted matter and have not burdened the pages with a detailed listing of sources. I invite correspondence with scholars who might care to have particular sources identified, and for their use I am also placing annotated copies of *The House of Harper* in the Pierpont Morgan Library, New York, and in the library of the R. R. Bowker Company, New York. Certain papers of Thomas W. Lamont, made available by his son, the late Thomas S. Lamont, were of especial value in detailing the story of the Morgan-Harper relationship.

Many of the illustrations that add interest to these pages have been made possible by the courtesy of individuals and institutions as listed below:

Mrs. Fletcher Harper IV for the portrait of Fletcher Harper, by Elliott (p. 2).

Brenwasser of New York for the photograph of the painting of the S.S. *Europe* (p. 6).

Mrs. William C. Colby for the miniature of James Harper (p. 8).

American Antiquarian Society for the card advertising the new firm of Harper & Brothers (p. 14).

Parke-Bernet Galleries for the photograph of *Two Years Before the Mast* (p. 20).

East River Savings Bank for the painting of City Hall, New York (p. 25).

Museum of the City of New York for the drawing of Mayor Harper's residence (p. 27), photographs of the Harpers' Cliff Street establishment (p. 33) and the painting "Central-Park Winter," by Parsons (p. 103).

New York Public Library for the Harper catalogue title page (p. 31), the page from *Thomas Nast's Almanac, 1873* (p. 136), and the picture of Columbia College (p. 164).

Harvard College Library for the portrait of Herman Melville, by Eaton (p. 38) and the memorandum of Allan Melville (p. 39).

Mount Vernon Ladies' Association for the Fletcher Harper letter introducing Winslow Homer (p. 95).

National Gallery of Art, Washington, D.C., Rosenwald Collection, for the wood engraving "Raid on a Sand-Swallow Colony," by Homer (p. 105).

Collection of the Montclair Art Museum, Montclair, New Jersey, for the drawings "Center of Attention," by Reinhart (p. 109), and "The Old Flute Player," by Pyle (p. 115).

New-York Historical Society, New York City, for the picture of the unfinished Brooklyn Bridge (p. 129).

H. W. Tetlow for his photograph of boy holding *Harper's School Geography* (p. 166).

Pierpont Morgan Library for photographs of original drawings for *Trilby* (p. 174) and *Peter Ibbetson* (p. 175) by Du Maurier.

Miss Helen Leale Harper, Jr., for the memorandum covering a loan made by Mrs. Lillie Harper (p. 182).

The Mark Twain Company for the Clemens letter to Harvey (p. 191).

Mr. Mark Saxton for the photograph of E. F. Saxton and Aldous Huxley (p. 228).

The *Publishers' Weekly* for photographs of E. J. Cullen being honored (p. 247), and the drawing of names of booksellers (p. 264).

Mr. Garth Williams for the drawing of "Stuart Little" (p. 279).

Mr. Maurice Sendak for the drawing from *Where the Wild Things Are* (pp. 280, 281).

POSTSCRIPT TO THE 1967 EDITION

As this book goes to press a change in Harper management is being effected whereby Jones relinquishes the chairmanship of the Board of Directors and is succeeded by Harwood, who will serve in that post on a full-time basis; Jones becomes chairman of the executive committee. Arnold has been named president of the company and his Evanston responsibilities are assumed by Wilson G. Kuhlman. Canfield continues his active participation in the editorial activities of the House as well as the chairmanship of the Board of Directors of Harper's Magazine, Inc.

Willie Morris is now editor of the *Magazine* and Robert Kotlowitz is managing editor. Fischer and Lynes are relinquishing these posts in order to devote more time to their own writing while continuing as contributing editors to the *Magazine*.

INDEX

(Numbers in *italics* refer to illustration material.)